I hope you enjoy
the adventures of
my amazing Hands!

To My FRIEND, HOUSEKEEPER,
AND FRIEND IN THE LORD

(HOPE YOU ENJOY READING ABOUT

MY
AMAZING
HANDS

MY *Amazing* HANDS

180 Short Stories

JAMES E. MCCARTHY

 FriesenPress

One Printers Way
Altona, MB R0G 0B0
Canada

www.friesenpress.com

Copyright © 2023 by James E. McCarthy
First Edition — 2023

All rights reserved.

No part of this publication may be reproduced in any form, or by any means, electronic or mechanical, including photocopying, recording, or any information browsing, storage, or retrieval system, without permission in writing from FriesenPress.

ISBN
978-1-03-916995-1 (Hardcover)
978-1-03-916994-4 (Paperback)
978-1-03-916996-8 (eBook)

1. BIOGRAPHY & AUTOBIOGRAPHY

Distributed to the trade by The Ingram Book Company

Introduction

My Amazing Hands have done extraordinary things . . . things that most people would consider a highlight in their life if even *one* of them occurred.

I have been fortunate enough to have many such things permeate *my* life.

I will tell you about . . .

- some extraordinary people My Amazing Hands have met, like Wayne Gretzky and Vince Gill.
- some extraordinary places they have been to. I sat where Elvis sat in the movie *Fun In Acapulco*.
- and some extraordinary occurrences. I got shot at while up the Eiffel Tower.
- and stories of 177 more things My Amazing Hands have done!

My Amazing Hands . . .

- have shaken hands with thirty-five celebrities . . . besides Wayne.
- have performed on television and on the radio and have been in two movies. One of them was a speaking part.
- have been on the front page and elsewhere in newspapers.
- have performed on the Casino Rama Entertainment Centre stage and elsewhere to audiences of more than 3,500.
- played with a mariachi band in Mexico.
- made three music CDs and recorded at RCA Studios in Toronto.

My Amazing Hands also . . .

- held a hymnary while I sang in church, both solo and with the choir.
- were proud to hold the Bible while I preached the sermon a couple of Sundays that the pastor couldn't attend.
- choose the hymns for all Sunday services, and in my current position as Music Director for the church, lead the congregation in song.
- performed various acting roles in many live theatre performances.
- lighting and sound effects for many others.

My Amazing Hands . . .

- directed three amateur theatre plays; two in Wasaga Beach and one in Collingwood.
- sat in the director's chair at Stratford Shakespearean Festival and visited 'understage', where costumes are made, and the art of sword-fighting is learned.
- while there, rode the elevator upwards, then stood reverently, at centre stage!
- **and, My Amazing Hands were . . . SANTA CLAUS! . . . for a weekend! . . . in a mall!**

My Amazing Hands . . .

- have owned a Porsche, a Bugatti, a Parisienne Custom Sport, a limousine, and a convertible.
- have also owned a twenty-four ft. yacht, together with a variety of other watercraft from paddleboats to sailboats

My Amazing Hands . . .

- are licensed to fly Cessna, Cherokee, Piper Cub, and Beechcraft aircraft. They have even piloted a huge glider.
- are licensed to drive motorcycles of all sizes from 90cc up to and including a Honda 1200cc Gold Wing Touring bike.

My Amazing Hands are STILL licensed to drive motorcycles.
And lots and lots more.

MY AMAZING HANDS

My AMAZING HANDS are now in their eighties, and they STILL haven't slowed down (well— maybe a little bit).

And My AMAZING HANDS are STILL, genuinely, AMAZING!!!

I sincerely hope that you will enjoy the adventures of MY AMAZING HANDS!!!

This is the Canadian version.

There are no chapters in this book. ONLY AMAZING YEARS!

THESE SEVENTY-NINE AMAZING YEARS CONTAIN A TOTAL OF OVER 180 ADVENTURES.

I sure do hope you enjoy them!

Jim McCarthy

1942

Little did I know the adventures that My Amazing Hands would have while I grasped my mother's tender hand at Stratford General Hospital when I was born.

The first photo taken of me was one of my hand-maidens, my nana, giving me my daily bath in a small basin in her backyard in the sun.

It was 1942, WWII raged, and my dad was fighting Hitler somewhere in Europe.

I wish I could show you the photo. It showed that I, too, was ready to fight! My left hand was tightly drawn into a fist, ready to punch Hitler—and my right hand was showing Churchill's Victory sign for when I did punch him.

On the home front, we honoured the efforts of heroes like my dad.

I sure wished Nana would put some powder on my bottom. I was getting chilly!

1943

My earliest recollection was playing on the kitchen floor in Grampa and Nana's house. I wasn't walking yet, just crawling everywhere. There was a furnace damper on the floor in their house. The two chains that came up through the floor that led to the furnace would open or close the damper. More than once, I got my hand slapped for turning the knob that activated the chains. I'd *laugh*!

In winter, I had a sleigh with a handle, and Mom would pull me through the snow. I was so bundled up that I couldn't move. Have you ever seen Ralphie's younger brother, Randy, in *A Christmas Story*? That was what I looked, and felt like.

***

Like most brave Canadian men at that time, my father, Earl D'Alton Corrie McCarthy, served in WWII.

He was in the Engineering Corps of the Canadian Army. He built Bailey bridges, so vehicles carrying troops and supplies could cross rivers and streams to advance on the enemy. I think he was primarily in Holland, although I never discussed his wartime service with him, regretfully. I remember seeing some photos.

I do remember asking him if he ever got shot at, and he told me, "Only once. I got my plate of food from the food truck and was going to sit down with my buddies under some trees and have lunch. Suddenly a bullet zinged into my plate. I ran for cover. We looked but couldn't see anybody, so we assumed it was a sniper. There were a lot of snipers left when the Germans retreated."

Then he winked at me and said, "I skipped lunch that day."

Dad came home from the war on leave, periodically. When he did, it was a time for celebration for both families. And, of course, I was included in that abundance of love.

Mom and I shared a bedroom, but when Dad was home for a couple of days, they let me sleep in nana and grampa's room. What fun!! I thought it was a real treat, sleeping cuddled up with Nana and Grampa. I was too young to know the REAL (wink wink) reason.

Too soon, Daddy left again, and I had to sleep back in with Mommy . . . but she was nice and cuddly too . . . so I didn't mind a bit!

As he was scarcely there during my formative years, I associated the uniform with 'Daddy.'

We lived on Ontario Street in Stratford, part of Hwy #8, on the edge of town, and this road was very busy. I wasn't allowed to go past the sidewalk. There was a grass boulevard, or verge, between the sidewalk and the street, which kept me safe. At first, I was closely monitored, but I was a 'good' boy and obeyed my mom's rules.

Often, uniformed troops would march down the pavement. I remember standing on the sidewalk, waving my little mom-made flag and watching them march past. Now and then, I would see a soldier that I thought looked like my father, and at the top of my lungs, I would yell, "Daddy! Daddy!" That brought many snickers and chuckles from these brave men. Even at such a tender age, I unknowingly brought a bit of cheer to an otherwise bleak time.

1944

As I matured, Mom, Nana, and I, in my stroller, went on walks, often down to the beautiful park on the Avon River. There was an old cannon 'guarding the park' at the entrance, and I was sat on it.

I'd throw my hands up in the air, and I'd LAUGH!

I thought that was great—I was higher than they were. (Of course, they held me tight so I wouldn't fall).

I believe that cannon is still there! Would it be foolish of me to climb up on it just one last time? To the right, there was a wooden footbridge over a railway track. Mom or Nana would hold one of My Amazing Hands, and we would run up the planks to the top of the bridge, then run back down again.

Great fun for me . . . tiring for Nana . . . but she would do anything for me!

Though she died many years ago . . . I STILL love her so!

The park had a playground area, and I would always get a ride on the swings.

Then we would go down a winding road on a big hill to get to the river, where My Amazing Hands would feed the snow-white Trumpeter Swans, Canada Geese, and ducks of every kind. Nana would save stale bread crusts to feed them, and because the tourists who visited this park also fed them, the birds got pretty tame (and rather plump).

Every fall, the park's caretakers herded the birds to a nearby empty warehouse where they spent the winter. They were brought back to the river in spring after having their wings clipped.

I remember a steamboat puffing along the river, full of sightseers. I also remember it went 'toot, toot' as the captain blew the whistle and steam came out. That absolutely delighted me!

The Avon River was dammed up, making a vast, relatively shallow lake—ideal for canoeing. Further along the bank, there was a canoe rental place. Many couples took advantage of this, as the gentleman could serenely paddle his lady love up and down the river to one of the many secluded nooks on the lake.

There were many overhanging willow branches where couples could stop and flirt. Sometimes, they would carve their initials and the date inside a big heart on a tree trunk!

I often wondered—how many men bring a knife on a date? I also wondered how many canoes overturned while he tried to steal a kiss.

And— how many marriage proposals those willows have witnessed!

Further upriver, there were some motorboats. I remember they used to go very fast. The people in them would wave back to me when we waved to them. I got so excited!

Mom and Nana would order groceries by phone from Pogson's Grocery on Romeo Street. They would get delivered in a cardboard box. After they were unloaded and put away, Mom put the box on the linoleum kitchen floor for me to play with. I would get in and put one of My Amazing Hands behind me like I saw the men in their motorboats on the river do and make a b-r-r-r-r noise.

That was MY motorboat!

Every now and then, I'd 'toot-toot' while tugging an imaginary lanyard with one of My Amazing Hands.

I'd reach out front and pull myself around the kitchen floor. 'B-r-r-r-r-t.' 'Toot-toot!'

Sometimes, I'd get really lucky, and I'd get two boxes. They transformed into a tourist boat for me. I would put the two together, end to end, and put the tourist (my teddy) into the front one. I would sit in the back with one arm outstretched behind me, pretending I was the captain, steering a tourist boat up and down the Avon River, accompanied by very loud 'VROOM-VROOM' boat noises.

I would ride in one 'boat' and tow the other. Great fun!

Then I was taken upstairs to change into play clothes, and when we returned to the kitchen, the boxes would be gone. I was told that the delivery man needed them back and Teddy would be sitting alone in the middle of the floor.

MY AMAZING HANDS

I swear he was crying.

Ten minutes on the sidewalk with my tricycle and the boat would be forgotten—until next grocery day.

***

When I was a VERY young boy, about two, my dad took me 'horseback riding.' My Amazing Hands did it the hard way—bareback (with Daddy standing beside the pony, holding me)!

I could tell the horse was afraid of me by the wild look in his eye! He *knew* that I was the best cowboy that ever rode the range!

1945

I used to love going shopping with Mom and Nana. I got to ride in the back seat of our old '37 Chevy two-door coupe. Seatbelts were unheard of in the forties, so I had the run of the back seat. The car's trunk was very small, so parcels also had to be put in the back seat, and I would be moved to Nana's knee on the front seat to make room. It was a treat because Nana always smelled so sweet. I loved to cuddle with her, and I can still feel her soft, soft cheeks as I kissed her—and her soft, smooth lips when she kissed me.

That is one of my fondest memories of Nana.

Even though they owned the car, Nana and Grampa couldn't drive, so my mother did the honours.

Every Sunday, Mom would back the car out of the old wooden garage and hand-wash it . . . whether it went anywhere or not . . . because birds raised their young in the eaves of the garage, and Nana and Mom were too kind-hearted to evict them.

I remember that for many years a pair of robins raised their young in a nest built in the small window in the upstairs bathroom. It didn't bother the birds that people came and went, even though the window was only waist-high. Of course, it was great to watch them every spring, repairing the nest, then laying the eggs, then the fledglings, mouths wide open and chirping as loud as they could whenever Mom or Dad robin would return with a juicy worm or bug.

Then one day, they would be gone from the nest. However, they often were seen in the garden, finally getting their own dinner.

Mom would dress me in my best—a dark blue velvet outfit with short pants—now and then. First, though, she would stand me on a chair to scrub me clean. Then she would carefully comb my shiny black hair into one huge curl. It ran across the top of my head from front to back.

She put me in my stroller or sleigh, later my three-wheel trike (a gift when I became a 'big boy of about three). My Amazing Hands quickly learned how to ride it, and we would journey to my Grandma and Grandpa McCarthy's house . . . my dad's parents.

Grandpa McCarthy used to make me wary, as he had bushy, thick eyebrows. That is until his face broke out in this big, friendly smile as he handed me a cookie.

He was an engineer on the Canadian National Railroad.

My grandma was an 'always smiling,' robust woman.

She and my nana both wore girdles. I remember I would throw my arms around them to give them a big hug . . . keep in mind that I wasn't very tall . . . my arms reaching around their backsides.

I didn't know what the hard thing that I hugged was. It wasn't soft like the rest of their bodies.

Now I know—girdles!

Grandma was a great cook, and I always got to 'lick the bowl' when I visited her.

I was intrigued by the device she had for coring and peeling apples. She just had to skewer the apple, put it in this machine, then turn the handle, and like magic, it was cored, peeled, and ready to eat. Grandma used to let me turn the handle!

Many years later, I was poking around the back room of this really old hardware store in a small town, and there it was—an apple coring device exactly like Grandma's.

Of course I bought it, still have it, and use it—bushels of apples later.

Another great little appliance in Grandma's kitchen that held me spellbound was a meat grinder. She would take a beef or pork roast out of the 'icebox', cut it into chunks, add weird things like apple and onion chunks, shake salt and pepper and other seasonings all over the pieces, and then she would stuff them into the top of the grinder, tell me to "turn the handle, sweetie," and this red stuff would come out, to be collected in a bowl.

The ground-up meat would be put back until just before supper. Then Grandma would fetch it, roll it into balls a little bigger than my 'bonker' marbles, squish them down flat, cook them in the big old iron frying pan, then plop them onto our plates while they were still sizzling.

THEY TASTED EXQUISITE!!

So, while I was at that same old hardware store . . . I asked, found, and bought one! I just can't get my supper to taste the way Grandma's did, though! I sure wish I could!

There were times when my aunts and uncles would also be visiting their parents when we were there.

Often it was for a special occasion, like someone's birthday. My uncles used to pick me up and swing me over their heads.

A-A-G-G-H-H!!

I was terrified. Mom used to intervene, though. She saved me (again).

As mentioned earlier, when I became a 'big boy,' I was given a tricycle. At first, Mom and Nana watched me very closely, and I was only allowed to ride it on the sidewalk in front of Nana's house.

As time passed and I matured, I was allowed to ride further down the street.

The sidewalk ended at the edge of my grandparent's property to the east but extended an entire block to the west, ending at a side street. On the corner across this side street was Kroehler's Manufacturing, where Grampa made furniture. A loud whistle blew every weekday at 11:55 a.m. for lunch and again at 4:55 p.m. to signal the workers to finish up, as their shifts ended in five minutes.

But . . . for me, it was a signal to drop what I was doing, jump on my tricycle, and pedal down to the end of the sidewalk to meet Grampa as he'd be getting off work for lunch and at the end of the day. Grampa and I would make our way home, where Nana and Mom would have our meals ready.

Beside the house, there was a copse of willows surrounding a small pond that must have been spring-fed, as there was always a couple of feet of crystal-clear water in it. There was what I called 'fish' in the pond. I had never seen tadpoles before. Mom made me a 'fishin' pole' from a branch, with about four or five feet of twine and a safety pin with a bit of yellow and red yarn tied to it. I spent much of my youth—fishin'! I don't recall catching anything, but I had fun all by myself, as there weren't any other kids around my age in the neighbourhood. My Amazing Hands held the fishin' pole!

There was an apple tree in the middle of our backyard. The apples were edible and delicious in the fall when they turned red, but, being so young, I didn't understand that they were sour when green. I found out the hard way when I took a bite! Same thing with the gooseberries. Nana had a gooseberry bush at the end of the garden path, and the berries were sour in spring, but oh, so sweet in the fall!

Mom told me when My Amazing Hands were allowed to eat them, but only as many as I had fingers.

That's how I learned to count to ten! Those ripe, freshly picked, backyard-grown gooseberries were so *G-O-O-O-O-D!*

I can't understand why they aren't very popular anymore. I love them!

1946

My life has been filled with music. I started, as most singers do, at a very early age.

I had no idea of the musical adventures that lay before me.

Let me tell you what I mean....when I was about four, my mother stood me on the kitchen table to sing for her. I sang the best I could at that age—inventing many words that I didn't know. The entertaining bug bit me hard when I got those first accolades. I wanted to entertain all the time, and I sang and sang. While singing, I clapped my little hands along with the music. My audience loved it!

I had no idea how BIG of an influence music would have on the rest of my life!

My mother, Dorothy McCarthy, played the piano . . . just at home, for the family's enjoyment . . . and she was quite good! I don't recall that she ever played in public, though. It was just for us. I also remember that the piano seat would spin around to raise and lower, and I loved riding up and down on it— till I got dizzy—staggered—and then fell. What fun for My Amazing Hands!

She was very pretty, too.

Dad sang a bit in the car. He had a couple of songs that he knew, and he repeated his repertoire whenever we went for a drive.

One song I vividly recall him singing was 'There's A Long, Long Trail A-Winding.' It sure made the miles fly on long trips. I looked up the song on YouTube and heard John McCormack sing it to me as I wrote this.

Okay! I'll admit it—I cried.

Dad had a darned good voice, too. But he was too shy to sing in front of anyone but his family.

I sure do miss you, Dad! And you, too, Mom! You were GREAT parents!!

I don't recall my sister having much interest in music, but my brother, Ken, was also very musical.

We were church-going folk, and as soon as I was old enough ... around five ... I used to go to Sunday School with Mom every week. Because I loved to sing and would do so every chance I got, it wasn't long before the pastor asked Mom if I would sing a song in church. I think it was 'Jesus Loves Me.'

Unaccompanied!

That would be the first time I would sing solo before an audience. Mom drilled me all that week, standing me on the kitchen table. Of course, I had it down pat.

Finally, Sunday morning came. Mom dressed me in my most elegant clothes, and I was so clean I sparkled. The pastor introduced me, and my mother took my little hand and led me in front of the podium. And ... I sang ...

THE WRONG SONG ... !

Before my horrified mother, the shocked pastor, and the laughing congregation, I sang ...

♫ ' **I Want To Buy A Paper Doll That I Can Call My Own**' ♫

Yup ... I did!

It was my first solo gig before an audience, and I messed it up!

But ...

I entertained my audience! And—I loved it!

I often sang in church after that. My mom was always prepared to hustle me off the podium if I sang the wrong song again. I never did.

When I grew older, I joined the choir and sang many solos.

My mother taught me how to read music scores, and I 'tinkled' on the piano, but it wasn't for me.

I did learn 'Chopsticks,' and I could play *some* piano. One of my favorites from when I was a kid that I still sing today (karaoke style), is 'The Old Lamp-lighter.'

Mom also taught me how to tap dance. I remember it well ...

Hop shuffle step, step, step
Hop shuffle step, step, step
Hop shuffle step
Hop shuffle step
Hop shuffle step, step, step

I was about four.

I never was a very good dancer (except for the slow 'cuddly' songs), so this didn't go very far.

But I could sing!

When our mom died in 1983, my brother inherited her old piano.

He can play rings around me on it. But I don't think he knows *'The Old Lamp-lighter.'* I bet I could still show him how to play it—on the piano—with two fingers! That . . . and *'Chopsticks!'*

Just like Mom taught me!

I did buy an organ many years later, and My Amazing Hands learned to play a few simple things on it, but it just wasn't for me. It's a great place to display family portraits, though!

***

One day, Grampa brought home some sticks and brown twine from his work! Mom used the twine to make a cross with the sticks, then joined the sticks with this twine by cutting a small notch at the ends.

Then she made a paste from flour and water and got some old newspaper. And she made me a kite.

She even knew how to make a tail for the kite out of more twine and paper.

There was an open field behind the house that went clear over to the next street, and there was a thin tree line about halfway. Occasionally, we would see deer there—I thought they were cows when I was young. It was a perfect place for a young boy to fly his kite, tied to the ball of twine from the furniture factory . . . daily . . . for hours.

My Amazing Hands held the string that controlled the kite!

Eventually, the city put a street beside Nana and Grampa's house, across the field, to the next road.

MY AMAZING HANDS

A gas station, later a restaurant, was built beside their house on the other side of this street, and a potato chip manufacturing company was built on the east side. My Amazing Hands waved at the ladies that worked there, and I was usually given bags of fresh potato chips through the window. They were super fresh, and they tasted GREAT! Thank you, ladies!

Nana and Grampa's house is gone now; a car wash sits on that corner.

For a long time, the big maple tree on the property remained. I remember climbing that tree until Mom, Nana or Grampa yelled at me to get down. My Amazing Hands picked a leaf from that tree a couple of years ago and framed it. Sadly, the tree is gone now!

The framed leaf now sits in my living room on an antique table that belonged to Nana and Grampa.

Shortly after Dad returned from the war, he took advantage of our great government's assistance to these wartime heroes. He got his pre-war job back with the CNR and took advantage of 'wartime housing.'

However, we had to move to Chatham, Ontario, until a CNR position became available in Stratford.

So we moved to Willomac Avenue in Chatham—a wartime-built house. My parents and I liked Chatham, so we decided to live there. Dad even asked MY opinion, which made me feel SO grown up.

Besides, my sister, Cheryl Lynn (we all called her Sherry), was born on August 14, 1946, and my grandparents' house in Stratford just wasn't big enough for everyone.

I loved my baby sister.

I laughed when she cooed and chuckled at me as only babies can.

Then she would grab the forefinger on one of My Amazing Hands and sh-shake it.

Yes, I loved my baby sister.

1947

My first schooling was in kindergarten, a temporary home in an ex-military Quonset hut.

The year was 1947 . . . just two short years after the war ended.

For the most part, kindergarten was uneventful until one day that I recall vividly. The teacher had let us out for recess, and I was late getting back in because we were playing hide-and-seek, and I didn't hear the bell. My five-year-old brain figured that if I hid outside, the teacher wouldn't notice that I was not in my seat, and I could just go home at noon when class was dismissed. But she easily saw me hiding in some bushes, through the window.

I didn't tell my parents, and the following morning, I went off to school as if nothing had happened.

The teacher asked where I had been the previous day, and I told her I had gone home sick. She said that I would need a note from my parents. She said she would let me stay, but without a note, she wouldn't let me back to class the next day.

OH-OH!!

I couldn't ask my parents to write me a note, so I decided to write it myself, after conferring with my buddies, who were also five. I couldn't find any writing paper and didn't know how to use pen and ink, so I got inventive and carefully tore a strip from the unprinted top of the daily newspaper. My Amazing Hands came through for me again as it printed (in capital letters that I thought would elevate the value of the message) . . .

AN EARACHE!

I did it very carefully, using all my very best 'pencil-man-ship.' I confidently presented my 'note' to the teacher the following morning. At five years old, I didn't understand why she couldn't stop laughing as she pointed to my seat.

Or why Mom and Dad asked how my earache was as they broke out laughing when I came in for supper that evening?

Whew! I barely escaped!

My Amazing Hands saved me!

1948

One of the Quonset huts became a church, and my parents took me to church there EVERY Sunday.

Dad became an Elder, and every Sunday, he would usher people to a seat, distribute programs, pass the collection plate and keep everything running smoothly for that day's services which commenced at eleven sharp.

One morning, Dad hustled us all along at home so we wouldn't be late. It would NEVER do to have an Elder's family late, especially since this was a special commemorative Sunday celebrating the anniversary of the first year that the church had existed. We left the house at ten-thirty. It was a short fifteen-minute walk to the church. Dad forgot his Bible, so he sent us ahead while rushing back to retrieve it.

Mom and I arrived at the church at **11:45—45 minutes late!**

But... Dad arrived at **11:55—55 minutes late!**

He had forgotten that the clocks had to be moved AHEAD one hour, as it was the start of Daylight Savings Time.

To make embarrassing matters even worse...the local newspaper had sent a reporter to cover this momentous event. An article appeared on the front page of the second section of the next day's edition.

In the article, they mentioned Pastor Abbott, of course, but they also listed the Elders—Bob Smith and *EARLY* McCarthy.

My dad's name was Earl.

Somehow, the letter 'Y' had been added to his name! We didn't know if it was done on purpose or as a joke, or . . . perhaps it was just an inadvertent . . . tho' very apropos. . . error!

1949

My Amazing Hands were seven years old, and I was in love!

The object of my affection was a seven-year-old girl in my class named Susan Peat! She was a beauty with long, blonde hair, usually in pigtails that hung down in front, each with a brightly coloured ribbon tied in a big bow. She also had a lovely smile. And the cutest habit of tilting her head to one side as she smiled. You just KNEW that beguiling smile was meant only for YOU!

When she would catch me adoringly staring across the desks at her (she was seated on the opposite side of the room), her face would explode into this amazing grin as if a ray of sunshine had burst suddenly upon it.

I was too shy to do more than smile weakly back.

But I told Mom and Dad and Nana and Grandma and my sister and anyone else who would listen that I have a GIRLFRIEND!

I sure wish I knew where she is today. I often wondered if she still has that fantastic smile . . .

And still tilts her head when she smiles.

As if it's meant ONLY for ME!

My Amazing Hands would love to finally hold her hand!

And playfully tug on . . . THOSE BEAUTIFUL PIGTAILS!

1950

I don't remember too much happening in 1950! I was eight years old, and my sister, Cheryl, who we called Sherry, was three.

She had just learned to ride my tricycle.

One day My Amazing Hands were playing fetch with our dog, Jeff, in the backyard when I heard shouting and car horns tooting out front. I ignored it the first time, but when it happened again a few minutes later, I went to the front of the house to see what was happening. There was my sister, happily ignoring the traffic, having fun riding her tricycle up and down—ON THE STREET!

Realizing the danger, I ran to Sherry, grabbed her with both arms, scooped her off the tricycle . . .which I kicked safely to the curb . . . and rushed her to the safety of the sidewalk!

Mom appeared out of nowhere and, sitting down on the grass verge beside the sidewalk, started crying as she simultaneously (it seemed) scolded her, praised me, and hugged us both.

Mom called me her little hero! But, what the heck, why wouldn't I save her?

I loved my little sister!

1951

On May 18, 1951, my brother, Kenneth Wesley, came into this world.

No one could possibly have predicted that this tough little guy, constantly squalling for more food with tightly clenched fists and displaying an awesome set of lungs, would grow up to be such a talented man.

His childhood was normal.

He was usually accompanied by our family pet, Jeff . . . a beautiful male Border Collie.

Years later, when I was in the RCAF, I was home on leave, and we decided to paint the interior of Mom and Dad's front porch. As we painted, we sang. That was the first time I really *heard* Ken sing, as we enjoyed a current song, '*Tijuana Jail*,' with our newly-found brotherly harmony. Of course, we have sung many, many songs together over the years since then.

I was in the early stages of learning to play guitar, which sparked Ken's interest.

Today, he has been married for over fifty years and has raised a beautiful daughter.

And he MAKES guitars . . . from scratch. They are gorgeous and sound amazing.

Oh, by the way . . . he used to raise pigeons in later years, as I did.

***

The first celebrity My Amazing Hands was pleased to meet was Canadian stage, television and film actor **William Hutt**, when he lodged with Grandma and

Grandpa McCarthy in 1951. My Amazing Hands shook his right hand, but other than thinking that he was very tall and talked funny, at age nine, I wasn't too impressed!

The Stratford Memorial Theatre of Canada opened in 1879. Hutt was one of the premier actors there for many years. At that time, all performances were in a giant tent. It expanded when a permanent building was built in 1957. In 1992, I'll tell you a story about my experiences there.

1952

I attended Victor Lauriston public school for grades one through six. Elementary school was easy for me. I excelled, consistently achieving A's and A+'s, with only an occasional B+. I was ALWAYS the teacher's pet. Consequently, I advanced from grade four to six, skipping grade five.

As I have mentioned, I started meeting celebrities when I was very young. My Amazing Hands were about to meet a future baseball superstar—Fergie Jenkins.

Here's the story....

In 1952, when I was ten and living in Chatham, I joined Cub Scouts. When I got older, I would be a Boy Scout, and many years later, when my own sons were youths, I was a Boy Scout leader.

However, in THIS story—I volunteered to sell apples on Boy Scout Apple Day.

The Cubmaster paired me up with another boy. My Amazing Hands and HIS soon-to-be amazing hands loaded apples in our baskets. Then, we were driven to the street where we were to knock on doors and collect money by selling them.

The Cub who collected the most money got a special award.

We took turns knocking on the doors and had collected a bit of money when my partner noticed that there were milk bottles on the front steps of some of the houses with tokens or coins inside them.

These aluminum, triangular-shaped tokens could be purchased from the milk driver at a discount and were designed to be balanced on the top of an empty quart bottle instead of coins inside the bottle. Fergie suggested that we take the money but leave the tokens, and each of us would leave an apple.

We split the money and put it in our collection cans. We were honest . . . we didn't take <u>any</u> for ourselves. We wanted to win that award, though . . . for most money collected . . . for our Cub pack.

We almost reached the end of the street when the Cubmaster's car pulled up, and he signalled us over.

He didn't say a word, but drove us back to the fire hall where we had initially gathered. We turned in our collection cans and the unsold apples. Then we were thanked for our work and sent home.

The cub I was paired with was Fergie Jenkins. Fergie is a Hall of Fame pitcher whose primary team was, almost prophetically, the Chicago Cubs. He was a Cub twice—once with the Boy Scouts—and once with Major Leagues Baseball! My Amazing Hands shook Fergie's soon-to-be amazing hand. He was another celebrity that I knew personally.

My Amazing Hands would have many more adventures over many more years!

***

The Thames River flowed through Chatham on its way to Lake St. Clair. That was where I learned to fish.

On my birthday, I was given one of those kid's fishing rods, and my dad took me and a can of worms to a dock near the downtown area, where he showed me how to thread the worm on the hook. For the very first time, My Amazing Hands cast out the bait. The only fish able to live in this polluted water were catfish. And, because the water was so severely polluted back then, they had sores on their leathery body and were missing an eye or sometimes both, and all their tails and fins were in rough shape.

Dad taught me to cut the line (with my brand new pocket knife—just for fishin') and kick the fish off the dock and back into the water, being careful not to touch the fish with our bare skin. He showed me the proper way to tie a hook onto the line, thread on a new worm, and away we went again!

Little did I know the hundreds of fish that My Amazing Hands would eventually catch. In future pages, I will tell you of: monster muskies, delicious salmon (that I smoked in my smoker), trout, smelt, bass, pike, pickerel, etc.—all caught by My Amazing Hands over the years!

1953

Grade six ended my education at Victor Lauriston Public School, and . . . I entered grade seven at King George Public School in Chatham, Ontario.

To get to King George, I had to cross over the CNR tracks near the train station where Dad worked, so I got to say "hi" to Dad and the train crew most days! On my way home, if Dad was nearby, he would often lift me into the locomotive's cab. This, of course, was a steam engine – years before diesel locomotives became the norm for the railway switching work in the yard. My Amazing Hands were taught by the engineer which levers would make the train go forward, reverse and stop. One of My Amazing Hands even pulled the handle that blew the steam whistle! I could drive a Puffing Billy!

WOW!

I was the envy of all the kids and treated with a LOT of respect at school.

***

In March of 1953, when I was ten, the Kiwanis Club of Chatham held a music festival. Mom entered me in my age group. The song in my category was 'Mr. Sailorman'.

There were quite a few children entered in this category, and when it was my turn to sing, I did (I thought) a magnificent job.

I had practiced the song diligently, and I was after first prize, as I considered myself a pretty good singer; after all, I regularly sang solos in church.

Remember, I was ten.

I sang the song brilliantly, then waited while all the other contestants took their turn. Mom said I should win! She said that I sang it the best of everyone!

My mother? Biased?

Of course not!

Visions of that first-place trophy standing on our living room table danced in my brain. I was a cinch to win! However . . .

The judges wanted to hear four or five of us sing it again!

What? I wasn't expecting to have to do it again! It threw me for a loop.

I had never before sung a song twice before the same audience! I was SO nervous—then it was my turn to sing again. The piano started. And I sang it again . . . nowhere nearly as brilliantly as I sang it the first time! My Amazing Hands came in THIRD!

THIRD!

UGH!

I was SO disappointed! I vowed to myself that I would NEVER get caught unprepared to sing, ever again, . . . and I kept that vow for many years, but then . . .

Aw-w, but that is a story I will save for a future year of this book.

1954

Grandpa (John Augustus) McCarthy Jr. was born in 1875. He was a locomotive engineer for many years until he eventually retired from the Canadian National Railroad.

His son (my dad) followed in his footsteps... he, too, worked for the CNR... as a brakeman.

Grandpa enjoyed working around his home and especially loved woodworking in his basement.

When I was just a youngster, I doubt if I was even five, he had me helping him around his house.

Sometimes it meant learning how to hang a picture, or pulling those darned dandelions, or painting a porch.

John Augustus McCarthy Jr and his wife, Charlotte (Lottie), raised six children:

1. John Augustus III
2. Doris Charlotte
3. Cyril Thomas Britiffe
4. Earl Corrie Dalton
5. Elizabeth Ann
6. Barbara Ethel

He died in 1954 at age 79. My grandpa was a very kind man. All of us, his family, missed him!

MY AMAZING HANDS

***

When I was twelve years old, I got a job!!

I went door-to-door at all of the stores on Chatham's main street, looking for <u>anything</u> that I could do to make some money. Clement's Shoes hired me to clean up the place, put away the newly delivered footwear on Fridays after school, and deliver purchased footwear to their customers on Saturdays. Fortunately, my bicycle had a big wire carrier mounted to the handlebars.

My Amazing Hands also learned how to hold a cigarette that year.

On Friday nights, after I finished working, I would lock myself in the bathroom in the store's basement, as it had an exhaust fan.

I would sit on the throne and puff away and cough and cough, acting like I was a big shot now.

I was starting to mature.

Just around the corner, by the bridge over the Thames River, was The Spudnut Shop. For the uninitiated, spudnuts are delicious doughnuts made with grated potatoes and potato flour—deep-fried and delicious! I recently heard about somebody making them from sweet potato flour. I'm told the sweet potato kind are absolutely to die for! I'm going to get a recipe off the web and try them.

You won't regret eating spudnuts if you like doughnuts! They've even got a hole!

I was paid on Saturdays, after the deliveries were completed, and I would spend some of my earnings at The Spudnut Shop before I headed to the river, where I'd sit on the dock and 'pig out'!

After the spudnuts—a smoke—My Amazing Hands held my cigarette!

1955

I completed public school at King George in Chatham. I think that there must have been some kind of graduation ceremony, but it couldn't have been much, as I can't remember anything special.

Dad got bumped from the Chatham yard, so we moved back to Stratford. However, we knew that it was only temporary. A brakeman in Goderich was about to retire, and Dad was eligible for and desired, the position.

So, at 13, I started my high school education by attending Stratford Central Secondary School. We were staying with dad's sister and family on their farm, so I rode the school bus early every morning and then back every afternoon.

My after-school and weekend social life was spent with the cows. I learned all about barns, stanchions, silos . . . and manure! Most mornings, before school, I would have to go to the pasture at the back of the farm and, with the help of our farm dog, would drive the cows to the barn to be milked. One cow let me ride her back to the barn. My Amazing Hands learned how to milk a cow by hand and with a milking machine.

I would carry my Uncle Jack's rifle to the back pastures, where My Amazing Hands learned how to shoot a gun by killing groundhogs. A farmer friend of my uncle had a row crop tractor with its close-together front wheels. It flipped when the wheels sank into a groundhog hole, overturned, and crushed him. So I had my uncle's full approval and encouragement to use his .22 to shoot these critters in the fields so no one else would get hurt. Consequently, My Amazing Hands learned how to hunt.

I learned how to ride a horse, perched bareback on one of a pair of my uncle's Clydesdales – now retired from a lifetime of pulling plows and wagons. My Amazing Hands held the reins that controlled these gentle behemoths from a past era.

They were replaced by a powerful tractor, which I was taught to drive.

At harvest time, My Amazing Hands learned how to drive a harvester.

A couple of months later, the railway job that Dad had been waiting for became available, so he transferred to the Goderich yard.

And the family moved to The Prettiest Town In Canada!

Right next door to the Huron County Jail! The huge, solid stone jail was built between 1839 and 1842.

It ceased functioning as a jail in 1972 (it's now a National Historic Site), but it was fully functional when we were living next door in the late fifties. We often heard activity on the other side of the massive stone wall, which we assumed was an exercise yard.

***

I attended Goderich District Collegiate Institute from 1955 to 1958 and became friends with Paul Smith, who not only was a new buddy of mine in high school but was also an excellent drummer.

He was VERY popular, especially with the ladies. He was extremely talented and looked a lot like the actor Sal Mineo (*Rebel Without A Cause, Exodus, Escape From The Planet Of The Apes*) with his black, wavy hair and snappy clothes. Just like Elvis! A real heartthrob!

He was in a band called 'The Be-Bops.' which consisted of Paul on drums, Wayne Mills on lead guitar and leader of the group, and Wayne 'Weiner' Weller on rhythm guitar and vocals.

I SO wanted to be involved.

But at that time, I couldn't play anything, and I was a scrawny, 'tho brainy— kid who wore glasses!

I was still unloved but at least tolerated.

I heard that Millsy went on to fame playing in Rompin' Ronnie Hawkins' backup band at Le Coq D'Or in Toronto. I saw him years later in London,

Ontario, as he was entering a bar where he was performing, but as I was on my way out of town, I didn't have time to do more than say hello.

I heard that Wayne Weller got sick and died. Too bad ... he was a good singer and a nice guy! Paul went on to play drums with other groups, including a group called The Assembly.

Regrettably, I didn't get a chance to see them perform.

Paul was also the lead drummer in the Goderich Town Band. Our next-door neighbour, Harold Jefferson, played trombone in this band. Smitty told me that the band was looking for new members, so I went to the next band practice to look into it. Grampa had told me how he played cornet in a marching band back in Wales when he was a young man. This was all brand new to me, but I wanted to join my buddy, Paul, and I knew it would please my parents and Grampa.

The band leader asked me what instrument I wanted to learn to play.

I promptly answered— 'A CLARINET.' I didn't know that the two words, cornet and clarinet, were entirely different instruments. We laughed at my mistake when I arrived home and showed my parents the chosen instrument. I enthusiastically tried to play the clarinet but couldn't tolerate the reed vibrating in my mouth. It was like nails on a blackboard.

So, as quickly as I acquired my new instrument, I returned it at the next band practice, and I requested what I really meant—a cornet. The band leader told me they didn't have cornets, so I went home with my new instrument—a trumpet! He explained that a trumpet is played the same way as a cornet.

When I got home, Mom said it would be fine, so I went along. I learned to play, and as my 'lip' developed, I joined the town band, playing the third trumpet part. I was 'promoted' to the second trumpet part a year later. I was never good enough to play the lead, though. Speaking frankly—I didn't care.

The Goderich Town Band was a marching/concert band, and *singing* was my thing...

But this is a book about My Amazing Hands. So....

While we were still in high school, Paul phoned me one day and told me to come over to his house.

When I got there, he played a 45 record for me called *'Bongo Rock,'* and then handed me a set of bongos that he had and asked me to play along. I did—and it was fun. I had a natural talent for rhythm, so My Amazing Hands quickly picked up how to play the bongos.

MY AMAZING HANDS

Paul also gave me a pair of drumsticks and showed me how to properly hold them and rat-a-tat a simple pattern on his snare drum.

My Amazing Hands picked it up right away! I had a great time that day! Little did I know the mighty oak that would grow from those simple acorns that day because . . . that weekend . . . The Be-Bops were playing in an 'open-to-the-air' dance hall just outside a neighbouring town.

Of course, I was there.

Suddenly I heard my name over the PA system. Someone was calling me to the stage. I figured that one of the band members needed a bottle of Coke opened or had dropped something off the stage, or a similar errand for me—their groupie. Then, to my utter amazement, they announced that they were going to play '*Bongo Rock*' for the first time, featuring ME on the bongos.

YA-HOO!

I played '*Bongo Rock*' and another song called '*Bongo Party*' . . . both were recorded initially by Preston Epps . . . whenever and wherever the Be-Bops played.

We performed at many venues, including school dances and proms, in more than one town. I loved my ten minutes of stardom wherever we went! Everyone in high school knew me! Guys talked to me! Girls smiled at me! A lifetime of musical fun had sprouted.

YES-S-S! (pumping fist in air)!

In retrospect, I wonder . . . if I hadn't been in the RCAF when Paul was playing with The Assembly, and I had gone to see *them* . . . would I have been called up on stage to perform '*Bongo Rock*' one more time? I know—a dream!

Sadly, my buddy, Paul, died in 2013, survived by his wife, Dorothy. I have spoken to her on the phone, but we've never met.

Paul also is survived by a son, Thomas (TJ), and a daughter, Cindy.

I haven't met them, either.

I remember you, though, Paul . . . <u>VERY</u> well.

YOU introduced me to MUSIC!

Thank you, my dear . . . very, very much missed . . . friend!

1956

Ron Feagan and I attended Goderich District Collegiate Institute at the same time and were the same age. However, as I had skipped grade five in public school, I was one year ahead of him.

Ron was short—about the same height as me . . . around five feet, seven inches or so. But—I was pretty nerdy and wore glasses in high school, whereas Ron was stocky and very strong.

He was also a true gentleman to everyone.

I recall chatting with him at recess once about his love of horses and horse racing. One of My Amazing Hands shook his hand and wished him much future success.

Ron later became Canada's premier harness racer, amassing over 3,000 wins.

He was known as the 'King of the Sulky' racers.

He was the first Canadian to <u>win 200 races in a single season</u>.

In 1966, Ron was the youngest driver to break the two-minute mile record.

He was the top-earning driver in Canada on twenty-four occasions.

Ron also loved to play hockey. He played junior hockey with future greats Larry Jeffrey and Paul Henderson. And he could hold his own on the ice, too.

Sadly, Ron died suddenly at his home on January 13, 1979, at age thirty-six.

I mentioned Larry Jeffrey! Larry also attended Goderich District Collegiate Institute at the same time as me. Of course, he went on to have a successful career in the National Hockey League. He is a couple of years older than I (he was born in October 1940), but considering that I skipped a grade, he was just one year ahead of me in high school.

My Amazing Hands shook his hand to congratulate him whenever I heard that he had done something spectacular on the ice, and I knew him well enough to say "Hi Larry" when I passed him in the halls.

And he *ALWAYS* said, "Hi Jim!" back!

I recall that Larry was a tall, soft-spoken, gentlemanly guy. Remember, though... that was OFF the ice!

I wasn't interested in hockey other than watching the occasional Leafs or Red Wings game on the television with my dad. So Larry's world and mine rarely came into contact... but I heard some on-ice tales about him!

"Don't mess with that Jeffrey guy... OR ELSE...!"

Larry began his National Hockey League career playing left wing with the Detroit Red Wings in 1961.

He was a lefty.

He played for Detroit, Toronto Maple Leafs and New York Rangers from 1961 to 1969.

And (drum roll, please)... Larry was a superstar for the Toronto Maple Leafs in 1967 when they won the Stanley Cup.

He retired from hockey a year or so later. Apparently, the Toronto Maple Leafs did, too, as they haven't won anything since!

He retired back to Goderich, where he operated a beef farm. He also owned a concession booth open during the season at Goderich's popular Bluewater Beach.

The last I heard, he had died, age 81, on July 18, 2022, in his hometown of Goderich. A true gentleman; it was an honour to have known Larry Jeffrey!

***

Smitty and I used to go for bike rides whenever the mood took us. One day, we rode out of town to see a school buddy, Eddy Laithwaite. He was always fun to visit, as his grandfather had sculpted several concrete statues on the front grounds of the farm between 1920 and 1952... easily seen from the road.

There were statues of political figures driving oxen; Balaam, the Mighty Monarch, and his pet donkey; Jiggs from the old cartoon 'Bringing Up Father,' with his pipe and top hat; two bull elk fighting; a young flapper from the twenties and numerous other characters, all made of concrete, including a beautiful arch entranceway made entirely of cemented rocks.

Eddy wasn't home, so we decided to carry on down the highway.

One of us remembered an old house further down the highway that was HAUNTED! When we got there, we dared each other to go over the gate and up the lane to investigate further.

So My Amazing Hands got me over the gate, and up the laneway we crept.

It was just at 'twilight.'

I, braver than Paul, went first.

It was early spring. The landscape was dirty, with dead leaves and branches from the fall. Nothing green was growing yet. As we made our way around the side of the house and through some dead brush, we spotted a window that was lower than the others. So we dared each other to go inside!

We slid the window screechingly open, and, as I had bravely ventured up the laneway first, I felt that the honourable thing would be to let Paul 'lead the way.' Heh! Heh!

Reluctantly, he swung himself through the now-open window and into the house. However, I lost my balance as I hoisted myself through the window. One of My Amazing Hands reached out to an old organ to steady myself but unknowingly pressed down on the keyboard instead. It must have been one of those old pedal-pumping organs called a harmonium, because when I pressed down on the bass keys, it let out a loud ghostly G-G-R-O-A-N-ing sound.

Paul uttered a wailing scream and literally—flew—out the window! I don't think his feet touched the ground. Perhaps it was the oncoming darkness playing tricks with my eyes, but I KNOW I didn't see him climb over the gate. Pretty sure he was **airborne!** When I got close enough to see, Paul—still yelling—was upright on his bike, and his feet were going a buck-ninety!

THE CHAIN HAD COME OFF!

He jumped off his bike and started to run—pushing it down the highway—as I jumped on mine. When I caught up to him, he was already a couple of farms down the road, where he had stopped and was putting his chain back on.

It took a few minutes—he was shaking so badly.

I never told him about the harmonium.

He was certain, and told *everybody,* that the old farmhouse was haunted!

MY AMAZING HANDS

***

Near the school, there was a quarter-mile track. It was only used for athletic events, so I often went there after school to do some laps. Linda, a tall girl a couple of grades ahead of me, would often run there as well. If I didn't have anything to do at home, I usually jogged five miles or so, took a fifteen-minute break, then jogged five more miles. I wasn't a speed runner, I was a long-distance jogger, and it was just for my own satisfaction.

Linda and I would jog over to Clinton, about ten miles away, if the track was in use.

About halfway there, a farmhouse near the highway had a well pump.

My Amazing Hands pumped us some fresh, cold drinking water, and there were lots of shade trees, so we could stop and rest.

It also had an old-fashioned outhouse—a one-holer with a half-moon on the door.

Thank you, Mr. Farmer!

There was an old country restaurant in Clinton where we would split a milkshake, and after we were rested and refreshed, we would jog back to Goderich—stopping, of course, at the watering hole on the way back.

Linda and I were jogging buddies—and friends.

***

When I was fourteen, I was pretty cool. I wore peg-leg pants and turned my collars up. Me 'n the guys used to walk uptown every day during our hour lunch break. Andrew's Dairy Bar on West Street was a favourite hangout.

Old Amos Andrews was extremely patient with us kids.

After we got our milkshake or hamburger or ice cream sundae, he would let us hang around in there, devising plans to get into and more plans to get out of—*trouble*. And many budding romances had their roots there.

Andrew's Dairy Bar gave me something that I will keep with me until I die . . . a unique way to sign my signature.

Part of growing up is shedding the commonplace and devising your own personal way of doing things. I decided that I wanted to have my own unique signature. So I 'doodled' on the steamed windows at Andrew's Dairy Bar while consuming a milkshake!

You might think there's not too much you can do with a 'J.' It's just a stick with a hook on one end.

WRONG!

My Amazing Hands devised a way of drawing the stick sideways first, then across, then down with a nice flourish on the bottom, then curve it to finish it off and be positioned for the following letter.

Ni-i-c-c-e-e!

The M was easier to design. A nice curl to start the first of three bridge abutments . . . with the last one flowing downstream. My new, revised signature was now complete and personalized.

I noticed other guys (and girls) inventing their own personalized signatures in the days that followed. I guess I started something at Andrew's Dairy Bar that day.

Every second or third day, we would go to Fincher's.

That was the whole name of the store . . . just plain Fincher's.

Dennis Fincher owned it. He sold cigarettes and didn't pay much attention to how old you were. He also had pinball machines. And pool tables—both Boston and snooker. That's where I, and dozens of other local males our age, got our education . . . equally important as what we learned at school.

At that time, an essential part of growing up was . . . smoking!

Both Mom and Dad smoked. Mom smoked Matinee Mild, and Dad was a Player's Plain man.

So obtaining a couple of cigarettes so me and my buddy could smoke wasn't too difficult.

We arranged it so that one of us would swipe a couple of cigarettes. (I filched a couple of my dad's Players because I wanted to smoke 'like a man,' not those weak, women's Matinee's). We swiped some matches, then went to this conduit manufacturing place where we hid in a gigantic sewer pipe, away from prying eyes (appropriate, eh?).

Well, My Amazing Hands lit up our smokes, and, you guessed it, we coughed and choked for at least fifteen minutes. We told each other how great it was and how much we enjoyed it.

Ah . . . growing up. Such fun!

My smoking habit lasted 26 twenty-six years . . . until 1982.

No tobacco of any kind has touched these lips since June 22, 1982.

Fast forward in this book to '1982,' if you want to know how I quit a pack-and-a-half-a-day habit—cold turkey—with no ill effects—without doctors or drugs. I was SO proud of myself!

Dad used to go home every day for lunch at eleven, and I often saw him driving down Britannia Road on his way back to work, just as I was crossing this street with my friends on our way uptown. I always waved, and he tooted his car horn to me.

Being kool, we <u>always</u> smoked on our way downtown.

One day, I was busy flirting with the girls and didn't see Dad driving by. He tooted his horn. There I was, cigarette hanging out of my mouth, having just puffed out a gigantic smoke ring! I was caught!

All afternoon I stewed away about the lecture I would get when I got home that night! So I devised a plan . . . I rushed home as quickly as I could when school let out. Mom was home alone—my sister and brother weren't home yet.

Most important—neither was Dad!

So off-handedly, nonchalantly, cool as a cucumber, I announced to my mom: "I tried smoking at noon today, Mom, on my way downtown! I coughed a lot and didn't care for it much!"

Then I retired to my bedroom and waited . . . .

Sherry got home, and then Ken got home. Then, after an eternity, I heard Dad's car in the driveway.

He came into the house, and I heard him say hello to Mom. Then he said, "I saw Jim smoking at noon today when I was returning to work."

"Yes, I know," she said. "He told me he tried it but didn't like it. I don't think we have to worry about Jim smoking!"

It worked!

I was VERY careful with my smoking after that, and I don't think that they were any the wiser until I came home, smoking, after I joined the Air Force in 1959.

1957

I asked a very pretty girl to allow me to escort her to the high school prom, and she accepted . . . but I didn't know her last name. I knew her first name was Eleanor, and I was told her surname was either Drake or Olson. I couldn't find anyone who knew her and could tell me which it was. On prom night, my dad drove me to pick her up at her home just outside of town. I knocked on the door, it opened, and there she was. Absolutely gorgeous! One of My Amazing Hands gave her a corsage, and her mother helped pin it on her lovely dress.

We rode in the back seat. My very first date. I was fifteen. So was Eleanor. I was SO nervous. So was she. She told me, shyly, that it was also her first date! We arrived at the school, found some friends, and joined their table. After some dancing, we decided to go outside for some fresh air.

A teacher at the door, acting as a chaperone, asked to be introduced. I crossed one of My Amazing Hands fingers behind my back and blurted out . . . "Eleanor Olson."

I WAS WRONG!

I was SO embarrassed, just standing there as she introduced herself with her correct last name.

On the ride home after the prom, I couldn't get up enough nerve to even hold her hand with one of My Amazing Hands. She ran into the house.

I later asked her on another date, but she said something about me not liking her enough to even know her name, turned me down, and she never spoke to me again. And I saw her chatting with other girls and pointing at me!

This probably had something to do with why I found it so difficult to get any other girls to go to dances with me!

Oh, well!

***

A couple of buddies taught me about bass fishing in the Maitland River. The Maitland was a vast, but shallow, river with an occasional deep 'fishin' hole. A long way upriver, some natural falls stretched across the expanse of water. That was the best spot to find my old fishy friends from Chatham—catfish. These catfish, unlike the ones from the Thames, were not only edible, but they were also delicious.

And the cuts in the rock bottom created great spots to attract largemouth bass.

However, the very first thing that we had to do after we made our way through the thicket that was on both banks, was to build a semi-circle of rocks at the river's edge.

There were SO many giant bass in that river back in the fifties that, as we caught them, we would keep either the one we just caught or the biggest one in the rock-ring and let the smallest go.

At that time, the limit of 'keepers' was six, and we were afraid of the game wardens who, we were told, regularly patrolled the river bank there. (In reality, none of us ever *did* meet a game warden in all the years we fished there).

We had no idea what gruesome torture the dreaded game wardens had in store for us if we took home more than the daily limit.

But, man-o-man, freshly caught, cleaned and scaled, then fried by Mom in butter . . . with a bit of lemon and seasoning . . . fare fit for a king! Or My Amazing Hands!

***

The Canadian Pacific Railway had a train station near the beach. It was also near the concession stand and the huge grain elevators. That was the end of the line for the CPR after crossing the Maitland over the huge aqueduct bridge. The fishing was especially good in the deep hole . . . at the far side of, and near a foot of, the bridge. The railway ties were spaced about ten inches apart on the bridge. Should you slip and fall between the ties, you had nothing between you and the water far below.

I vividly recall the first time I walked over the bridge. Man, I was scared, but I didn't want my fishing buddies to know. Of course, they tried to scare me even more by telling me that they could hear the train coming and that they had heard about a kid that got trapped on the bridge and had to jump. The bridge had little platforms that jutted out that I knew we could go out on if a train really *did* come, but we hurried across just the same.

My Amazing Hands held tight to the railing. They kept me safe!

It was worth it! The fishing really WAS excellent in what we called 'The Black Hole.'

And in spring, Steelhead Trout would spawn there, and they were great fun to catch, and delicious to eat.

***

As I have previously mentioned, my Dad worked for the CNR. He was a switchman, also known as a brakeman. He would ride on the train, hop off to throw the switches so the cars would go to a siding, then jump on the cars to turn the wheel that applied the brakes. Sometimes, I would ride the train down the big hill that led to the grain elevators.

Corn, wheat, and soybeans, grown on the farms, would be loaded into hopper cars, then shipped to the Goderich train yard.

Dad's train crew would transport these loaded cars down a long hill to the grain elevators at the harbour.

There they would be shunted onto side rails, where a different crew would off-load them into the elevators waiting for the huge ocean-going freighters to take the grain to ports in the USA and Europe.

Dad's crew would then take the empty cars back up the hill to be taken by a freight locomotive back to the farmers to re-load and do it all over again.

My Amazing Hands would often drive the locomotive as they did in Chatham. The locomotive taking the cars back up the hill went VERY slowly, with their hefty, tho empty, load. Sometimes, I would ride on the front of the locomotive on its uphill trip. It wasn't going very fast, so I had time to hop off, pick some wildflowers for Mom, and hop back on.

They always brought a big smile to her face and a kiss for me! She was my favourite girl!

***

My Amazing Hands needed more money!

The few dollars I picked up delivering shoes, together with the 'what-we-can-afford' weekly allowance from my parents, just wasn't enough for a growing fifteen-year-old boy/man. I was old enough to be allowed certain freedoms, like going to the show every Saturday night with my buddies using my own money. But now I was also going to dances, smoking, buying goodies for girls, flip-top white bucks, and peg-leg black or khaki chinos! And I STILL needed more money!

In other words ... I needed a good-paying part-time job.

Then, I went bowling with Mom and Dad one warm summer evening. A guy I knew from school was playing pinball at one of the machines in the back corner, so I let them bowl a game without me, and I went over to say hello.

He said he only had a few minutes to chat, and then he had to get back to work. I asked what he meant, and he told me that he was working at the bowling alley every evening as a pinboy. He was just on a ten-minute break that the owner insisted each boy take each hour.

This five-pin bowling alley was called 'LITTLE BOWL', named after the owner, Harry Little.

This wonderful man was terrific with the young boys ... making certain that they were well looked after while they were working for him. He was a friend as well as a boss. Everybody liked him!

After checking with my parents that it was okay with them, Harry hired me. I worked three nights a week so it wouldn't affect my school work (I was still top of my class, so it didn't interfere at all).

A pinboy's job was to set up the pins and clear the deadwood after each ball. He normally was in charge of two lanes ... there was a cutaway between the lanes where he perched.

The bowler threw up to three balls. There were five pins. Hidden in the floor were five pegs that would pop up when the pinboy stepped on a lever.

It went like this...

One ball was thrown. If it was a 'strike,' My Amazing Hands put the ball on the ball return and started it rolling back to the ball storage area. He would then step on the lever to pop up the pegs, pick up the pins, reset them on the pegs, then jump back up to the perch between the lanes. If not a strike, the pinboy would just clear any deadwood that had bounced back onto the lane.

The bowler would bowl again, and if he got a 'spare,' he would send the balls back and proceed as I have described for a 'strike.'

Lastly, if a third ball was thrown, the same procedure—except a skilled pinboy would pick up all three balls at the same time by slamming them against his chest.

Now, the pinboys were allowed to go shirtless, as the bowling alley wasn't air-conditioned, and, man... it sure got hot back there—especially if the men's or women's leagues were playing. They bowled quickly—hot and heavy action. We had to keep up and not get hit by one of those fiery-fast balls.

Slamming the balls against your chest every night meant that, before long, the dirt from the balls would be permanently 'tattooed' into your skin. To this day, I STILL have a faint brown patch under my left nipple where I slammed the balls against my chest those many years ago, so that I could send three balls at a time down the return chute.

Oh well... hazards of the job.

That explains why there weren't any <u>PINGIRLS</u>, though, doesn't it!

Bowling was charged by the ten-frame line, and the pinboy was paid by the lines he set up.

The Little Bowl bowling alley is STILL THERE TODAY... SIXTY-THREE YEARS LATER!

I wonder if My Amazing Hands could STILL get a job there setting pins? I'm experienced!!!

1958

I took Driver's Ed in high school, passed the course, and a couple of weeks later, on my sixteenth birthday, I got my driver's licence. While I was there, I noticed a sign that said that if I had driven a motorcycle a minimum of fifty miles, all I had to do was sign a piece of paper, and I would get an 'M' on my driver's licence.

I had never even sat on one at that time, but . . . I was now qualified to drive one.

So, when I learned to drive one in the mid-sixties, I didn't have to take a test. And it was pretty cool to show my buddies! And, of course, the ladies were impressed!

While I haven't driven a motorcycle in a while now, I STILL have that 'M' on my driver's licence! And the ladies are STILL impressed!

Back then, Dad let me drive the family car, but only when he was with me. So, my only mode of transportation at that time was still my bicycle.

My buddy, Paul, was given a really groovy birthday present. A ten-speed racing bicycle . . . the type with the skinny seat and down-turned handlebars. On the other hand, I had this big comfortable regular-looking bicycle that my parents had given me a few years before. Ho-hum!

Paul impressed the girls! I did not! So . . .

I decided to paint my bicycle.

I took it down to our cellar and looked for some sharp, shiny black paint that I was SURE I had seen Dad using. But all I could find was this flat pink paint that he had used in my sister's bedroom.

So My Amazing Hands painted my bicycle pink.

PINK!

And I rode it to school the next day!

It did what I wanted it to—the ladies noticed!

The whole school knew me as the guy with the fantastic pink bicycle!

And it never got stolen, like Paul's did!!

***

Dad was an amazing handyman and taught me so much that, in later years, I was able to completely re-build my house—all on my own.

One day when I was shopping with him for home repair items at a local hardware store, I saw a cool two-sided throwing knife. I really wanted that knife, so I promised Dad I would wash his car twice if he bought it for me. He did! (I would have washed the car anytime anyway. All he had to do was ask me!)

I did a fair bit of fishing in the local Maitland River, and I only had one serious mishap.

A friend and I lashed some logs together to make a raft. The plan was to pole out to the deepest part of the river, where the REALLY BIG fish lay, and spend time QUALITY fishing for the lunkers that we were certain must lurk in the deep holes out there. I had my two-sided knife with me, and I stuck it into the log floor in the middle of the raft so either of us could grab it quickly if we hooked into and 'boated' one of these lunkers.

We might have to stab it before it flopped back into the water and escaped.

Suddenly, the swift current in the middle of the river swirled the raft, throwing both of us off balance.

I was barefoot with my jeans rolled up. In the scurry to keep the raft a-right, I took a quick step and, you guessed it, sliced the inside of my foot.

OUCH!

Blood spurted from the wound. So . . . I used My Amazing Hands to staunch blood flow with my T-shirt while my buddy poled the craft to the nearest shore.

My T-shirt was tied around my foot as we made our way out of the riverside thicket to my car.

Then, taking the back streets so that we could go faster than was probably the legal speed limit, we made it back to my house, and, always my hero, my mother, made a quick phone call, then off we went in our car to our family doctor.

He was accustomed to repairing young boys in those days, so half a dozen stitches and having my foot painted red with mercurochrome later, I was good to go.

But Mom wouldn't let me go fishing for two weeks (she wanted to let my wound heal).

My buddy used the raft again and *told* me he caught an 8lb largemouth. Out in the middle of the river!

Yes, he *told* me about the big fish!

But he didn't *show* me the big fish!

H-m-m-m!

Later in this book, in 1979, I'll tell you about a REALLY *BIG* fish *I* caught—A *HUGE* MUSKY!

So, I get the LAST laugh!

***

I had a sixteen-year-old's vision of becoming an expert knife thrower. I had seen expert knife throwers on The Ed Sullivan Show many times and thought, "I can do THAT!"

My Amazing Hands were getting pretty good at doing it, too!

Our house had a car-port, at the end of which Dad had built a small shed for his gardening tools which had a wooden door. I discovered that if I propped open the shed door, I could throw my knife from the porch, which opened into the kitchen. It was the perfect distance, so the blade stuck into the door almost every time.

I got some paint from the basement and painted a target on the shed door inside. You couldn't see this target unless the door was wide open. So my dad didn't see anything amiss when leaving for work the next day. He didn't notice when he arrived home from work either—tired out from a long, hot day in the sun! And he didn't notice when he stepped around the corner of the house that day on his way to the back door, as he usually did.

Suddenly... THWONK!!!!

With a flash of light, something flew in front of his face . . . narrowly missing his nose, and stopped . . . quivering . . . deeply embedded in the wood on the inside of his shed door!

MY THROWING KNIFE!!

My dad didn't swear very often. . . he's a good Christian man . . . but . . . that day, I heard expletives from him that I didn't think had been invented yet!! He told me to 'git runnin' as he slowly took off his thick leather belt!

Now, my dad loved all of us kids and never hurt us, other than an occasional swat on the backside with the palm of the hand. However, that day . . . he flicked at my butt WITH THE BELT to make me start running . . . and then he took after me. He chased me down the driveway, down the street, and then down the adjoining street. Every time I slowed down to beg him not to kill me, he would give me another flick of the belt, and I'd speed back up again. I didn't know Dad could run so fast!

Finally, I couldn't run any longer, so I turned around and hugged him. Then we both broke out in laughter.

I have no idea where the knife went. It just disappeared!

***

I was at Andrew's Dairy Bar chatting with some buddies one day when some friends dropped in wearing their Air Cadet uniforms. We chatted about Air Cadets, which sounded like a lot of fun. I noticed that the ladies sure did like the uniforms! I wasn't too sure about marching and taking orders, but I enjoyed marching in the town band and thought I might also enjoy marching with my buddies in the military.

And Air Cadets would take everyone for plane rides throughout the summer.

So . . . I signed up, received a uniform, and joined my buddies on the parade ground a couple of nights a week after school, and every Saturday morning, weather permitting.

This triggered my parents to think this might be my future. If they only knew the military adventures that My Amazing Hands and I would have! In just a few short years, My Amazing Hands would have lunch with top-ranking officers from the three military branches—Army, Navy, and Air Force—from each country in NATO!

MY AMAZING HANDS

This was because I had a Top Secret security clearance in the Royal Canadian Air Force at Air Transport Command Headquarters at Trenton authorizing me, and me alone, to show 16 mm. film of tri-service NATO military maneuvers at a top-level conference.

And I'm going to tell you all about it in 1963—the year it happened.

1959

On June 1, 1959, when I turned seventeen, I joined the RCAF.

My Amazing Hands already knew how to salute – learned in Air Cadets!

So, as I boarded the train in Goderich, I saluted goodbye to my mother and father, sister Sherry and eight-year-old brother Kenny. I thought to myself . . . well . . . here you go, Jim! You are totally on your own now to sink or swim in the adult world!

I swam!

After a L-O-N-G train ride and a L-O-N-G bus ride, I finally arrived at the base where I would receive my basic training - RCAF Stn Saint-Jean, Quebec.

I completed a ten-week course, where I learned to make my own bed, iron my own clothes, pee in a room with fifty other men, march, and drink beer at the wet canteen. (I was seventeen. I was allowed to drink on the base at the wet canteen, but not okay off-base where the drinking age was twenty-one).

The airwomen had a separate section on the base, and we hardly had any contact with them. But I DID see a young lady that I really liked . . . when I took classes in the building beside the swimming pool.

She was swimming with her friends and looked GREAT in her bathing suit!

We went outside and flirted with the ladies when we took a break. That weekend, I went with some others to the small village. Surprisingly, the pub served us. My Amazing Hands had occasionally snuck one or two of Dad's beers out of the house. Often these were shared with two or three buddies. Those were small bottles, too. However, the beer in the pub was QUART BOTTLES! And we bought ROUNDS! Drunk city!

There was a bus that ran from the town to the base.

When I managed to get on the bus, I stumbled into an empty seat. When my eyes refocused, I discovered that the young lady in the seat in front of me was the airwoman I had admired at the pool.

But when I opened my mouth to say hello ... I PUKED ... ALL OVER THE BACK OF HER HEAD!

Then I passed out!

I never did tell her how beautiful she was! So I remained a virgin! But ... hey ... I was 'totally on my own!'

1960

Training completed, I was tested for aptitude, then transferred to RCAF Stn Clinton for training in electronics. I was just twelve miles from Goderich, so I visited home frequently.

I purchased my very first car from Nana. You guessed it—the old '37 Chevy. It had running boards, and I would take my friends from the base to Goderich or Grand Bend to swim in Lake Huron. If there were more than the car's capacity, the extra people would ride on the running boards! Picture it—my Amazing Hands ripping down the highway at fifty miles per hour (not metric back in those days), with three or four guys or girls on the running boards, clinging to the center posts Please don't ask me how we became so lucky, but we never got caught by the cops . . . and had no accidents!

WHEW!

When the transmission broke, I didn't have the money to pay to have it fixed—but one of my friends had worked in his dad's garage and knew how to fix it. We bought a second-hand transmission from the local scrap yard, and he showed My Amazing Hands how to install it. And when we road-tested it . . .

It worked GREAT!

That was the start of my 'being able to do things for myself.'

I was always a quick learner, so learning about electronics came to me easily. However, I was classified as eligible to learn Radar Air—all about the radar units on aircraft. But my fingers weren't nimble enough to do the intricate fine-tuning required. So, as my aptitude tests indicated that I also qualified for clerical work, I was transferred to RCAF Stn Aylmer to learn that trade. However, there was a delay before the start of the course.

So, while still at the base at Clinton, they assigned me to the guardhouse (jail) and made me a security guard. I worked with the Military Police doing menial chores, like checking the dependent's ID on Sunday morning as they passed through a gate to go to and from the church.

One day, when I went to the guardhouse to get my day's assignment, I was told to stand out of the way until further orders. A couple of minutes later, I was ordered outside to join a small group of airmen. They were told that My Amazing Hands were in charge. We still didn't know what was going on.

We were driven in a van off the base and down Front Road, a side road that connected Hwy 4 to Hwy 8. Our van stopped just north of the base, and we got out. Another van was stopped just in front of us. Personnel were starting to search the woods on the right-hand side of the road.

I was told to take my men, fan out, and search the fields on the road's left-hand side. Then, we were told why all the secrecy! Fourteen-year-old Steven Truscott had been charged with the murder of twelve-year-old Lynn Harper the previous year, and we were looking for anything suspicious.

An MP (Military Police constable) accompanied us and gave me more details.

While *we* didn't find anything during *our* search, I understand something pertinent was found in the woods on the other side of the road.

Steven Truscott was being held in the Goderich Jail.

One day, I visited Mom and Dad at the house they were still renting right beside the jail. There was a big stone wall, about 20 feet high, which we assumed was the outside wall of an exercise yard.

As I pulled into dad's driveway, I saw a kid about my age who had climbed this big old maple tree in dad's backyard. It grew beside the wall.

I shouted at him, and he called back that his brother, Steven, was in the yard and he wasn't allowed to see him. He asked if he could visit with his brother for a little while. Dad said it was okay.

I never saw him again!

1961

I took the Clerk Administration course at RCAF Stn Aylmer, Ontario.

I didn't know it at the time, but this suited me more than electronics! I was a quick learner and ended up with the highest grades and fastest typing speed (of all the males), sixty-five words per minute! It may not sound like much, but when you consider that the typewriter was an old Remington, non-electric, the kind where one of My Amazing Hands had to throw the carriage over to get to the next line and to make multiple copies, you had to use carbon paper, and I was only seventeen with NO office experience—I did pretty darned good!

And My Amazing Hands can STILL type sixty-five WPM!

It was good enough that I was chosen to go to Air Transport Command Headquarters in Trenton.

And it was good enough that I was given a Top Secret security clearance.

And a promotion from Airman 2nd Class to Airman 1st Class.

YA-HOO!

***

My Nana was the 'social convener' for her church. She would deliver flowers to members of the congregation who were sick or in the hospital.

In 1961, Nana stepped off the town bus while delivering flowers, had a heart attack, and died.

She was 75 years young.

MY AMAZING HANDS

I was still at Aylmer at the time, and I was called out of class to take an urgent phone call! It was Mom!

When she told me about Nana, I crumpled to the floor and cried my eyes out! I loved her SO MUCH!

I requested, and was granted, time off to attend her funeral in Stratford.

Sadly, one of My Amazing Hands became a pallbearer's hand.

Syl Apps, who played hockey for the Stratford Indians, later the Toronto Marlboros, then the Toronto Maple Leafs was driving behind the bus. He saw Nana fall and stopped to help, but it was too late!

Thank You and God Bless You, Mr. Apps!

***

So, after completing training at Aylmer, I found myself stationed at Air Transport Command Headquarters in Trenton.

I was sent to one of the headquarters divisions to test my abilities.

They had already determined that I would be their new Classified Central Registry clerk. I just had to get my Top Secret clearance, which would take a month or so. They started by giving me a typing test... even though I had scored the highest of all the airmen.

A typing test... at least that's what the Flight Sergeant called it!

Flight Sergeant Brooks gave me a twenty-page document and asked me to make him three copies of it using carbon paper. It was a list of twenty different recipes for *homemade brew* of all kinds... beer... wine... spirits....

"No problem, Flight! I'll have them for you by noon tomorrow!"

At 11:27 the next morning, My Amazing Hands placed the original pages, plus the three completed copies, all error-free, on the Flight Sergeant's desk, together with the three carbon sheets. Unbeknown to all, My Amazing Hands had also slipped a 4th carbon copy, with the carbon paper folded in half, into my locker, to be taken back to my barracks and perused at my leisure. S-H-h-h-h!

I gave this copy to my dad! S-H-h-h-h!

***

Through sheer good luck, all three other guys in the room that I was assigned to were, like me, amateur musicians. Let me remember... there was Cal Smith., a handsome, blond-headed singer who also played bass—Pierre LaBrook (we called him Frenchy), a French-Canadian from Quebec who played lead guitar—and Rudy Kloofmans, a blue-eyed blond guy of Dutch descent who played rhythm and a bit of lead.

Cal used to drive to Port Hope regularly to visit his girl, and one night, a couple of years later, he lost control and died in a car accident on his way back to the base. We lost a darned good bass player and a really nice guy that night.

I guess you can see that a drummer was needed to complete this little combo. So I decided to learn to play drums.

I ordered a drum kit from a Simpson's catalogue. But I had one big problem. When they came a week or so later, I took them out of the boxes, but had no clue how to put them together. I hadn't beat a drum, not counting the bongos . . . or Smitty's snare drum . . . in my whole life.

But I wanted to be one of the boys and be in their band *so* badly.

When the word got out that I had drums but needed help assembling the kit, I got a visit from a really great guy . . . Ernie was his name . . . from the next barracks. He knew a <u>lot</u> about drums. He assembled my kit, showed me how to 'tune' the drums, then some simple rhythm patterns.

Thank you so very much, Ernie, wherever you are!

So now our musical barracks room was complete.

I learned to sing and play simultaneously, and I sang both solo and harmony while drumming.

All the barracks had an outdoor porch at the end of the room. But ours had something special. Our open porch faced the open porches of the airwomen's barracks across the sidewalk that separated it from the airmen's barrack blocks. And when we jammed, we took our gear outside onto this porch. So all the young ladies came out on their porches to see and hear us. And they were in various states of dress, or should I say 'undress.'

Another, very loud, YA-HOO!

I was about nineteen then—still a virgin (sigh!).

But—man, I've gotta tell 'ya— I lived and breathed drums!

I joined the Town of Trenton marching band as a snare drummer (one of three). I learned how to read drum music, including percussion (cymbals, cowbell, tambourine, maracas, etc.).

I also joined the RCAF Stn Trenton marching band. I stayed with the town band, as well. My Amazing Hands played snare and tenor drums and cymbals. We provided a military band on the base for various occasions, including parades and funerals.

They flew us in a variety of military aircraft—Yukons, Caribou, Hercules, and helicopters— to various military functions, such as the Warriors Day Parade in Toronto.

We learned to read and play the music while marching in formation. Slow step for funerals.

Some of the guys from the military band formed a group called Wally K's Orchestra, as he was the man who created and directed it. Wally looked like the American actor - Ernest Borgnine.

My Amazing Hands played big band music like the Dorsey Brothers, Count Basie, Glenn Miller, Harry James and others from the era. Some of the gigs were for more significant events, and Wally would add other musicians as required. The biggest gig we ever played was the Officer's Mess one New Year's Eve. There were fourteen musicians for THAT gig, mostly military musicians from other bases.

What an orchestra.

I still was the sole percussionist and male singer!

At that event, there were dignitaries, with their ladies, from all across Canada.

Waltzes, Tangos, Fox-trots, Two-steps, Jitterbug, and Rock 'n' Roll were enjoyed 'till the wee hours.

These officers—all dressed in their military finery . . . medals and ribbons flashing . . . demonstrated that they could easily lead on the dance floor as well as on the parade ground. Indeed, it was an unforgettable gala event. Not many of them happen anymore.

Some gigs were with a smaller 'combo'—a five-piece group—including Wally on sax, a trumpet player, upright bass, guitarist, and myself—singer, percussionist, and drummer.

We played everything from sheet music, but all of us could read sheet music very well, so we could ad-lib some hot jazz on musical flights-of-fancy, yet return to the written score at will.

We played for weddings, Buck 'n Doe's, parties, dance halls, legions, and hotels. And My Amazing Hands managed some memorable drum riffs and solo bits.

I sang all the songs, as a drummer was the only one in the group who could sing and play simultaneously! Sometimes a female singer would join me, and we would sing some great duets together.

Many years later, I ran into Wally after we both had left the RCAF. I was living in London, and he owned and operated a car wash in St. Thomas. I drove there, and we reminisced. And he even washed my car. Thanks again, Wally. It was GREAT to recall the good times with you, my friend! You have given me some AMAZING memories! (And a very clean car!)

Rudy Kloofmans, my room-mate for a time, was already married, so now that he was established in the RCAF, he rented an apartment in the town of Trenton and brought his wife to live with him. One night, after we got together for another jam session, I mentioned how much I loved to sing, and I wished I could play guitar as well as he did so that I could accompany myself.

He said if I bought a guitar, he would teach me to play.

Now, I didn't know the first thing about buying a guitar. However, being a smoker at that time, I often dropped into the local red-fronted United Cigar Store (remember them?) for pipe tobacco or the occasional cigar. The next time I went, I noticed a small guitar on the top shelf for only fifteen dollars.

After checking with Rudy, I bought it, understanding that I could return it if it wasn't suitable. Rudy told me it was a three-quarter guitar, hence its small size, but it should do the job for me just fine!

So My Amazing Hands took lessons from Rudy every couple of days. I started with three simple chords to which I could sing a simple country song, then added chords to my repertoire as needed. Before long, I could sing and play rhythm like an old pro, with Rudy playing lead along with me.

The next step was to buy a full-size electric guitar, (a used Gretsch Country Club), and a small amplifier and microphone.

My Amazing Hands were playing guitar!

Thanks, Rudy! YA-HOO!

***

Around this time, I met a very pretty young lady... June P.

She was sitting all alone on the beach (A-w-w!), so I stopped the car and went over to "make sure she was alright"! She said that she was cold! (Another A-w-w!).

MY AMAZING HANDS

Well, it *was* a chilly day, and she *was* shivering (I *think* it was from the cold . . . maybe not)!

Not thinking of myself (yeah, right!), I offered to let her sit in my car to get warm. A few kisses later, and she was *finally* warm. She told me she lived in Trenton, so I drove her home.

And later that night, much later, I was no longer a virgin!!!!!!!!!!!!!!!!!!!!!!!!!!!!!!!!

And June was still shivering—but not from being cold!

So was I!

YAY!

I'll **always** VERY fondly remember YOU, June!

1962

When I reported for my shift one morning, I was told to report to the Flight Lieutenant's office.

I saluted him!

Then, out of nowhere, he asked me if I would like to go to France.

It floored me. When I got off the floor, (Ha! Ha!) I replied, "Hell, Yeah"! Then I quickly added, "Thank you, sir"!

Then he told me to go home and pack!

After a quick phone call to my parents, I was soon boarding the first Yukon aircraft to fly over the pond (Atlantic Ocean). This Yukon was destined to be THE aircraft (similar to Air Force One in the USA) in which kings and queens and prime ministers and presidents and high mucky-mucks across Canada and around the world would be flown to destinations worldwide.

But first, a few last things HAD to be tested.

That was where I came in.

A French Canadian named Marc, and I, had to pretend that we were the President of France and the Prime Minister of Canada, respectively. I later was SO thankful to have Marc, who, of course, spoke French. I just knew a *little* bit from high school. (Thank you, Mrs. Ogg).

There was ONLY first class on *this* aircraft.

The plane was to fly to Grostenquin, France . . . refuel overnight, . . . and return to Trenton the next day.

MY AMAZING HANDS

We were to submit reports on things such as: the comfort and quality of the seats; the quality of the meals; the deportment of the stewardesses and stewards; etc.

You get the idea.

An officer from the cockpit came back to talk to us mid-flight. He told us that one of the engines had quit running and wouldn't restart.

AND THIS WAS <u>NOT</u> A SIMULATION!

He assured us that the aircraft could easily fly on three engines.

My Amazing Hands filled out our reports as we travelled over the boring ocean, and the rest of the flight was uneventful. Upon landing, we were told that only a T-bird starter from Trenton could re-start the Yukon engines. One was ordered but wouldn't get there for a couple more days.

However, we were also told that we were getting a two-day pass. Then we were each handed an envelope containing the equivalent of $150 in French francs. We were told to 'have fun' but be back before midnight two days hence. This was around seven a.m. local time.

We decided we wanted to see the country, meet some people, and do something special. So we hitch-hiked to Luxembourg! Back then, everyone hitched a ride in Canada. All the time. And persons in uniform had no trouble getting a ride.

But, we were told by a guy who stopped to see if we were all right that NOBODY HITCH-HIKES IN EUROPE!

Oops!

When we got to Luxembourg, we ate at a very old, quaint restaurant. The food was delicious, and when Marc chatted in French with the waitress, and they found out we were Canadians, they wouldn't let us pay for the meal. They toasted our health with some sweet local wine. VERY nice people.

Remember, this was less than twenty years since the end of WWII. The Canadians were a dominant factor in liberating France and Luxembourg, and the people had long memories.

The Cold War tensions were in full swing, however—the French didn't like the Americans at all.

They had three prices in most stores and restaurants—the highest, the American Price, the Locals Price, and the lowest, the price that they charged Canadians.

O Canada!

We had an offer to go to Paris from a gentleman farmer and his son, who had a load of turnips they were delivering there. It didn't take us long to decide, and away we went . . . the farmer driving, with Marc and I in the front seat. He sat beside the driver, and they chatted away in French. I sat by the door and took in the countryside, while the son, about 16 or so, rode in the back with the turnips.

We stopped at a restaurant on the way there. We waited for an hour or so while the driver had a snooze in the back room. While we waited, the owners took our pictures and asked us all about Canada.

Then off we went . . next stop . . . PARIS!!

It was raining lightly in Paris, so we bought raincoats. Again, we were charged special Canadian prices.

We decided to sight-see, so we hailed the first available taxi. It was around noon. Marc chatted with the driver for a few minutes, and he negotiated an excellent deal for us.

The driver would drive us all over the city, showing us all the attractions, then leave us at the end of the afternoon at a hotel near the Eiffel Tower. We saw the Louvre, but, sadly, only from the outside. There just wasn't enough time to tour this famous art museum. We drove down the Avenue des Champs-Elysée, around the Arc de Triomphe, and saw the ladies in the windows in the famous red light district (tongue firmly planted in cheek!)

The driver waited while we had our pictures taken in front of Notre Dame Cathedral and on the bridge over the Seine River. Regrettably, we didn't have time to go into the cathedral. But he waited so we could take a short walk along the banks of the Seine and chat with the street vendors there.

My Amazing Hands took my shoes and socks off, rolled up my pant cuffs, and then I dipped my feet in the Seine River, just so I could say I did so, carrying on the McCarthy tradition!

It was now late afternoon, so we exited the taxi. The hotel that we were dropped off at was perfect.

It was really, really old, yet VERY close to one of the legs of the Eiffel Tower. It had an old hand-cranked elevator with an equally old operator who would crank you up to the floor of your room and back down again.

Kool!

The next morning, after a great night's sleep in what could only be a feather bed, we had some bacon and eggs at the hotel, then walked over to a leg of the Eiffel Tower.

An amazing thing—I met some folks there who were neighbours when we lived in Goderich.

They were on holiday. Talk about coincidence!

Wow!

After a short wait, we bought a ticket and went up some old iron stairs to the first level. We stopped to catch our breath while looking at the fantastic view from the railing. Being young and adventurous, we planned to go right up to the top of the Eiffel Tower. However, three or four gendarmes stopped people from going up the stairs to the next level and prevented them from going back down! They herded us to the centre, away from the railing. We wondered why at the time but soon had our answer! Marc spoke to the gendarmes in French and discovered that the reason was that the Algerians, who wanted their independence from French rule, were demonstrating by doing a 'snake dance' in their traditional costume down below.

They would spasmodically shoot their rifles into the air as they danced.

You could hear the 'zing' of bullets whizzing through the steel legs of the Eiffel Tower. We were safe, though, as long as we stayed on the platform, in the centre, and off the stairs. A couple of hours later, the gendarmes had dispersed the Algerians, and it was safe to go down.

Our train was leaving soon to take us back to Grostenquin, so regrettably, we had to cut short our endeavour to reach the top.

We were told that there was only one more train at the Paris train station, as a train strike was imminent.

But we made it back to the airbase, on time, with no more incidents.

All four engines ran just fine when we boarded the Yukon for the flight home.

However, to be safe, the pilot had decided to take the longer but safer route—France to England to Ireland to Iceland to Greenland to Canada . . . landing for refuelling at Gander, Newfoundland . . . before continuing to Trenton.

My Amazing Hands had just experienced a ONCE-IN-A-LIFETIME, GREAT adventure.

***

Around this time, I met my first real love, Glenda Turcotte!

I was at the Other Ranks (OR) club on the base with a few of my buddies one Saturday afternoon. That was one of the weekends that we weren't playing. They held dances there every weekend, open to civilians by invitation. A couple of lovely young ladies were seated at the next table.

I struck up a conversation with this beautiful blonde who told me her name was Lillian Turcotte. I had a couple of dances with her, received her address, and told her I'd pick her up at eight, planning to return to the O.R. Club with my new date that evening.

My group had a scheduled practice at four, as we had to play a military event that weekend. So after the band's practice, I headed to Belleville to pick up Lil.

I had my drumsticks with me, and I was with another buddy, Ernie B., and his girl, Valerie, in his big, old 1957 Buick Riviera. I was in the back seat.

When we arrived at her house, My Amazing Hands went 'rat-a-tat-tat' with the drumsticks just to be kool . . . instead of knocking on Lil's front door. Her dad, Louis, answered the door, and he was not impressed!

Then Lil came out with this gorgeous dark-haired woman.

She introduced me to her sister, Glenda.

Being a gentleman, I intended to let the ladies into the car first, but they wouldn't hear of it. They wanted me in the middle.

The ride there was uneventful . . . just chatting . . . but the drive home . . . .

After dancing all night with first one sister, then the other (and all of us imbibing), we had the same seating arrangement on the way home, with me in the middle.

I was trying to be a gentleman but suddenly got a sharp jab in the ribs on my left side. I turned to Lil . . . and she gave me a great big kiss!

As I was kissing Lil, I got a sharp poke in the ribs on my right side. I turned to Glenda, and, well . . .

SHE WANTED A KISS, TOO.

And it was like that all the way back to their house . . . jab on the left . . . kiss Lil. Poke on the right . . . kiss Glenda. Over and over.

Poor me!

I made a date with Glenda for the next day—then another, then another. Sometimes with Lil and her escort, sometimes with Gail (another sister) and her husband, Keith. When we went anywhere, it didn't matter who with, we would sing and sing in the car.

Usually, we sang songs of the day . . . rock 'n roll, ballads, etc.

However . . .

Glenda and her family also introduced me to singing country music.

For the first time in my life, I was singing Hank Snow, Hank Williams, Conway Twitty, Johnny Cash, Merle Haggard, and many more of the greats, . . . AND I LOVED IT!

They introduced me to 'The Old Log Cabin For Sale,' 'Crazy Arms,' 'Four Walls,' 'I Walk The Line,' 'Hello Darlin,' etc.

Time would disappear when we went somewhere . . . thanks to Glenda and her family!

Then . . . one night My Amazing Right Hand offered her a gold ring as I got down on one knee

and
PROPOSED!

AFTER KEEPING ME KNEELING—IT SEEMED LIKE FOREVER
—IN SUPER SUSPENSE—
SHE SAID, "YES"!
THIS BEAUTIFUL, EXCITING, LOVEABLE, INTELLIGENT,
LOVE-OF-MY-LIFE SAID,

"YES!"

1963

ON AUGUST 10, 1963

DOROTHY GLENDA TURCOTTE
&
JAMES EARLE McCARTHY,

WERE WED!!!!

We had a GREAT wedding!

**My Amazing Right Hand slipped a wedding band
on her left ring finger, and, a few vows later,
we were husband and wife!**

Both families were there.

Due to the distance (groom from Goderich, bride from Belleville), it was the first (and for some, the only), time that the two families had a chance to meet each other.

Leaving the church, we were driven around town, horns tooting and tin cans clattering, making as much noise as possible, while pedestrians waved and cheered. Then, we made our way to the reception hall, rented from the Lion's Club for the occasion.

A very talented live band thrashed out some good old country tunes—both fast and slow. They even managed a square dance once everyone had consumed enough alcohol to release some inhibitions.

That was when I chose to croon a love ballad to my new wife,— Glenda McCarthy!

One of our wedding gifts was a cute little Beagle pup that somebody had named "Prince." We took him with us on our honeymoon. About twenty miles from Belleville, there was a small town which boasted a small, but friendly and VERY comfortable motel where I had booked the 'honeymoon suite.'

The next day, after a very late start (wink wink), we had breakfast, then proceeded to Kingston, where we toured historic Old Fort Henry. It was built in 1812 as a bastion of defence from the Americans.

Just what every Canadian newlywed couple wants to do on their honeymoon . . . visit an old fort . . . accompanied by a dog! (lol)

Actually—we were just putting in time, as we were given the use of Glenda's (and now my) aunt and uncle's house in Brockville, as they were just starting THEIR vacation and were on their way to the cottage that they had rented on the St. Lawrence River for a week.

Frankly, we were so much in love that it didn't matter to us WHERE we went—we went together!

***

After a couple of months of renting an apartment in Trenton, we purchased a forty-foot-long, eight-foot wide trailer and now resided just off the Trenton air base in Skyview Trailer Park. Skyview was right on the Bay of Quinte. In fact, if you drove into the trailer park, down the single roadway with trailers on both sides, you would go straight onto a dock and into the bay.

And there was a lovely little weed bed offshore, just enough that you couldn't cast *quite* far enough to catch the pike and bass you could see splashing just out of reach, while catching low-flying insects.

So My Amazing Hands built a punt. It was eight feet long by about four feet wide. The size of a sheet of plywood. Co-incidence?

I was just learning about woodworking!

I was given some paint, so it ended up a grayish-green colour. Perfect for fishing and duck hunting.

A local marina had a small used 3hp outboard that I bought cheap. It had a small gasoline tank attached, but it used so little gas that it would last all day. Not fast, but it didn't have to be.

Then my twenty-six-year-old, faithful '37 Chevy quit!

It literally fell apart, almost all at the same time, it seemed. There was so much wrong. It wasn't fixable, so I had it hauled to that great old car scrapyard off somewhere down a back road. I waved goodbye as it disappeared down the road, strapped to the back of a trailer driven by a big, burly guy chewing on an unlit cigar stub.

A few days later, Glenda needed some medicine, and I was tired out from a day of marching, so I went into town ... slowly ... in the punt! The round trip took over two hours. I could have walked it in one.

However ... one of my friends, who still lived on the base, had a motorcycle. He drew temporary duty at RCAF Stn Resolute Bay for three months and didn't have anywhere to store his baby — his bike!

He asked if he could leave it at my trailer. He also said I could learn to ride it if I wanted to.

Well, beside the trailer park was a soccer field with a dirt track. I could access it through my backyard. I had another friend who knew about motorcycles, so he gave me lessons. If you refer back to 1958, you will see that I already had the big M on my driver's licence.

So I could drive my buddy's cycle—LEGALLY (well, ... sort of)—while he was away.

He thanked me for letting him store it—I thanked him for letting me ride it!

Later ... I bought a little Honda 90cc from a guy who was transferred to B.C. ... and a helmet for Glenda. Mobile again; I caught lots of fish with the punt. However, I just about killed myself with that little Honda. Another day, a month or so later, I had to take a trip downtown. I left the punt at home and took the wee motorcycle. It had been drizzling, so the roads were wet. Hwy 2, when it gets near downtown Trenton, makes a fairly abrupt left curve, then it goes down a hill, then over a bridge at the Trent River and on downtown. Just before the bridge, there is a side street to the left. I noticed a flatbed truck that seemed to be slowing, going down the hill. I tried to slow down also, off the gas, and just lightly on the brake.

It didn't slow down, but the truck did.

He was going to turn onto the side street. I couldn't stop in time. All I could do was lay the bike on its side and hope for the best! I looked up as I passed the truck, still on the bike, on its side, and saw the bottom of the flatbed passing about a foot over my head.

After the truck passed, I hit a pot-hole in the road, and the little Honda bounced upright again, with me still in the saddle!

My Amazing Hands steered me to the side of the road, then shook for a while.

And I prayed my thanks to God because, He undoubtedly, saved me that day!

***

We lived close to a Dairy Queen outlet.

Occasionally, after I got home from work, Glenda and I would walk down to Dairy Queen to buy 'supper' and some ice cream.

One day, they were testing a new food that had just been added to their menu – onion rings!

We had never eaten them before!

M-m-m-m! We had never tasted anything so good!

That weekend, my brother, Ken, and his wife, Sharon, came for a visit. We immediately headed down to Dairy Queen to have some onion rings.

They became addicted to them also and came to visit us much more often!

***

One day, I took some documents to an officer inside one of the hangars.

After the delivery and getting the required signature, I saw a couple of guys I knew. They were standing beside a fat rope attached to the steel ceiling beams.

"What's going on?" I asked.

"Frankie here says he can climb to the top of this rope and touch the ceiling!"

"Looks pretty easy to me," says I.

Suddenly everybody was talking, then shouting, and a small crowd gathered. Then the friendly betting began.

These guys didn't know me very well because I worked on the other side of Highway 2 at Air Transport Command Headquarters. These guys all worked on the hanger line at RCAF Station Trenton.

So, most of the guys there were betting on Frankie.

I didn't know if I could climb that rope or not. If I fell from the top, I would seriously hurt myself—if I didn't KILL myself. But . . . I was young and dumb and thought I was indestructible. Frankie climbed the rope first.

He gave it a great try but only made it about three-quarters of the way up before his arms gave out, and he slid back down. Frankie obviously worked out, but all that muscle added a lot of weight.

I was just a skinny-ass kid of about 135 pounds. And my only 'muscle' was between my ears!

But I had My Amazing Hands, that pulled me up . . . hand-over-hand . . . up ten feet . . . twenty feet . . . fifty feet (I was starting to sweat) . . . sixty feet . . . seventy feet (I didn't dare look down) . . . eighty feet . . . (we all had 'guesstimated the ceiling to be about a hundred feet high) . . . (my left hand was starting to tremble) . . . ninety feet (people looked SO small down there) . . . one hundred feet . . . almost to the ceiling!

How high was this damn ceiling, anyway?

FINALLY, I reached out with one of My Amazing Hands and not only touched . . . but actually SLAPPED the ceiling so everyone on the ground below could HEAR it!

A hush fell over the spectators for a few seconds, then a huge round of applause, with shouting and whistling as I slid back down the rope.

My Amazing Hands brought something extra nice home to my wife that evening, and lots of onion rings, bought with my winnings!

Thank you, Station Trenton hangar line workers from a nerd at Command Headquarters.

***

I loved music—making it and singing it. Still do!

But I also had other interests, like —fishing and hunting. Also, I took up archery.

An archery club was on the base, and all the equipment was supplied.

So I attended a meeting where the recreation staff recruited anyone interested in learning the sport. I was VERY interested, and My Amazing Hands became skilled at accurately shooting a bow.

While the provided equipment was great, I wanted my own, so I purchased a forty lb. pull Ben Pearson Pinto recurve bow. I also bought a clip thing called a 'bow quiver' that mounted to the bow and held a couple of arrows.

Try something . . . pick a small object, about the size of an apple . . . ten or fifteen feet away.

Pretend to shoot it with your index finger.

Now, close one eye and then the other without moving your hand.

You will find that one eye is pointing your 'gun' at the target. The other is not.

That is your DOMINANT eye.

Because the base-supplied equipment I used to 'learn' archery with was right-handed, I purchased a bow that felt comfortable to me—a right-handed one.

But my LEFT eye is my dominant eye.

I was always shooting my arrows to the right of the bulls-eye.

So, to fix this, I purchased a 'bow sight' that would align the cross-hairs, and it would put my arrows into the bulls-eye every time. Slick, huh?

I taught other people about archery, joined the Canadian Archery Association, and they designated me as a 'Qualified Instructor.' Consequently, I showed a lot of airmen and airwomen how to shoot a bow and helped them get their own personal equipment. I also helped to organize tournaments between RCAF Stations to make it even more fun. My love of fishing was incorporated, as I also learned how to bow-fish for carp—an environmentally destructive, unwanted fish!

***

In 1963, My Amazing Hands did the ultimate Amazing thing!

Here's the story . . .

As I've mentioned, I had a 'Top Secret' security clearance.

I worked daily locked in a small room with a steel door, with but one other access – a small window with bars. I worked with Corporal Carm Vachon. He was a terrific guy.

He loved to swim.

If it wasn't busy, he could leave me alone to run Classified Central Registry, and he would go to the station's indoor pool and swim some laps.

Officers, airmen and airwomen would drop off and pick up all manner of classified documents and small parcels at my small window. The documents were classified from Restricted up to and including Top Secret. All required a signature, coming and going.

Part of my job entailed changing the padlock and safe combinations daily, weekly, or monthly, depending upon what was in the safe or filing cabinet and the security clearance of the officer whose safe or filing cabinet it was.

So I got to know the officers and chatted with them as I changed their safe combinations.

Air Commodore Reginald John Lane was Air Officer Commanding Air Transport Command.

One day, he asked me if I was qualified to operate the 16 mm. projectors in the conference room. When I replied in the negative, he made a phone call to the Flight Lieutenant who was in charge of Classified Central Registry—my superior officer.

I was told to report to the station film labs for training the next morning.

At the end of the next day, I was the only airman at Air Transport Command Headquarters with a Top Secret security clearance authorized to operate 16 mm projectors. This was in 1963 and was the only way to view films back then.

My superior officer told me that there had been some major exercises recently involving North Atlantic Treaty Organization (NATO) troops, ships, and aircraft. Air Transport Command Headquarters was hosting a major conference to discuss these excercises. Films would have been taken during the exercises. They would now be shown and discussed.

That was why it was imperative that the film operator have a Top Secret security clearance and also be certified to operate the 16 mm projectors.

The conference room was in the same building I worked in daily but on the third floor.

To My Amazing Hands, it was just another day at the office!

The films were delivered to me at Classified Central Registry the day before by an officer who had an armed escort. This was while the geopolitical tension between the Soviet Union and the United States—including both the Eastern and Western Blocs—was still festering—a mere eighteen years since World War II.

And . . . there were a long series of terrorist attacks perpetrated by the Front De Liberation Du Quebec (FLQ). They were eventually responsible for more than 200 bombings and dozens of robberies between 1963 and 1970. Six people died during that period.

Consequently, on the day of the special conference, when I changed floors with the film canisters, I had an armed guard, even though it only involved carrying them up three levels. An armed guard wasn't unusual for me, though, as I had an armed escort whenever I had to transport classified documents, so I was used to it.

I locked the door to the projectionist booth behind me when I entered and proceeded to load the first canister of film into the projector. Then I took out my newspaper and waited. Before long, I could hear strange voices coming from the conference room.

I heard bits and pieces of many foreign languages. I recognized French, of course, and English, spoken with various dialects, and guessed at Italian and Spanish and many words in a totally unknown (to me) tongue.

A/C Lane peeked around the door to ask if I was all set and did I need anything?

When I replied in the negative, he told me that he wanted the first film very soon—after his opening remarks. He said to load the next canister right away, and he would use the PA to tell me what to do from there.

Things went smoothly, and around ten thirty, while they were taking a break, he brought me a coffee and asked if I could stay there instead of going to the Other Ranks Mess for lunch.

He said he would make sure that I got something to eat.

Of course, I said, "Yes, Sir!"

At noon, he returned and told me to come with him . . . he had a seat for me in the conference room.

I opened the door and stepped into the conference room. WOW!

I hadn't seen so much power in my life.

ALL of these men were dressed either in uniform or in silk suits. Rows of medals decorated EVERY chest. Sashes and cummerbunds were everywhere. Gold braid adorned shoulders, sleeves, and epaulets.

Some even had brass and silver-handled sabres. I couldn't even try to guess *their* rank!

The two gentlemen to the left of where I was seated were chattering away, with hands and arms flailing —and I didn't understand a single word that they said.

However, the two gentlemen to my right were finishing their conversation when the gentleman to my immediate right turned to me and, with a very heavy accent, said, "Hello!"

He told me that he was 'Frederick' and was from Denmark, as he adjusted the golden sabre at his waist!

Then he asked my name, and My Amazing Right Hand shook his!

When I replied stiffly, "LAC McCarthy, sir!" he said, "Non! Non! What do your friends call you?"

That totally put me at ease. After telling him, "I am Jim," with his limited English, he asked me about my family and told me about his.

He asked me if I was born in Canada and had ever travelled abroad. I told him about my trip to Paris.

A white-clad waiter brought us some small sandwiches and soup.

Then something I didn't recognize in a bowl, with rolls. Then . . .

I decided that I definitely didn't belong in THIS room.

I wanted to get back to familiar surroundings . . . so after shaking my new friend's hand with one of My Amazing Hands . . . I went to the projection room.

Ten minutes or so later, A/C Lane appeared with a waiter who brought me a piece of apple pie a la mode and some coffee on a tray.

He told me to be ready to start in a few minutes.

I was ready!

1964

My son, William (Bill) Roberts McCarthy, was born on Sunday, May 10, 1964.

He was named after my Grampa Roberts, who gave so much help and advice to Glenda and me during the first few months of our marriage.

My Amazing Hands held my newborn son when I was first introduced to him that Sunday at Belleville General Hospital.

Later, at home, My Amazing Hands changed his diaper. He and I have been great friends ever since.

My Amazing Hands would have more children to cuddle ere long!

***

I was a NASTE boy!

Sounds terrible, but it wasn't so bad. It is the acronym for the (N-A-S-T-E) . . . Nuclear Accident Support TEam!

As I've mentioned, the Cold War was in full swing.

Canada and the USA were regularly flying nuclear-capable weapons to the far north. Apparently, a LOT of these aircraft were flying in the Trenton area, although they were too high to see. There was concern that one of these aircraft could have to make a 'forced landing' (aka—'crash landing') on Canadian soil! Hence, the NASTE boys would track the radioactivity should this occur.

So, in case the aircraft involved in the accident was transporting highly classified documents and/or other material, they needed ME to transport these things as I have a Top Secret security clearance. Ergo, I was 'asked to volunteer' to join the NASTE boys.

My Amazing Hands received training in using a Geiger counter, and we were either trucked, bused, or helicoptered to a theoretical crash site.

Then, we used Geiger counters to identify and stake off any radioactive areas.

But during our preliminary training, we were taken to a small Quonset hut behind one of the hangars.

It was divided into two sections.

In the first section, we stripped to our skivvies. Then we dressed in a pair of coveralls to be taped at the ankles and wrists.

You were 'buddied-up.' You taped him . . . he taped you.

Galoshes were worn over a pair of running shoes and also taped. Rubber gloves, taped at the wrists, completed our ensemble. An oxygen mask was taped around the face, and a small oxygen tank was carried on the back.

Then we were 'invited' into the 'second' section by a chuckling corporal.

Unbelievable!

The second section was where we got to test how well we had taped each other!

TEAR GAS! The room was full of TEAR GAS!

Pretty much immediately, you could tell which guys were taped by a friend and which were taped by a stranger!

To make it even MORE fun, an obstacle course had to be endured. Wearing all this paraphernalia, we had to go around obstacles (tables, small chairs, boxes), making our way, slowly, to the other end of the room, where there was a small bridge of stairs to climb over before we could go through the small door and out into that blessed sunshine and FRESH AIR!

I took my turn buying a round the night before for the rest of our class at the Other Ranks club on the base, so the guy that I partnered up with was a friendly face, and I didn't have any issues going through that room, but it was STILL an absolute delight to get outside, rip off the mask, and suck in some fresh, sunshiny air.

Some of the guys had to be helped through the middle room.

And there was a small change room with clean skivvies for those that required them. (Wink! Wink!).

I guess you know that the wet canteen got another visit by our bunch again THAT night.

We were first helicoptered out on an exercise a day later. It was the middle of summer.

I can't describe how hot it was inside this outfit.

And I had 'volunteered' for this! I couldn't get out of it now!

Except, I got an idea...

I noticed that a couple of guys were simulating casualties, and they got removed on a stretcher RIGHT AWAY, in an ambulance or an ambulatory chopper, and taken as quickly as possible back to RCAF Stn Trenton.

A few days later, the NASTE boys got called into action again.

However...

My Amazing Hands had contacted the officer in charge of the NASTE boys. I suggested to him that if they wanted a more realistic scenario that provided even more practice for the medical staff, a NASTE boy should also be used in their simulation. I volunteered!

So when we got called into action, I got dressed, taped, and transported, but I immediately dropped to the ground . . . simulating being unconscious. (Not too hard to do on that hot day.)

I was lifted onto a stretcher, then loaded in a field ambulance, then into a chopper, then flown to Trenton, loaded into another ambulance and transported to the hospital. I was expected.

They had a couple of male orderlies and a couple of VERY attractive female nurses waiting in an outer garage-like room to cut the tape and assist me out of the coveralls.

Then, to my great surprise, after removing my watch and wallet, the orderlies each grabbed a hose and thoroughly hosed me down. THAT cooled me down in a BIG hurry. B-r-r-r!

Then, they took me inside, and those pretty nurses removed my clothes . . . ALL of them . . .

AND THEY WASHED ME AGAIN!

But this time, the water was warm. Thank you, nurses!

Then they gave me a pair of one-size-fits-all pyjamas and wrapped me in a warm bathrobe, and someone from the motor pool drove me home.

I "forgot" to tell my wife about the nurses!

1965

My Amazing Hands held my second oldest son, James Earle McCarthy Jr., the day he was born, May 3, 1965.

It was a great Monday when I first saw his little face smiling up at me. I was probably doing one of those 'goofy Daddy faces' back at him!

He has had a rocky ride with many ups and downs, but he has ALWAYS been there for me.

And he's always been and still is . . . smiling!

His Amazing Hands have made him a great turkey hunter and a great fisherman.

Jim doesn't do a lot of emails. So when he does—HE MEANS IT!

Here's an email I received from my fantastic son recently:

> **"If there is one statement in your book that pertains to me when it comes to you, it's this . . .**
>
> **. . . One time, someone asked me who my best friend in the whole world is.**
>
> **. . . I responded with this, right out of the blue and from the heart . . . My dad!"**

I was left speechless! Thank you for your kind words, son!
I'M VERY, VERY PROUD OF YOU, JIM!

MY AMAZING HANDS

***

One windy day, a friend took me for a sailboat ride on the Bay of Quinte. I had never been on a sailboat before, and I was smitten!

He told me that ten small sailboats moored at the on-base yacht club belonged to the Air Force. To use them, all you needed was to join the sailing club and get some basic instructions on sailing.

So I joined this on-base club, took the instructions, and got involved.

My Amazing Hands took us sailing on the Bay.

I was also able to participate in racing around buoys for fun and ribbons (I never won, but I had lots of fun trying.)

After further training, I joined the Ontario Sailing Association and became a 'Qualified Instructor'!

My Amazing Hands were teaching others to sail.

What fun!

1966

Now that I had a wife and two small boys, I took stock of myself, my family, and our future.

I was being reminded more and more often that I had been stationed at Air Transport Command Headquarters for over five years, and I HAD to move on.

Only two bases in Canada and two overseas required an airman with my qualifications.

Overseas meant struggling with a new foreign language for myself, my wife, and the boys. It also meant not seeing either of our families for long periods. That wasn't acceptable, so I quickly ruled it out.

The only two bases in Canada were Resolute Bay, which meant I would be stuck in a frozen northland without my family for three-month increments, and Comox British Colombia. Again, that meant that Glenda and I would not see our respective families for extended periods. And we would have to start over in this new environment, 'cold turkey!'

And the minimum time before I could be transferred again was two years. So, as much as I loved my job, I had to face hard reality and request my discharge.

I got out of the Air Force about as quickly as I got in.

My Amazing Hands were honourably discharged from the RCAF on June 10, 1966.

During the preceding winter, Carl and Susan, a lovely middle-aged couple, rented the trailer next to ours for the season. We became friends instantly.

Carl had opened and operated a go-kart track in Welland on the huge, mostly unused parking lot of a grocery superstore. He showed me some pictures as he told me about it. He had six 'karts' and dozens of old truck tires laid out 'the track.' Susan ran the pay booth, and patrons (usually kids, depending on the time of day or evening) would buy their tickets, pick a kart, and line up at the starting line.

Carl ran the track with a teenage 'helper,' who would usually start the race with a green flag, count the 'laps,' wave the winner home with a checkered flag, and get the karts ready for the next 'race.'

Carl also sold Polaroid photos of the winners with their plastic 'trophies.'

It looked like a fun way to make a buck, so when Carl told me that he would like to open another track in Niagara Falls that summer and offered me the opportunity to run this one. It didn't take Glenda and me long to decide to move the trailer there after my discharge.

He offered me a salary plus half-ownership after two seasons. It sounded much better than overseas, Resolute Bay, or Comox, so I took the offer.

But it took so much of our time. There wasn't much time left for our boys or visiting family.

So when Glenda got pregnant, we decided to move to Goderich, where I had family and prospects of finding a regular job.

***

In 1966, my Grampa passed away at the age of 81. He had numerous heart issues before his death.

William James Roberts was born in Wales in 1885.

He and his wife, Edith (my nana), had two children, Edward (Ted), born in 1909, and my mother, Dorothy Isobel. She was born on November 2, 1919.

When I was just a little tyke of two or three, Grampa used to pick me up and put me on his knee and (even though he definitely wasn't a singer) sang, 'When The Midnight Choo-Choo Leaves For Alabam,' bouncing me up and down in rhythm with the music.

I was a 'Young Rapscallion' or a 'Scalawag.' He called Mom 'Dory.' We called him 'Gamper.'

In my mind, I STILL can 'see' his old, flat, gray cap that he wore to keep his balding head warm.

And how he used to roll his cigarettes, by hand . . . until Mom bought him a new-fangled gadget that would roll one long cigarette that you could cut into five regular-sized ones with a razor blade.

Every time I would visit, either alone, with my parents, or later, with my wife and kids, I would get out the old roller and roll him up a can of his favourite tobacco—'Old Mill.'

Grampa was a cabinet maker by trade and worked most of his life at Kroehler's in Stratford.

He developed heart trouble after he left Kroehler's.

After Nana passed away back in 1961, my parents helped him sell the house, settle his estate and move in with them in Goderich, so that Mom could nurse him in his later years.

Bless you, Mom and Dad, for your kindness!

And Grampa . . . My Amazing Hands salute you!

I named my first-born after you in recognition of the help and kindness you gave to Glenda and me when we dated, got engaged, married, then became new parents.

I've always loved you and looked up to you!

1967

I needed a full-time job, so I started knocking on doors.

Dominion Road Machinery Company in Goderich was impressed with my credentials and hired me to work in the Parts Department. This company made Champion brand road graders, and dozens and dozens of parts went into their manufacture.

My job was to ensure that there were enough parts on hand to supply the demand from the assembly line on the main floor. So I constantly went down to "babysit" the parts flow to the guys on the floor. My Amazing Hands would count parts, check parts, receive parts, return parts, call suppliers, etc., etc., to ensure it all ran smoothly. I got to know the guys as we chatted intermittently throughout the day.

The finished grader was driven out and parked in a "holding shed" at the end of the line.

One day, I happened to be there when one was completed, and the foreman asked me if I would like to drive it out. He talked me through starting it, checking the various mechanisms, driving it out, and parking it.

All the guys were whistling and cheering and applauding!

While I don't pretend to know much about road graders, I can, legitimately, say that My Amazing Hands drove a Champion road grader! WOW!

***

On Tuesday, May 23, 1967, my sweet little daughter, Jillian, was born. She was such a good baby and grew up to be a very pretty young lady.

My Amazing Hands held this sweet girl when she was just a few minutes old. It was, however, a difficult birth for Glenda. Mother and daughter were taken to Western University Hospital in London, Ontario, by ambulance for treatment and recovery. All I had at the time was the little Honda 90 motorcycle, as we couldn't afford a car.

So the next day, after getting time off from my job at Dominion Road Machinery Company, I jumped on my little Honda, and off I went . . . down Hwy 8 to Clinton, then south on Hwy 4 to London.

It was such a small, light "bike" that every puff of wind, every draft from every passing car or truck made the bike waver, so I couldn't get any speed up for fear of losing control.

I should have known better than to be concerned, as My Amazing Hands got me there and back . . . slowly . . . but safely. I got to satisfy myself that my wife, Glenda, and daughter, Jillian, were okay.

My Amazing Hands got to hold baby Jillian again.

And didn't lose my parts department job! Instead, they encouraged me. What a GREAT company!

***

With the next paycheque, after taking care of our needs, I traded the Honda 90 in for a Honda 125!

Shortly after that, I purchased another inexpensive car . . . on a payment plan, of course, as the motorcycle just didn't fit the needs of a growing family.

In 1967, I also joined the Goderich Town Band.

I was the lead drummer, playing snare drum.

We used to play 'sit down' concerts at places like the town bandshell, school auditorium, cenotaph, etc.

We also played while marching, at various events, like the Santa Claus, Memorial Day, and various other town parades and events.

During one of our weekly practices, it was announced that our bass drummer was moving away.

The conductor asked if anyone knew someone who could take over the bass drum.

MY AMAZING HANDS

Now my dad was over six feet tall and in pretty good shape. He was a switchman for the CNR – his job entailed jumping on and off trains as they shunted boxcars around the Goderich yards.

I didn't think he would have any problem handling the bass drum.

One evening, I brought the bass drum, harness, and mallets home from band practice.

Dad was already in bed, as his job meant rising early, so I smuggled the drum into the basement with no one the wiser.

The next day, just after supper, I told Dad to wait for me in the backyard, as I had something to show him. He thought I was referring to his garden, as both my parents were avid gardeners.

You can imagine his surprise when I brought out the bass drum. He was even more surprised when I helped him try it on, then got my snare drum and put it on.

He didn't know what I was going to ask him to do!

My Amazing Hands got him to join me, then father and son marched around and around our backyard—drumming!

I learned he had a great sense of rhythm.

The neighbours came out and hung over their fences to cheer us on. I announced that HE was the new bass drummer for the Goderich Town Band.

He couldn't have been more surprised.

WE couldn't have been prouder!

As time went by, I taught him how to read the bass drum line of sheet music and twirl the mallets. The drum sat on a stand when we were doing concerts. I taught him how to cross the mallets over the top of the drum and play one cymbal on top of the drum while maintaining the bass drum beat with the other hand during concerts.

Dad kept the beat perfectly!

One of the other band members had a young, blonde daughter, about seven or eight years old.

I remember her name was Elizabeth, and she was a tiny, cute little gal.

She used to march between her dad and my dad, playing the triangle.

The long and short of it!

1968

My Amazing Hands joined a group called The Country Boys.

The leader of the band, George, was the local Superior Propane salesperson during the day.

We played a variety of gigs around the area.

We had a drummer, an electric bass, George played lead guitar, and I played rhythm.

However, because we were all versatile, we would switch instruments... I'd jump on drums for a set, and the two guitars would alternate the lead parts. Then, we'd all change around again. We'd alternate the vocals, too. In some songs, I'd take the lead... in some songs, I'd sing harmony... in some songs, I'd sing bass (putting my chin on my chest and hoping for the best croaking sound).

The electric bass player, Hudson, stayed put. He didn't sing. Just played bass. But we paid him the same anyway because he was a nice guy... and a darned good bass player! People loved us. Great times! And great country music!

I was also drumming in another small group called the Pros and Cons that a few of us had put together about that time. Jeff S., the local chiropractor's son; Hudson W., a preacher's son; and two railroader's sons —my brother, Ken, and I—made up the group. Jeff was the frontman and lead singer. He also played tambourine. Hudson played bass. Ken played guitar. I, of course, played drums and harmonized (but no bass vocals).

MY AMAZING HANDS

We did a couple of gigs . . . I remember when we played on a hay wagon in the street for a car dealer's gala introducing his new car line. We also played in the 'square' in Goderich. The 'square' was actually an octagon—eight streets running north, south, east, and west (and named accordingly), with streets in between. The town courthouse was in the middle, with eight walkways leading up to it. In between was a beautifully treed grassy area.

That's where we set up—on the grass. I don't recall the occasion, but quite a few folks were listening to our music.

We even got our band name, and individual names, on the front page of the *Goderich Signal-Star* newspaper. It's hard to describe the special feeling you get when you see YOUR picture and name on the front page of your local newspaper. Mom and dad were very impressed with their offspring . . . we could tell!

I kept the original article from 1968 and partially restored the picture that accompanied it. My Amazing Hands are drumming in the photo, and Ken was playing his guitar! This was the first band that my brother, Ken, and I both played in.

And we were both on the FRONT PAGE! How GREAT is THAT!

1969

Ken married his high school sweetheart, Sharon Ryan, on September 19, 1969.

After the wedding party left the church, we drove around the square, Goderich's downtown, with a motorcycle escort. About fifteen of Ken's biker buddies decided to let the town know about his marriage by revving up their motorcycles and tooting their horns.

My Amazing Hands were waving—wishing the happy couple a great start to a superb marriage!

Time travel ahead to 2019. We celebrated their fiftieth wedding anniversary! YA-HOO!

***

I recall that I used to take my family down to the beach at Goderich, where I once again met my old schoolmate, NHL star, Larry Jeffrey. Larry had recently retired from the NHL due to injuries and had purchased the concession stand at the beach. I took the family to the booth for burgers and to say hi to him. My Amazing Hands shook his amazing hand once again. He remembered me from high school.

While there, I showed the family the famous Goderich Grain Elevators. Back when Dad was shunting boxcars around, he arranged for me to have a guided tour up those elevators to the very top. I still remember them. They were HUGE!!!

MY AMAZING HANDS

***

Mom and Dad got me involved in the Goderich Amateur Theatre again.

The troupe was putting on a play but didn't have a sound effects guy. Mom 'volunteered' me, as I had recording equipment (an old reel-to-reel tape machine) and a microphone.

In the script, someone leaves. You hear them driving away, then a tremendous crash. Then the actor re-appears, dishevelled and dazed, holding a broken steering wheel.

So . . . I went to my parent's house. My Amazing Hands ran a long extension cord out to the street.

Then Dad backed my old car out of the driveway, revved the engine, then drove away past me and my microphone. I was recording it ALL. Next, still recording, I had him frantically toot the car's loud horn. Then . . . .

He had an old set of lawn furniture, an all-metal table, and chairs. He smashed them together, a little at first, then more, ending in a crescendo of loud crashing.

It worked GREAT in the play . . . precisely what the director was looking for.

And Dad and I had a heck of a lot of fun.

The neighbours sure were curious, though, . . . so we sold them tickets to the play.

Our parents both worked backstage—dad constructing and painting 'sets'—mom working on makeup and wardrobe.

Eventually, they took a crack at acting . . . and they were GREAT!

When the theatre group decided to put a float in the annual Christmas Parade, they played the 'mom and dad' characters, while the rest of the members provided the children and danced, in costume, alongside.

My Amazing Hands filmed it all.

In one play, a character played a man who was shot dead on stage. Someone phoned for an ambulance. My brother and I played ambulance attendants. We came on stage with a stretcher, loaded the actor, then carried him off. The first night, we arrived on the scene, lifted him onto the stretcher, raised him, —AND DARNED NEAR DROPPED HIM.

As he put out a foot to save himself, then sat up, the audience roared with laughter! It's a good thing it was a comedy, even though it wasn't written with laughter at that point! We thought we should do it again the next night, but the director cut that idea short.

The other nights were uneventful. We took our bows along with the rest of the cast.

So . . . I was smitten with amateur theatre after Mom and Dad got me further involved.

1970

Working as a parts clerk in a local factory barely paid me enough to get by, and Glenda had her hands full with HER full-time job—looking after the kids and me. The part-time money that I made playing music helped, but it STILL wasn't enough!

So . . .

We moved to Belleville, my wife's hometown, and I got employment there, managing a Beckers convenience store. This job paid enough to meet our needs and provide the children with everything required to fit in, while attending the local schools.

***

I formed another musical group known around Belleville, Trenton, and the surrounding area as Jimmy Jay & the Jaycees and I played in hotels, legions, dance halls, and, of course, on the base. I didn't think that Jim McCarthy was a name people would remember if they saw it on a billboard outside a bar, so I took the nom de plume—Jimmy Jay.

The guys in my band were John and Chuck, hence the Jaycees. John played bass and sang harmony, Chuck was the drummer, and I played guitar and sang lead.

I bought a new guitar—a Gibson—and a new amp. I also bought a wah-wah pedal and a couple of other 'effects' pedals to modernize our sound. And we became card-carrying members of the Belleville Chapter of the International Federation Of Musicians. Joe Burchill was the Secretary of the chapter.

That didn't get us any more money, but it sounded good for advertising and in the newspaper.

There was a whole new generation of musicians and dancers.

It was the Hippy Generation. Go-go dancers were just starting to appear.

The girls would wear mini-skirts and turtle-neck sweaters, or snug-at-the-neck blouses, with fringes sewn on so that when they did *"The Twist,"* or "*The Swim,*" and swivelled their hips, the fringes would swirl around their body.

Very sexy!

The go-go dancers would either be in separate 'cages' or on stage with the band.

Glenda, and Johnny's wife, Brenda, became go-go dancers and danced to our music. They did a great job; both were good dancers and good-looking ladies. It wasn't lewd . . . just fun.

We were popular in hotels especially. The ladies made our band somewhat unique, and we often had our picture in the local paper, along with our names.

WOW!

One unique gig was when we performed one Friday evening in the front window of David's furniture store in downtown Trenton. There were two big windows with the entrance to the store in the middle.

My Amazing Hands played in one window, and the girls danced in the other. Their window always had a bigger audience. (Wink! Wink!).

David's ran a full-page newspaper ad on the back page of the local newspaper, with a picture of the band and the girls. Go-go dancers gradually became less popular because the audience wanted more. Obviously, we didn't want our wives to _do_ more, so they gave way to strippers.

Strippers—far more daring than go-go dancers—travelled from bar to bar, as did the musicians. They had their own, separate, booking agents. In most venues, the band would play for about thirty minutes, then introduce the stripper, who would usually dance to three songs . . . a faster one to strip off her outer clothes. Then a mediocre tempo one where she would show off her dancing skills while losing even more costume, and then a final, sensual song, a bump and grind, where she would be mostly naked.

MY AMAZING HANDS

They wore pasties and a G-string in the early days, but they got removed as time went by Those stages were often quite small, so the dancer would perform while standing beside the lead singer.

I was the lead singer! *YAHOO!*

You might say they were appealing (a-peeling) to me.

I'd be lost in a song, glance over, and the dancer would be gone. She'd be at my feet, lying on the stage, doing her bumping and grinding.

And they would pay me, too!!

A tough job, but somebody had to do it!

S-h-h! Don't tell my wife!

1971

My son, Peter Samuel, was born on Wednesday, February 3, 1971.

Glenda and I had agreed when we first started to raise a family that she would name the girls, and I would name the boys.

So, naming our *firstborn* after a man I respected—a man who helped Glenda and I get our marriage started on the right track, William (Bill) Roberts, my Granpa, just seemed the right thing to do.

And I guess I was showing a lot of vanity when I wanted to name the next male child— Jim Jr. —after myself. But I was proud of my name! Still am! And I wanted him to be proud, too!

I was standing on the riverbank in Belleville when I decided on my next male child's name.

I was on my way home from church.

Our doctor's ultrasound told us that our baby would be a male. I had my Bible in my hand, so I opened it randomly to let the Lord choose his name. I opened it to Peter. Great! I liked Peter as a strong, masculine name, and 'Pete' was a good nickname.

I opened the Bible again to choose his second name.

Then ... I lost my balance, stumbled, and lost my place ... after a quick glance told me where it *would* have opened. I guess the Lord didn't want Peter's second name to be 'Proverbs.' Lol!

The third time, it opened on Samuel.

MY AMAZING HANDS

Peter Samuel McCarthy!

A strong, masculine name, and . . . it has a nice ring to it.

Everyone I spoke to—wife, family, and friends—approved of my name choice.

***

Looking toward my family's future and wanting to finish high school, I attended the *Loyalist College Adult Re-training* program.

My Amazing Hands completed high school, then college, majoring in Accounting, at the college.

But to keep the wolf away from the door, I also had to work. So I would retire early, get up at five, then, after a quick shower and breakfast, I was off to the Red Lobster restaurant, where My Amazing Hands would clean the grease off the grills and chimneys around six.

Then I would pedal downtown to the *Belleville Intelligencer* to count and bundle newspapers at nine a.m. so the trucks could distribute them. I had purchased an inexpensive used bicycle to use around the city when I didn't need the car.

My third job was playing music most weekends.

***

An interesting thing happened to My Amazing Hands in 1971!

I got asked to sit in with a band that needed a drummer for a big band and jazz night being held at the *Belleville School For The Deaf*. At the last minute, their drummer had an emergency.

They played 'by ear' (no sheet music), but that wasn't a problem for me.

So, I got there and set up with the rest of this five-piece combo. I didn't know what to expect . . . our audience was, for the most part, stone-deaf. We kicked off the night and played like we usually did. To our great surprise and delight . . . we got many dancers up on the floor.

You couldn't tell this audience from any other —except for one thing— nobody spoke!

Except for an occasional grunt, the audience was silent.

You guessed it . . . they conversed using sign language!

I spoke to this lady later that night (she told me she could read my lips), and she said that the dancers *'felt'* the vibrations from the music through the floor and their shoes into their feet.

She said music by My Amazing Hands was perfect for deaf folks . . . right on the beat!

1972

My grandma, (Charlotte O. Corrie) McCarthy, died in 1972 at age 89.

Grandma was an amazing woman.

Born in 1883, she married John Augustus McCarthy Jr, and they raised six children:

1. John Augustus III
2. Doris Charlotte
3. Cyril Thomas Britiffe
4. Earl Corrie Dalton
5. Elizabeth Ann
6. Barbara Ethel

Lottie, as friends and family lovingly called her, worked tirelessly to maintain her family home on Nile Street in Stratford, Ontario.

She even took in boarders . . . actors from the Stratford Shakespearean Festival. (Remember 1951?).

My grandma made it a home away from home for these famous people, and she was rewarded monetarily, of course, but also with the pleasure of having these world-renowned actors rehearse lines with grandma as a very willing sounding board.

There was always lots of love and laughter at Grandma McCarthy's house!

And she loved it . . . as we all loved her!

When I was pretty young, I recall being "shush-ed" out of the way because Grandma was vacuuming, sweeping or dusting.

She moved into a nursing home in her later years.

Grandma, we miss you!

***

I had an interesting thing happen 1n 1972!

We performed at a hotel in Cobourg—a venue we had played in many times before.

The first few tables at the front of the seating area would be taken by ladies whenever we performed.

They would flirt mercilessly with the guys in the band as we were performing and usually had a cold beer waiting for us when we took our break, to entice us to sit with them.

It was almost a contest.

Of course, they knew each other, and this 'contest' appeared to be just fun.

I have to be honest, though . . . the attention was flattering.

One night, this one young lady showed a LOT of interest in me . . . she kept me supplied with beer all night, requested many songs, and sat beside me during all of the breaks.

I didn't recall having met her previously, and I didn't think I encouraged anything.

At the end of the night, it took a while to pack up the band equipment and load it into our vehicle for the trip home. I don't remember seeing her around.

We got in the vehicle and drove home . . . the whole band . . . together.

A couple of days later, I was out somewhere with my wife and children.

We lived in a townhouse, an hour's drive from where we had performed a few days previously.

I pulled into the parking lot; my wife got out of the car and walked toward our home with the children running in front of her.

I started to unload our purchases.

Then . . . this guy in the car parked beside me rolled down his window and called me by name.

I noticed a female in his passenger seat. It was my 'fan' from the Cobourg hotel.

He asked me to get in, opened the driver's door, and moved across to the passenger seat as the young lady got out and moved to the back seat.

He introduced himself as her husband!

I didn't know what to do!

So . . . I just waited him out . . . let him make the first move.

It wasn't what I expected.

First . . . he asked her if this was the man she was in love with.

She nodded her head in the affirmative.

Then he turned to me and asked if I was in love with her.

I said, "In love with her? Hell, I don't even know her, other than she bought me a couple of beers at the hotel where we were performing a couple of nights ago!"

I asked him, "Didn't you see who was in my car with me? That was my wife and children . . . that is my family . . . and I love them . . . and only them!

I hope you and your lady get this sorted out, but believe me, I'm not interested in your wife!"

I got out of his car, got my groceries from mine, and went home.

We played in that same hotel once a month for a few years.

And the young ladies still sat at the front. And they still bought the beers for the bands.

But . . . I never saw him or his wife again. I genuinely hope that they sorted it out, reconciled, and are still living happily somewhere with a passel of kids!

Gotta hand it to the guy, though . . . confronting me like that took guts.

I guess he felt that she was worth it!

***

I had the afternoon to complete chores at home, do homework then have an early supper when the kids got home from school.

Then I'm off to Loyalist College in the evening.

I had only completed grade 11 of high school education and wanted so badly to complete grades twelve and thirteen and graduate.

So . . . I attended Loyalist College in the Adult ReTraining program, and not only graduated, but when I remained on at Loyalist to further my education— My Amazing Hands made the DEAN'S LIST in Accounting!

JAMES E. MCCARTHY

***

My Amazing Hands met Jerry Lee Lewis—at the Grand Theatre, Kingston—upstairs in the Green Room after a performance. Here's the story....

Glenda and I had arranged to drive to Kingston with my drummer and friend, Robbie, and his wife, as we all enjoyed Jerry Lee Lewis' music. I sang his songs at pretty well all of our gigs. He was still pretty popular at the time.

There were to be two shows, at seven and again at nine. We had ordered balcony seat tickets over the phone a couple of weeks previously for the earlier show.

However, there was a major thunder and lightning storm that left the theatre with just emergency lighting for quite a while. It was announced that because of this, they were combining the two shows into just one show at eight o'clock, so we had time to kill.

I went to have a smoke and noted my student pass card for Loyalist College in my jacket pocket.

I got an idea.

I thought it would be cool to meet Jerry Lee Lewis in person. So I went out to my car, got my student card, a notepad and a pencil from my schoolbag, and spoke to the guard at the entrance to the backstage area. Not the rear stage door at the back of the building, but the door that allowed access from the main auditorium to the backstage area inside.

I told him I was a reporter for the Loyalist College newspaper and wanted to interview Jerry Lee Lewis.

He couldn't let me back there at that time, as it was too close to show-time—but he told me to come back after the show.

I went back to my seat and told the other three that I had arranged for us to have a private interview with Jerry Lee after the show. I got a lot of "Oh, sure!" and "Yeah, right!"

After a fantastic show—exceeding our expectations—we packed up and left the balcony.

I hurried everyone to get downstairs as quickly as possible, as I didn't want to keep Jerry Lee waiting.

We made our way through the emptying theatre, and there was my new buddy, the backstage security guard.

MY AMAZING HANDS

He recognized me and waved us through a small crowd of fans, and there we were... suddenly backstage!

WOW!

My wife's eyes were huge!

My buddy and his wife were looking at me with total respect!

I asked a nearby stagehand where Jerry Lee was, and he directed me to a set of stairs that led to the Green Room.

Everyone assumed that we were Jerry's personal friends, so we were ushered up the stairs into the Green Room, and right up to Jerry Lee Lewis.

My Amazing Hands shook his Amazing Hand!

I asked for, and received, his autograph.

I still have it! I kept it all these years.

I introduced Robbie and his wife.

Jerry Lee kissed her cheek.

And when I introduced Glenda, she, too, received a kiss from Jerry Lee Lewis. Wow!

The energy to perform must have tired him out, as he collapsed in an easy chair, closed his eyes, and fell asleep!

I commented to someone about it, and they said he often did so.

So....

Yes, I knew Jerry Lee Lewis. I spoke with 'The Killer' and shook his hand. And let him kiss my wife.

Jerry died on October 28, 2022, at the age of 87.

He succumbed to one of the various illnesses from which he suffered.

I still sing his songs.

'*Whole Lotta Shakin' Goin' On*' is still one of my often-requested favourites.

Oh... I almost forgot to tell you all about Red Sovine!

He sang '*Phantom 309*,' '*Roses For Mama*,' '*Teddy Bear*,' and many other Country Trucker songs.

Did I *really* meet Red Sovine that night?

Smoke with him on the back steps of the theatre?

Eat popcorn with him that we bought at the theatre across the street?

DID I???

All of the answers are YES! YES, I DID!

While waiting for the show to start, I slipped out for a smoke and a stroll. I wandered around the building to the stage entrance at the back.

I saw a man sitting on the stairs. I thought he might tell me something interesting about the show, so I said hello, and we chatted. Then we each bought a box of popcorn from the theatre across the street and shared it while on the steps.

One of my My Amazing Hands shook his, and we went back inside . . . me in the front door, he in the rear.

I had no idea who he was until the Master of Ceremonies introduced him when the show started.

Introducing . . . "RED SOVINE."

And there was my smoking and popcorn-sharing buddy!

A VERY nice guy!!

1973

I was sitting at home one night in my T-shirt and shorts, wrestling with the boys and the dog, when suddenly there was a knock at the front door.

Glenda was busy getting supper ready, so I, accompanied by my excited kids, answered it.

There stood two very distinguished-looking gentlemen dressed in suits and ties. They introduced themselves as Ramon and Doug Walmsley from Dixie Lee as I was handed a business card. They told me they got my name from a friend at Loyalist College and said they had a business proposition to discuss with me.

The two men glanced at my attire and surroundings, children clinging to my legs, and asked if I could meet with them the next day. I told them it would have to be in the afternoon as I wouldn't be available until noon. (I had early-morning work to do at Red Lobster! Remember?) We agreed to meet at their offices.

So, the next day, after cleaning the grills, getting the newspapers to the carriers, getting showered, having lunch, getting all suited up, and driving to their offices, I finally got some quiet time with the owners of the Dixie Lee Fried Chicken franchise.

I was told that Ramon Walmsley was the company's owner, and his brother, Doug, was the general manager. The two gentlemen explained that the company sold chicken and fish, with accoutrements, to the public, whereas Kentucky Fried Chicken, their competitor, didn't sell fish.

They had maintained company-owned and operated outlets, as well as privately owned franchises. They were expanding rapidly, and more locations would be opening shortly! The business was growing so quickly that it needed an operations manager.

A professor at Loyalist College suggested that they talk to **ME!**

My Amazing Hands met the criteria of a young family man who had top grades, majored in accounting, was clean-cut and eager to get involved in business and make his way in the world. It was decided that I would start immediately by working in the local Dixie Lee store for two weeks. After that time, if it was mutually agreed that it was a good fit for us both, I would start immediately—as operations manager for Ontario for Dixie Lee Fried Chicken.

The two weeks flew by, and I learned all about the retail end of the business.

I worked in the kitchen mixing, cooking, washing, and frying, and soon knew **all** about chicken and fish and potatoes, and the Dixie Lee way of preparing, serving, and selling our products!

And mopping floors and vacuuming rugs, and cleaning and dusting. The staff there loved me!

I wore a white apron and one of those cute little hats. I packed the boxes to make up the snacks, dinners, and buckets and even gave personal attention to the customers. As I wore a 'company' badge with my name and title, 'Operations Manager,' they loved the personal attention they got from a 'company big-shot.'.

They didn't know I was a trainee, and I certainly didn't tell them. If an extra piece of chicken happened to get into their dinner, it could have been ***anybody's*** error. (tongue-in-cheek!)

Two weeks later, My Amazing Hands received its first paycheque, and it included a little bonus 'for the kids'.

Thank you, Walmsleys!

I was told that the construction of a new, company-owned store would be completed in a couple of weeks in Napanee, just a short drive from Belleville. Now I know why hiring an Operations Manager was a priority. I went there the next morning, met the newly hired manager, and we developed a plan for hiring and training staff.

Non-perishable supplies had already been ordered for the opening, and I had arranged a meeting with the company that would provide frozen fish and chicken. I attended their factory and saw the process from the time the chickens arrived, were put on the conveyor belt, killed, plucked, eviscerated, inspected, cut into nine, and put in iced boxes.

The nine pieces would be two thighs, two drumsticks, two side ribs, two wings, and a breast.

The order would be packed on ice with eight chickens per carton.

The fish came frozen, wrapped in slabs, and then were kept in chest freezers.

The staff would remove the slabs, as required, the night before and, when thawed, would cut portion sizes that were checked regularly on a portion scale.

My Amazing Hands got VERY good at guess-timating how to cut the portions to the correct size!

The batter was pre-mixed, but the fish were dipped and fried on demand for super freshness!

The store had a refrigerated unit to hold the perishable, non-frozen items.

My Amazing Hands learned how to cook.

The Napanee Dixie Lee Fried Chicken store opened on time and was a great success! Again, after a very nice bonus for a job well done, I was sent to Stratford to open a store there.

And I was still making a few bucks 'on the side' playing and singing with Jimmy Jay & the Jaycees.

And having a ball!

One day, I received a message that Doug wanted to see me at the corporate offices.

He told me the company was considering opening a location in Nassau in The Bahamas.

He wanted to know if I was available this coming weekend to fly down with him on Friday evening, returning on Sunday evening. We will look for a suitable site on Saturday. I knew Doug preferred not to drive, so I put two and two together and told Glenda that I wouldn't be home for the weekend.

I picked up Doug at his home on Friday, left my car there (Glenda didn't drive), and off we went to Toronto Pearson International Airport.

Doug looked after the tickets, we boarded, and we landed in Nassau six and a half hours later. Doug had already made hotel reservations, and after a couple of drinks at the bar, we were both tired, so we went to bed.

Yes, we DID get some prices of possible sites, spoke to suppliers, etc.

Thus it was confirmed to the tax guys that this was a commercial trip . . . not a recreational one.

So, the business out of the way, Doug and I donned our bathing suits and hit the beach.

Bikinis were everywhere!

I walked down to the fishing wharf in the early evening and watched some of the deep-sea fishing vessels offloading their catches.

Some of those fish were HUGE!

Being a freshwater fisherman, I had no idea what species of fish they were.

My Amazing Hands fed me some absolutely awesome fresh red snapper for supper and helped me sample a LOT of super-fresh tropical fruit cocktails. Delicious!

We bar-hopped that night!

I was happy to sit and listen to the fabulous Caribbean bands and their music. WOW!

We left Sunday morning for the seven-hour trip to Toronto, then a two-and-a-half-hour drive back to Belleville. And after dropping Doug off and trading cars, I still had to drive home alone. I was bushed!

Glenda and the kids were overjoyed to see me, especially as I started handing out presents when I first stepped through the door.

I was supposed to be in Stratford for a training session on Tuesday. I slept in on Monday, but I drove to Stratford and had Tuesday's session, as promised.

I sure hoped that Doug wouldn't ask me to do <u>that</u> again. (Yeah, right!)

He never did!

1974

My wife was expecting again when an opportunity came to purchase a variety store in Clinton at a good price, so I moved the family there. We called it J&G (for Jim and Glenda) Variety and Aviary.

Being the first store coming into Clinton on Hwy 4, we got a LOT of Air Force trade from the base personnel. Also, we got a lot of customers from folks who were going north on Hwy 4 on their way to northern destinations.

We sold convenience store items, a lot of pop, and cigarettes—and did well.

The convenience store was in front, but . . . go through a curtain, and you were in our home. Travel costs to and from work were NIL!

Gotta like that!

Didn't have to pay anything for rent, either!

There was an outside entrance to our house at the side of the building, and on the other side was what used to be a garage but had been refurbished as another room.

It also had a separate outside entrance.

I had always enjoyed pets, and budgies were a favourite. So My Amazing Hands started to breed them. I had a huge 'flight,' about ten ft wide by eight ft deep by eight ft high, where the birds flew free. There were perches on each side, cuttlebone and millet seeds hanging down, and seed trays on the floor. The mulch on the floor was cleaned weekly.

I contracted with Hartz Mountain to take all my young birds and 'culls.' Birds that didn't have the configuration to compete as "show birds" were "culls." They were eventually sold to the public in pet shops. I shipped my show birds to shows across Canada and won many ribbons and trophies.

I had about ten 'breeding cages.' I would take my best male and put it in the cage with a suitable female and breed offspring that I hoped would show well. If they didn't have it, they, too, became culls.

I expanded the aviary to include canaries, doves, fancy bantam chickens and even ended up with a pair of flying squirrels that had been injured.

At peak capacity, I had about 350 budgies.

I didn't do much musically during this time, just the odd gig when possible.

However, when they closed the RCAF Station at Clinton, I lost my primary customer source for the convenience store. Things started getting tight financially as my family was growing up and needing more and more of everything!

One of my regular customers was a neighbour, Bill, who owned Clinton Taxi. He asked me one day if I would drive for him when I wasn't busy in the store. He could use more free time, as he was getting up in years—and I sure could use the extra income. My wife could easily look after the store, so I drove a taxi.

Bill hung out at the taxi stand with me, and we played a LOT of cribbage while waiting for calls. Before long, he was leaving me there to handle things independently. The telephone to the taxi company was at his home—this is WAY before cell phones—so when a call for a taxi came in, Bill or his wife would call me on the two-way radio, and I would look after the customer.

As Clinton was a dry town back then, I got a lot of customers who would go for a short ride to Seaforth, where there was a bootlegger. One guy had me drive him around for an hour or so after a brief stop there while he did whatever in the back seat.

I sold the aviary as we were about to have another child, I was about to take my music on the road and it was too much for Glenda, being pregnant, to handle, along with our other children.

And we desperately needed the money!

***

Angela Dawn was born on Monday, October 21, 1974.

She was so cute laying there all bundled up in her mother's arms . . . I just couldn't resist a quick kiss on that little button nose. She was sound asleep, and I didn't want to wake her.

MY AMAZING HANDS

Then she grabbed one of My Amazing Hands by the finger . . . and I just couldn't leave.

Little did we know that she would grow into a very beautiful woman, marry a handsome policeman, and raise a pretty little girl of her own one day.

***

The Mercey Brothers used to play in The Elm Haven Motel on the edge of town fairly often.

My Amazing Hands shook each of their guitar-pickin' hands in greeting whenever we met.

One Saturday, after I caught their matinee show, I invited them to my home for supper, and they accepted my invitation.

We sang some of their songs, and I harmonized with them. Great fun!

The other day, I put "Larry Mercey" into a Google search and found him singing—*'I LOVE YOU CANADA,'*—on YouTube.

Go there and play it. You won't be sorry.

Larry's voice is even better after all these years.

I recently sent him an email, and he replied and told me that his brothers, Ray and Lloyd, are still alive and well.

I can STILL hear the brothers singing . . .

'Who Wrote The Words – Written On The Old Brick Wall!' and *'Hey, Uncle Tom – How Are You Getting On!'*

Larry's now eighty years old! And he is still singing.

And he *still* sounds great!

After chatting with them back then, they convinced me I was talented enough to go on the road and earn a living with my music—to sing and play in hotels.

So, I made phone calls and hooked up with musical booking agents, TOPS Country Music.

Although their offices were in Toronto, they booked me all over Ontario.

My career "on the road" started with a gig that needed a single act in Chatham at the Tecumseh Hotel.

Back in those days, the hotels had two separate beverage rooms; one "**For Men Only**" and one for '**Ladies and Escorts.**' There was a two-sided bar in the middle and a long stage that stretched over both rooms.

The hotel had an eight-piece house band that did half-hour sets. I was a single person hired to entertain when the house band was on break.

Man, that was one of the toughest gigs I have ever done.

Picture it . . . my first gig, and I'm all alone on a big stage . . . just me, my guitar, and a microphone. And I'm sitting in the middle facing a blank wall about twelve feet wide. First, I would look to the left to sing to the men's room—then to the right to sing to the ladies' room. Nobody really wanted to hear me . . . they wanted me off the stage so they could listen to the eight-piece band again.

However . . . I persevered, finished out the week, and went on to the next gig . . . in Sarnia . . . as a single . . . in the basement lounge . . . in a hotel . . . for a week.

And the family got fed!!!

I called myself 'The Jimmy Jay Show,' which I figured was an all-encompassing name, no matter which way the musical wind blew.

I went back to Clinton and convinced my buddy, Dave, to come on the road with me.

We decided to call our duo "Just-Us."

Dave played tambourine, maracas, bongos, and "eggs," and I played guitar.

We both sang, and we harmonized beautifully.

The "eggs" were hollow plastic with seeds that made music when you shook them. We'd let the patrons play them, and everyone had fun.

My Amazing Hands would also play them when we had a guest artist.

The booking agent insisted that we needed a promotional picture, so Dave and I went shopping for clothing classy enough for musicians "on the road." We bought matching Nehru shirts . . . shiny silk with tight around-the-neck collars and requiring cufflinks.

Pretty gol-darned classy!!

The first booking as 'Just-Us' was still with TOPS and was at the Riverside Motel in Bracebridge.

We drove up there on Sunday, arriving mid-afternoon.

I went inside, met the manager, and introduced ourselves as his entertainment for the forthcoming week.

After shaking one of My Amazing Hands, he said, "I sure hope you aren't like the asshole that was here last week!"

I asked him what he meant by that, and he said to me, "This place was bought recently by lawyers from Toronto as a financial investment. They spent a TON of money completely renovating the interior and the exterior. They replaced all the tables and chairs and combined the For Men Only and the Ladies and Escorts rooms into one large **LOUNGE**! They rebuilt the dance floor and even refurbished the stage."

Then he took my arm and told me to come with him and look at something, as he led me into the lounge and up to the stage.

The floor had been recently recarpeted, and an ugly gash was apparent in the carpet in the centre of the stage.

He told me, "That son-of-a-bitch that was here last week wore cowboy boots and used to scuff his boot on the floor to the beat of the music. Look at the damn hole he's left in the carpet. I didn't see it until this morning after they had packed up and left."

I calmed him down by assuring him that I didn't scuff my shoes and I didn't wear cowboy boots (at that time . . . I have worn them many times since, of course).

When I touched base with my booking agent, I mentioned this incident.

He told me that I was following a group that had recently signed with them, a group that was new to Ontario, having just arrived from Skinner's Pond, PEI.

So— I followed Stompin' Tom Connors on tour in Northern Ontario.

Tom used to stomp his left foot to help him keep the rhythm, as the bars back at that time were VERY noisy with clapping and cheering.

Someone suggested Tom should stomp on a piece of plywood.

He did, but would have to replace this "stompin' board" weekly, as he stomped a hole right through it.

Then he started to auction off his "stompin' board" for charity. He used to joke about the quality of the local lumber. When asked about it, he would joke, "It's just a stage I'm going through!"

I say I was "Stomped" by Stompin' Tom Connors because Tom was so well-liked that he would get held over due to his popularity, and we would be out of work for the week when that happened.

Sometimes TOPS would get something for us, but not always.

One motel had a live band one week and a stripper the next. They would often be willing to use the live band to provide music for the stripper instead of the jukebox, at a reduced price, of course.

We took what we could get.

Weeks when we couldn't get any work, we went home. The wives and kids were thrilled to have Daddy home for a week, allowing us to keep our affairs in order. But— there was no income that week!

We played in lounges all over Northern Ontario.

We performed in The Tri-Towns, which is now called Temiskaming Shores.

Tri-Towns consisted of New Liskeard, Haileybury, and Cobalt back in the day. Cobalt rejected the merger when Temiskaming Shores came to be.

We often returned to the hotel at Haileybury and got to know some locals.

After we chatted over beers one afternoon, one guy took My Amazing Hands out pickerel fishing on Lake Temiskaming the next morning.

We caught our limit, and the hotel cook served them to us for supper.

M-m-m! Delicious!

Just north of Haileybury, around the north end of Lake Temiskaming, on Hwy 65, in Quebec, near the Quebec/Ontario border is the little town of Notre-Dame-du-Nord.

The local watering hole was the White Oaks Inn. I remember going down a flight of stairs to get to the lounge.

This was the bar where the stripper and the entertainment alternated weeks and where we used to go when Stompin' Tom stomped us!

Our agent could usually get us in there with a phone call, as they liked us.

It was great to have a venue that would hire us, even though we hadn't been previously booked to play.

Nice folks there!

We also played up in North Bay and over in Sturgeon Falls, Timmins, Smooth Rock Falls, and Cochrane, to name a few dance halls. Cochrane was memorable, as it was the most northern point you could drive to— you had to take the Polar Bear Express railway service up to Moosonee.

We were playing in the first motel on the left after going around Lake Commando and entering the town. I can't recall its name, but it was very old and had this GIGANTIC moose head in the lobby when you first entered the building.

We travelled and set up there on Sunday, as most bands did.

On Monday, after lunch, I wandered into the bar and introduced myself to Dennis, the bartender.

While we chatted, an old Indian couple hobbled in. The husband was aged and wrinkled. He walked with some difficulty but maintained an air of respect.

His wife was long past the concerns for her appearance. The dress she wore hadn't seen soap and water in some time, attested to by the dribbles of dried egg yolk running down her ample bosom.

She only wore one nylon, with runs, on one leg. The other leg was bare and very dirty.

They took seats in the corner, and I saw Dennis sadly shaking his head after a brief exchange with the old man. When he returned to the bar, I heard him mumble something about it being too bad that he couldn't help them out anymore or he'd lose his job.

My Amazing Hands threw a twenty on the bar and told Dennis to spend it on the old couple.

A big smile appeared on their faces when Dennis brought them a large pitcher of cold draft and two glasses. The old man said something to Dennis, who told me, "Henry and his squaw thank you!"

That night, we noticed an interesting thing.

The room was divided roughly into two parts. Half of the room was white, and half was Indian. I asked Dennis about it, and he said it wasn't anything official. It just evolved that way. The Cochrane area was home to the Wahgoshig First Nation, formerly known as Abitibi—Indians.

After we finished our first set, the waitress whispered to me that one of the natives wanted to buy me a beer. I looked, and Henry was standing up beside his wife in the middle of the Indian section.

He beckoned me over. So . . . I went over, thinking that he might want to request a song. I was wrong . . . he just wanted to buy me a beer. He had guided some hunters the day before, and they were successful, so he got paid, and they gave him a bonus.

After the next set, Henry beckoned me over again for another beer. Then again, after the next set.

Dennis commented that he hadn't seen any musicians invited to sit with the natives, ever.

We were practicing on the stage the next day when Henry and his woman came in.

In his broken English, Henry told me to pick a date during the moose season, and he would take me out hunting.

He said, "We will shoot de moose. Mais, not just any moose—non, non, non, mon ami!"

With an expansive arms-wide gesture, he said, "We will shoot de B-I-I-G-G moose."

He told me not to bring anything, no rifle, no food, nothing!

He would provide it all!

Then they left.

Dennis, who happened to be there restocking the bar, told me that Henry was the best guide in the area.

Much in demand!

He said that Henry meant every word that he said. We would shoot a moose! We would "shoot de B-I–I-G-G moose."

We performed there all week. I asked if he had a business card, so I could reach him if I wanted de B-I-I-G-G MOOSE! He got a piece of cardboard and a pen from Dennis and carefully printed

> Henry MacDougall,
> Cochrane, Ontario,
> Gen Delivery

and beneath this, the word 'MOOSE.'

And, forty-six years later, I still have the 'card' that Henry gave me. In case I want to shoot 'de B-I-I-G moose!'

***

A couple of nights later, I looked at the entrance and noticed an unusual thing. Three men had just walked in and taken a table near the door. One of the men was a little person. They ordered drinks, then whispered something to the waiter. As he took and delivered drink orders, the waiter gradually made his way to the stage. He stopped to tell me that the little person near the door would like us to play some old country music.

We were about to take a break, so I picked my old country favourite, "*The Auctioneer*", as our last song of the set. Then, as we came off the stage, the little person signaled me to come to their table. He had a cold beer waiting for me and introduced himself as Sky Low Low. I remembered seeing him wrestling on television. He was very pleased that I recognized him.

He introduced me to his friends, who he said were also wrestlers, but I didn't recognize them or recognize their names. Of course, I let on otherwise—these guys are WRESTLERS! Mama didn't raise any dumb ones!

It turns out he loved country music, so we did an entire set of country music for him and his friends.

That earned me another cold beer, and he sent one of his friends to the car to get his poster, which he signed for me. So, in return, my Amazing Hands gave him a poster signed by both Dave and me.

I was just wondering if he still has OUR signed poster.

Of course, I still have his. After all, these guys are WRESTLERS!

On Wednesday, during one of our breaks, I was approached by a couple of guys.

One gave me his business card with his name and showed he was from RCA Records in Toronto. His title on the card was Director of Public Relations.

He said that he was told to come and listen to us by someone who had heard us perform and was impressed. He liked what he heard, so he asked me to call RCA to see if we could be in Toronto for a recording tryout, as they were actively searching for new talent.

The other guy also gave me his card and introduced himself as Don Gauthier with CBC TV.

He and the Public Relations guy knew each other.

It turns out that a locally televised variety show had a fifteen-minute spot to fill and asked my permission to video us to fill that spot.

The owner was excited about the free publicity and told us to quit early on Saturday afternoon, allowing the television technicians to get their cameras and equipment set up. They taped part of the evening's performance.

He said I could call the number on his card, and his secretary would tell me the date and time that the program would be broadcast.

My Amazing Hands are going to be on TELEVISION! YAY!

Dave and I decided to walk down the road to a lounge—about a half-mile walk—as we heard that there was a spectacular female singer there, and we wanted to catch her Saturday matinee show.

She was every bit as good as we heard she was and then some!

The place was packed . . . it was deer hunting season, and our hotel bar had closed early, remember?

Dave and I knew somebody, so we got a small table and chairs set up for us beside the dance floor.

I didn't notice then, but when I took some cash out of my pocket to buy the beer, the two business cards fell on the floor. The waiter must have picked them up, as we noticed him talking to the singer, and pointing at us.

When she went on her break, she came to our little table and introduced herself.

I almost choked on my beer when she said that she heard that an A&R man was here from RCA records.

Then she asked if it was me!

I got this beautiful lady a chair, and while I didn't claim that it was true, I didn't discourage her from thinking so!

After her break, before leaving for the stage, she asked if she could look me up at the RCA studios when she made it to Toronto again. I said, "Oh, yes! Please do!"

She said, "Thank you, sir! I will play a special song I wrote just for you."

So she left us and returned to the stage for her next set. Then I heard her announce that she would sing a special song just for Jim and pointed me out to the crowd. She was singing just for me!

WOW!

I wonder if anyone ever told her I was just another musician, playing just up the road.

And my buddy, Dave, kept calling me 'Sir' the rest of the day!

And that's how I met . . . I'm not positive . . . but in retrospect . . . I think it was . . . Shirley Eikhard!!

When Google happened, I looked it up, and—it *could* have been her. She would be nineteen years old, and just starting her amazing career.

So . . . a beautiful, talented superstar sang just for me . . . I'm just not certain who it was!

By the way, . . . I saw the camera crew filming us that night but didn't hear anything more about it.

MY AMAZING HANDS

At the time, I had no idea where they were from or if anything ever got televised.

I wish I hadn't dropped the television guy's card, but then I'm glad I DID drop the other one!

And My Amazing Hands were SO looking forward to meeting Johnny Carson, too!

Oh, well . . . we were feeding our families!!

As I've mentioned, the next day being a Sunday—we packed up and moved on. We drove south through Quebec on Hwy 101 to the White Oaks Inn in Timiskaming.

It was a huge building, well known in the surrounding area as THE place to go to have a great time.

The manager showed us to the room where we would be performing all that week, and, as usual, we set up and ran through a few tunes to ensure all was in order.

Of course, this room was for Ladies and Escorts, and we all had a great time throughout the week.

These French sure knew how to party!

Out of nowhere, Dave handed me the business card of the television guy. The waiter gave it to Dave as we left.

I fully intended to phone and find out if and when we would be televised, but I'll be honest . . . I forgot!

I wonder . . . is it still too late? Yeah, I agree . . . it probably is! Darn!

One night, a couple of fans, a man and his lady, invited Dave and me to join them at their table. I sat beside the man, and Dave sat beside his lady. They bought us drinks, and we chatted with them during most of our breaks that night. He told me that he was a foreman at a company in town that made wooden matches (Eddy Match Company, perhaps?) and explained to me all about how they were made while Dave chatted with the lady.

Dave whispered to me when we went back on stage that he wanted me to ask the guy for a guided tour of the match factory the next day. So, the next day I tried not to fall asleep from boredom while this guy explained in great detail how wooden matches are made.

Dave never did tell me where he was while I was on my tour, but he kept smiling at me all that night.

We never did see the couple again. Probably a good thing.

On Friday, we were outside chatting when a bus pulled up at the rear of the building. It had a band name, with lots of musical symbols all over it. We had no idea what was happening, so I went inside to ask the manager.

He told us that he had another group play outside for two shows—afternoon and evening on Saturdays.

It didn't affect us, though, as we were playing in the inside lounge, which was quite large.

We had accumulated quite a following of fans who had either seen us earlier in the week or heard about us and wanted to see us. Dave and I helped these guys unload their gear, and they set up on the covered patio. As we chatted with them, they said that they heard that we were pretty darned good.

They came into the lounge with their ladies to check us out that night.

It surprised the heck out of us when they said that they would help us to move our gear outside, set it up out there and play with them if we wished. Just combine the two bands.

What a great idea!

And the manager was all for it!

Around noon the next day, people started arriving.

There were grass-covered hills behind the motel, and people set up their umbrellas and tents all over them. An extensive dance floor area doubled as an outdoor rink in the winter, between these hills and the patio we had set up to play.

Our matinee was one to five. By one o'clock, the hill was covered with people, and they stayed all afternoon and into the evening.

You could see dozens of bonfires where they were BBQing their supper. And the dance floor was packed from the first tunes to the last notes of the last song.

Typically, a band plays forty-minute sets, with twenty-minute breaks... with the last hour being twenty- minutes on, twenty-minutes off, twenty- minutes on to finish on the hour.

However, that Saturday, My Amazing Hands jammed for four solid hours. No breaks were taken!

There were six musicians in that band, plus Dave and I, if I remember correctly. So if anyone needed a pee or beer break, we just shouted to the next guy and went. Of course, they had a drummer, so I could pound the skins whenever their drummer took a break.

I was playing harmonica also by that time and would wail away on one of the five that I had purchased.

Great fun!

My Amazing Hands played a whole lot of really great music during those eight hours.

Rock 'N Roll was going strong, Country, Soul, Blues, Ballads—every genre you could think of.

When we finished playing one song, someone would shout out another and the key, and away we would go again.

When he paid us that night (with a pretty sweet bonus, by the way), the manager told us that he estimated 1,500-2,000 people visited the White Oaks Inn that day. Sweet!

And our families got fed yet again!!

1975

—SOMETHING VERY EXCITING HAPPENED IN 1975—

Let me tell you about it . . .

I found a brochure backstage at one of our gigs offering recording services at RCA Victor Studios in Toronto and I still had the business card from the A&R man I met up north. So, I decided it was time to *finally* 'cut' a record. So, during a phone call to our agent (when Stompin' Tom 'gave' us the next week off), I asked if he could arrange it.

That was on Saturday.

Excited, one of My Amazing Hands called the studio right away. I was told that the studio was free on Monday around four o'clock, for about an hour—if that would work. He told me a choir was recording till then, but he would record us afterward. We would have to carry in and set up all of our equipment, record one song, then dismantle and remove everything. Then be gone – quickly.

He said it would be no charge to us, and he would suggest to the bigwigs that they give us a listen, "If you are any good!"

Dave and I thought that was great.

We thought we were better than just 'any good.'

We were at the studio about an hour early and carried all our equipment inside.

MY AMAZING HANDS

Then we waited in the hallway while the choir finished their recording. At 3:55, the choir finally left, and we were told to come into the studio and get set up. For us, it was like walking into heaven!

I'm sure we set up in 'record' time (pardon the pun).

We wanted nothing but perfection.

We put on the headphones, then suddenly realized . . . here it was. Our BIG break!!

I can't remember what song we chose, (probably 'The Auctioneer', my signature song) but . . . I know Dave and I busted our butts to do it the best we could in the limited time allotted.

The A&R guy, after we did the song for the third time, told us we were out of time and signalled us to come into the studio room.

He started up our song, and . . .

IT WAS TERRIBLE!!!!

So much for our recording careers. Heck . . . I didn't want to be a superstar anyway!

It sure let the wind out of OUR sails!

I guess we needed a room full of drunks—that's when we performed our best!

One of My Amazing Hands shook HIS hand, and we left!

Oh well!

We made a phone call to our agent who said that Stompin' Tom was being held over for another week, and they didn't have a job for us . . . so . . . we went home to Clinton.

After a short discussion, Glenda and I decided to sell the store and move back to Belleville.

***

A few phone calls later, I found work as the office manager with Standard Machine & Equipment Company—the company that demolished the Portland Cement Company in Point Anne, just outside of Belleville. Bobby Hull was born in Point Anne, and his dad, Robert Hull Sr., was a cement company foreman.

Hockey fans will know all about Bobby Hull, famous for his 23-year hockey career. I heard stories about the Hull family from the Point Anne natives who worked for the demolition company. All good!

My job was pretty simple.

Two of us worked in the office.

Dennis was in charge of sales—selling any salvageable items.

I tracked the employees' punch cards, phoned their hours to head office in the USA, picked up the pre-prepared payroll from the bank in Belleville and gave the men their pay envelopes at the end of the week. If something was needed, I was the gopher.

This was a great job—I had TONS of free time to do as I wished.

Of course, I had a guitar in the office and would play tunes sometimes (after the day's necessities were taken care of, of course).

But I was also friends with ALL of the guys. Remember, it was up to me to make sure the men got paid every week, and it was always correct. So, I would often put on my white hard hat and see what was happening in the yard when I was bored. These great guys taught My Amazing Hands how to operate all of the demolition equipment.

Now I could operate the huge crane that had a big demolition ball that I would swing back, then *SMASH* into the concrete wall. Remember, this is a cement factory, so they were very thick from the cement dust that had accumulated and hardened over many years.

I also learned to drive the giant fork truck used to move the massive kiln sections. I wish I still had the photos showing me standing inside a kiln. I'm approximately six feet tall, and it is almost three times my height... about fifteen feet in diameter. Each section was about twenty-five feet long.

An exciting story while I'm on the topic of kilns... a country in South America (I never did find out which one) purchased one of the four kilns that were on the site.

They sent a HUGE ocean-going ship to pick up the kiln sections and transport them from our site on the Bay of Quinte, through Lake Ontario, down the St. Lawrence River, and through the Atlantic Ocean on the eastern side of the United States to their destination country.

A giant crane was leased, with its operator and oiler, to lift the enormous kiln sections that had been transported to the water's edge by the massive fork truck onto the big boat.

This was a HUGE undertaking, involving LOTS of overtime for everyone.

In the wee hours, after they had just finished loading a section, I took some coffee up to the crane operator—his name was Les.

I told Les that I had driven the giant fork truck and operated the wrecking ball and crane.

He asked me if I would like to drive this gigantic crane into position beside the ship—ready to move the next section in the morning.

Would I? You KNOW the answer!

So I drove this HUGE crane a couple of hundred feet.

YES!

The cement plant also had an ENORMOUS smokestack that had to be demolished.

So—they set charges around the perimeter of the base and had a couple of steel cables leading to a big front-end loader and a D-10 bulldozer to pull it over.

The foremen let me sit with them in the bunker when they set off the explosive charges!

'KA-BLOOM'!

But, as the smokestack was built of layers of bricks that tapered from the bottom to the top, the outer bricks at the bottom disintegrated, but the upper bricks merely slid up and then down again.

The loader and the crawler maintained the tension on the cables, but to no avail.

Then someone suggested a time delay.

Charges were set, so a mouth shape was blown out first on the side that you wanted the stack to fall, then a time delay on the opposite side would flip it over. That worked fine, and after more overtime for all involved (including me, thank you), the smokestack FINALLY fell.

The story doesn't end there.

Ernie, who operated the massive D10 and to whom I would bring cold drinks on the *really* hot days, overheard me thanking the fork truck operator for teaching me to drive the fork truck.

He asked me if I would like to clear the rubble from the smokestack with the D10. DUH!

Yes, My Amazing Hands sure had fun clearing the rubble while learning to drive this behemoth!

1976

When the job ended with the Portland Cement Company site's total demolition, I became a car salesman at a General Motors dealership in Belleville called Elliott Motors.

Here's how....

I had heard they were looking for an office manager, but the position had been filled. However... the General Manager told me that I have 'the gift of gab.' So he hired me! My Amazing Hands did VERY well—signing many contracts with customers who wanted cars and trucks and school buses and recreational vehicles, etc.!

But my family was growing up, and we needed even more income!

I was hired away by Trudeau Motors, the Chevrolet dealer in Belleville, as the tower operator.

Thus, my knowledge of how car dealerships work was tremendously expanded.

My job was to receive the work orders after the service manager filled out the customer's information, including the work required for their vehicle. I would then allocate the repair to one of fifteen licensed mechanics.

The new vehicles were brought in whenever we had a free bay (unless it was sold, of course) for its pre-delivery inspection.

I sat in a little multi-windowed office on the second story of the work bays and had a clear view of everything below. The pay was good, and I got a LOT of respect... but I missed selling. So...

Elliott Motors, the other GM dealership where I previously sold vehicles, had been purchased by a GM dealership in Toronto. They changed the name to BAY Pontiac/Buick. They eagerly hired me back, as I had been a 'top three' salesman before, and now had a lot of additional automotive knowledge,

1977

Ken Trottier, a fellow salesperson, had a farm just outside of Belleville.

He was into trotters and pacers, and Ken Trottier Stables trucked his horses and equipment to various racetracks to compete with them.

Incidentally, for those who don't know . . . when referring to a horse as a 'trotter' or 'pacer', you are referring to its gait. A trotter's legs on the horse's left side move opposite one another. For example, when the left front leg moves forward, the left rear leg moves backward.

However, the gait of a pacer is different. Both front and rear legs on the left side of a pacer go forward simultaneously. I discovered that one day when we were chatting at the dealership, waiting for customers.

When I mentioned that I went to high school at the same time as Ron Feagan, he was VERY interested, although I couldn't tell him much about my friend Ronny.

I knew Ron to say hello to and shake hands with, but I really didn't know anything about his racing career.

Ken asked me if I would like to come to his stables to see his horses.

He asked me if I would like to come early the next morning.

So at six a.m. My Amazing Hands pulled into his driveway.

It wasn't long before I found out why so early when he handed me a pitchfork to help him 'muck out' the stables.

I think he had four horses at that time. He asked me if I had ever driven a sulky with Ron Feagan.

When I replied in the negative, he asked me if I would like to drive a sulky with him.

Of course, I said a resounding, "YES!"

He led a horse out of its pen and clipped it to the cross-ties attached to each side of the barn.

Then he harnessed the horse and got a jog cart—which was used to exercise the horse— instead of the light-weight racing sulky and attached the harness to the shafts.

Then he gave me a pair of goggles, showed me how to sit on the sulky, and explained some of the commands that the horse understands.

He explained that to properly exercise a horse, you take it in a clockwise direction around the track, slowly walking at first, then you speed it up into a trot as the horse warms up.

When you have warmed the horse up, you turn around and go counter-clockwise.

The horse knows that it is to trot as fast as it can when it is going counter-clockwise, as if it were in a race on a racetrack—and opens up into a speedy trot.

It's hard to describe the feeling when this very muscular horse, hooves pounding rhythmically on the track, is running full out, with its tail flying up in your face.

WHAT A RUSH!

Then you turn the horse around and cool it down, keeping it walking until it returns to normal. Then you return it to the barn, unharness it, and return the horse to its stall. Then you get the next horse and do it all again.

My Amazing Hands helped Ken exercise the horses a couple more times over the next month.

1978

I heard that the bigwigs from Parkwood Central, the company that owned Bay Pontiac/Buick, got together with the bigwigs from Bay Pontiac/Buick, either weekly or bi-weekly and were considering purchasing a light aircraft for company use—flying to and from these meetings.

That way, they would be more productive, instead of a tiring six-hour drive there and back for either party for the meetings, and without the necessity of staying overnight.

They would need a pilot.

I had always wanted to pilot an airplane. I knew I jumped the gun, but I figured that this would be an opportunity to make more money than I could just selling vehicles, as well as impress these men with my astuteness.

So . . . My Amazing Hands went to the local airport, and I became a student pilot.

However, before I could pilot an aircraft, I had to pass a medical exam—I did so on April 13, 1978.

My Student Pilot Permit was issued on May 30, 1978.

The instructor explained everything when I took my lessons as HE did the flying.

Eventually, I learned how to do the pre-flight checks, take off and land in a Cessna.

MY AMAZING HANDS

I learned how to use the radio and the controls—flaps, ailerons, rudder, and brakes.

In other words ... I COULD FLY!!

Just not alone!

We did bumps and circuits. That meant we would take off, circle the field, and land into the wind for take-offs and landings. After we landed, I would taxi, push the throttle fully forward, then take off again.

I would have to do these 'bumps and circuits' for an hour or so. The instructor was sitting in the co-pilot's seat in case something went wrong.

My Amazing Hands flew those little planes perfectly.

One day, we were doing bumps and circuits, and I had just landed when the instructor told me to pull up on the tarmac near where his car was parked. He needed something from the vehicle.

When I stopped the plane, he closed the door and said, "Take it around this time by yourself!"

I didn't realize the significance of what he said until I had taken off, turned left, then left again, then started the downwind leg of the circuit.

I looked down, and there was the instructor ... way down there on the ground ... waving at me.

I glanced to my right and just saw an empty seat beside me!

Then it struck me ... FOR THE FIRST TIME IN MY LIFE ... **_I WAS FLYING SOLO!!_**

When I landed and we went into the clubhouse, the guys there came over and grabbed me and cut a big swatch out of the back of my shirt. They wrote my name and the date on it and took me to a bar in the same building.

I had never been there before. I saw all the swatches of the shirts of the pilots that had flown solo for the first time there on display.

I watched proudly as my shirt joined the others on the wall!

Then they handed me an envelope! Inside was my Student Pilot Permit, issued on May 30, 1978. It said that I soloed on June 16, 1978. I no longer needed an instructor with me. I could rent a plane and fly all I wanted by myself. With or without passengers!

While I had first flown a Cessna aircraft, I could also fly a Piper Cub, which also had its wings *over* the passenger cabin, as the controls were the same on both aircraft. I later qualified on a Cherokee (wings under the passenger cabin). I even qualified on a twin-engine Beechcraft!

Flying the bosses never did materialize, but . . .

My Amazing Hands could FLY!!

I even piloted a huge glider, but that's a story for another day.

***

The Toronto dealership had an in-store contest that they had been running every year for the past five years and this year included Bay Pontiac of Belleville. However, we weren't competing against them, only each other in-store.

And each department within the store had separate parameters.

Obviously, the sales department based its parameters on sales.

The prize was an all-expenses-paid ten-day vacation in Acapulco, Mexico!!

And the race was on! OLE!

They decided to give the vacation to the top three salespeople.

Points were allotted based on the type of vehicle sold—big flatbed type trucks, recreational vehicles, and school buses received the most points.

Boy, I was glad I got that additional school bus and heavy truck training back when I did.

I was doing pretty good—about the middle of the pack—until one day, I received a phone call from a company near Port Hope.

Over the phone, I sold them three school buses, but only if they could be delivered immediately.

So I grabbed some drivers and three dealer plates, phoned my wife to tell her that I'd be late for supper, and we delivered the three school buses a couple of hours later. After picking up a cheque and signing over the bus ownerships, the drivers and I headed home.

The company paid us each a bonus, and I got a special round of applause at the next sales meeting!

More importantly, I got bonus points on the TRIP TO ACAPULCO tally board!

Thirty-five salespeople were selling new and used cars of all makes and models.

Also, new and used trucks, from pickups to big eighteen-wheelers; recreational vehicles, from the small camper trailers attached to bumpers, to huge self-contained units.

And, of course, school buses.

About a third of the salesforce surged ahead in Acapulco points, and I was in the top ten.

The top guy, Ken Trottier (who you will remember having read about in 1977, as he also owned Trottier Stables) surged ahead of the pack, as he was the only employee (he called himself 'manager') of the newly formed Leasing Department.

LEASING was a brand new aspect of vehicle sales and caught on rapidly. Ken leased out a LOT of vehicles, and he was credited in the Acapulco contest as selling them. He was the only employee at the time licensed to lease vehicles, so it was a gravy train for him—a shoo-in for the trip.

He was the only one IN the leasing department and had his own office.

But I didn't mind—Ken was a great guy!

The guy in second place, Steve Rexe, was a fantastic goaltender. He was the first-ever draft pick of the Pittsburgh Penguins and second overall pick in the 1967 NHL Amateur Draft. At the 1968 Winter Olympics, Steve was the backup goalie on the way to the Canadian bronze medal.

Sadly, he died on November 12, 2013—at the age of sixty-six.

He was also a salesman at the dealership when he wasn't playing hockey. All the sports fanatics in the area sought him out when they needed a new vehicle. He sold a LOT of vehicles to his sports fans and friends.

So, I KNEW I'd have to give a whole lot extra if I wanted to be third. I REALLY wanted to go to Acapulco, and the end of the year was getting closer and closer.

I started working from noon till closing, six days a week. I took as many phone calls as I could. I closed deals as quickly as possible to get on to the next customer. I made arrangements with other sales associates to split the commission if they would write a customer up, so I could get on to the next one faster.

The sales manager posted each sale, including the salesperson and how many points they had, on a board, so everyone knew where everyone else stood.

Coming down to New Year's Eve, another associate, Joe, was neck to neck with me.

The dealership agreed to stay open until nine p.m. that night to accommodate any last-minute sales from either of us. Joe sold one around six and snuck ahead of me. I frantically phoned everyone I knew, trying to get someone—*anyone*—to agree to buy in the new year.

Management said that it would count in the year's total.

An uncle of a friend, a farmer a couple of miles out of town, bought an old rusty pickup truck from the field behind the dealership, which hadn't run in years, for a couple of hundred bucks, as it had a plow on it that he could use on his tractor.

It counted as a used truck, and I snuck into third place at 8:45 p.m. on New Year's Eve.

At the first sales meeting in the new year, the sales manager announced the results: Ken Trottier in first place, Steve Rexe in second place, and Jim McCarthy in third place! YAY!

However, Bay Pontiac Buick, being the 'class' act that they were, announced that there would be a wild card . . . a fourth-place prize of also going to Acapulco . . . won by Joe!

My Amazing Hands shook the hand of the sales manager in gratitude. And the hands of Ken, Steve, and Joe—the other winners!

MEXICO, HERE WE COME!!

OLÉ!

The winners from each department met at the dealership when it was time to go on our Acapulco adventure. We loaded up in an available school bus and proceeded down hwy 401 to Toronto.

We went to Toronto Pearson International Airport, boarded an aircraft, and arrived in Acapulco in a few hours, where we were met by a friend of the owners who lived there six months out of the year. He assisted us through the airport and onto buses, which took us into the city.

He helped us to get our hotel rooms and had taxis waiting to take us to the Plaza de Toros (also known as Plaza Caletilla) for bullfighting.

WOW!

We saw brave matadors, picadores, rejoneadores, and banderilleros and heard the famous bullfighting music—lots of trumpets and guitars.

Then we were on our own.

But it was early evening when it was over, so most of us went back to the hotel to eat and have a nap.

However, we had to assemble every evening at what was called the 'Boss's Suite.' The bosses got the penthouse to stay in, and it was mandatory to gather there at nine p.m.—lots of room for all of us. Heads were counted to ensure everyone was all right and to plan the next day's activities. This constituted a 'business meeting.' The company could write it off against the business for tax purposes. Smart!

One of the other dealership groups had provided entertainment for that first evening.

The sales guys from Bay Pontiac Buick were told that we had to provide it for the next night.

The next day was spent on the famous Acapulco beach, soaking up some sun while drinking lots of Corona and eating that delicious Mexican food. Just relaxing.

Ken, Steve, and I hired a sightseeing guide who took us to the famous La Perla Restaurant. Our guide seated us at the same table where Elvis sat to watch the cliff divers during the filming of *'Fun In Acapulco'*. At least that's what he claimed and who was I to dispute a Mexican guide's claim?

We saw the La Quebrada cliff divers, and they were outstanding! They were a group of professional high divers based in Acapulco. They performed daily shows for the public, which involved diving thirty meters (100 ft.) or forty-one metres (135 ft.) from the cliffs of **La Quebrada** into the sea below.

The ocean waters came rushing into this rocky inlet, then ran out again with each wave. The divers climbed the cliff opposite the restaurant where we were seated. Most stopped halfway up the cliff at a small shrine to pray before continuing up as high as they dared. They timed their dive to hit the water when the water was deepest. Daredevils, for sure!

Afterward, the guide took us to see the fantastic Flamenco dancers and singers at Hotel Acapulco.

It was a great, fun day.

We hired a travelling Mariachi band to sing and play for the evening's entertainment.

I borrowed a guitar and sang and played a couple of tunes with them. It was great. I never *dreamed* that someday I would perform with a Mariachi band in Acapulco, Mexico!

MY AMAZING HANDS did it again!!

Being an avid fisherman, I just couldn't go to Acapulco without going deep-sea fishing. I was thrilled when they announced that it was on tap for the next day.

We took a taxi to the far side of the bay, where a couple of boats had been reserved for us.

It was fun, and we drank a lot of Corona.

Our boat had a couple of sailfish following our bait but, alas, no takers.

However, those lucky guys in the OTHER boat hooked and landed an okay-sized sailfish.

They described it as HUGE!

Let's see ... the bosses were all on the other boat. Coincidence? Hm-m-m!

Now, if WE had caught a sailfish in OUR boat, it would have been HUGER, no matter how big it *actually* was. Lol!

The only downside was that, while fishing, I stupidly just wore a T-shirt and bathing suit. As we were seated on the boat most of the day, my thighs and arms got severely sunburned.

A group from the other dealership provided the night's entertainment that night. I wish I could describe it here ... but all I can say is that it caught and held our full attention. Highly entertaining!

The next morning was spent sunbathing, then a stroll down the beach where I ate my favourite seafood—fresh red snapper—cleaned, cooked, and on my plate—right on the beach.

Not only my foot, but my entire body was in the Pacific Ocean when I took a swim.

I bought presents for my family and a big, black, fancy sombrero for myself.

My AMAZING HANDS and I had a ball!

VIVA MEXICO!!

Like Elvis, we had '*FUN IN ACAPULCO.*'

~ OLÉ ~

1979

In my lifetime, I have owned many boats. Everything from a relaxing canoe that gave a very slow, easy ride—to many exciting high-speed powerboats.

In 1963 I told you about my first boat, which was homemade (by me, from plywood, using My Amazing Hands). This six-foot-long punt was powered by a tiny three-HP gas outboard. I painted it camouflage, and I used it for fishing and in a blind to hunt ducks and geese.

Later I owned three or four runabouts that I had outfitted for trolling. I caught many, many fish from the tasty little perch to the huge and powerful muskellunge.

I have deep-water trolled for salmon and steelhead trout, and when I was in Mexico, I deep-water fished for sailfish and other saltwater species.

My biggest freshwater fish was a musky that My Amazing Hands caught in Stoco Lake, north of Belleville in Ontario. It weighed thirty-eight and a half pounds and was five foot, three inches long.

Not a record, but indeed, a nice fish.

A friend, Keith Trudeau, owned Stoco Lake Lodge at Trudeau Park on Stoco Lake and asked if he could have the fish to display at the lodge if he paid the taxidermist.

Musky aren't edible, and I couldn't afford to have it mounted just then, so I gave it to him.

Keith prominently displayed my fish behind the counter, and it stayed there for many years.

I recently phoned the lodge to see if it was still hanging.

Keith's son runs the lodge now and gave me Keith's phone number.

When I called him, he told me he has the fish hanging in his rec room in his finished basement.

Another friend of mine was Bill McMullen.

He lived on a small spread (he called it The McMullen Ranch) with his wife and two young boys.

Bill raised horses on his ranch—that's why he needed a pickup truck . . . he had a couple of horses boarding there. He also had three of his own—two mares and a stallion. He needed a dependable vehicle to pick up bags of feed and bales of hay regularly.

It was around the middle of April on a warm, lovely spring day when he saddled up the stallion, 'Pepper'—helped me mount up—then turned us out into the pasture.

He told me that Pepper was the gentlest of the three and said, "Just walk him around until I join you, riding the mare!"

So I did.

All went well at first . . . but . . . I didn't know it, but this was the first time that year that the horses had been saddled and ridden. Pepper was 'feeling his oats' and decided that he was going to go for a run in this open pasture . . . with me hanging onto the reins for dear life. He took off at full gallop—ignoring my shouts and heaving on the reins.

I was starting to get a real burst of adrenalin when . . . without any warning at all . . . we were AIRBORNE. This huge, friendly critter KNEW that a narrow creek was flowing across the land, water gurgling madly.

I DIDN'T.

Arms and legs flailing about, I managed to grab a handful of mane with one of My Amazing Hands, I grabbed the saddle horn with the other, and . . . we made it safely over the creek!

I pulled the snorting, head-shaking stallion to an abrupt stop, dismounted, then stood there shaking while waiting for my heart to catch up to the rest of my body.

A few seconds later, Bill and one of the mares came sailing across the creek just a short way down from us.

Fortunately, there was a bridge over the creek on the other side of the field, so I didn't have to decide if I wanted to jump this behemoth back over or if I wanted to take my chances wading back through the turbulent water, dragging my horse by the reins.

I followed Bill, both of us mounted, over the bridge, and we walked the horses back to the stable.

Then Bill chastised me!

He said I "shouldn't have ridden Pepper so hard on his first outing in the big pasture that spring. The horse could have pulled a hamstring, stumbled, and we could have been hurt."

Hurt . . . I almost had a heart attack!

I guess all was forgiven, though, when Bill and his wife invited my family out to 'the Ranch' a couple of weekends later for a visit and supper. Imagine my surprise when Bill told them that we would be back in an hour after the wives and kids had met, then took me by the arm, and we headed out to the stable. Pepper was already harnessed and tied to the 'hitchin' rail along with one of the mares.

Bill lived about two miles west of Stoco.

He told me he had an errand at the Stoco Hotel and had decided to ride there.

This was just a quiet country road, and it was kind of soothing to just gently jog along to the sway of the horse and the soft 'clop-clop' of the horses' hooves.

My Amazing Hands tied Pepper to a hitchin' rail at the local country hotel that was there just for that purpose. Then we went in.

Bill's 'errand' was to have a couple of beers with his friends, then we headed back.

It was one of the most peaceful, delightful Saturday afternoons I have EVER spent. Bill's wife was an excellent cook, Bill was a great friend, and the kids had fun playing together.

Even Pepper enjoyed the trip to town.

I continued to go trail riding even after we moved away, but the publicly available horses are all, understandably, pretty tame.

I'd love to take another crack at jumping that creek while riding Pepper now that I know it's there!

1980

In 1980, Glenda and I separated.

I moved to Toronto.

Sally, who I met in Acapulco and stayed in touch with, had separated from her husband—and had a spare room in her apartment.

I moved in.

I knew a couple of guys, Jay and Louie, that played drums and keyboards but didn't sing.

After an evening's tryout with them (I played guitar & sang), we got hired at a restaurant in Chinatown called the Golden Dragon, to play Friday and Saturday nights in a small room near the entrance where folks used to sit waiting for their table to be prepared.

After a week or so, Sally got hired as a 'greeter.'

She had previously worked as a bartender, so she could mix drinks when necessary.

She wore a Chinese cheongsam—a colourful blue silk short-sleeved dress, tight at the neck and went to mid-shin. However, the dress had slits on both sides. Lots of leg would show when the lady wearing it walks or sits.

It looked great on Sally as she had long, silky legs.

The waitresses were all Chinese and also wore a cheongsam.

They needed a bartender to mix drinks, so I was hired, and Sally and I both worked there daily from three till nine.

So, with playing and bartending, I was still supporting my family.

At first, I had a tough time, being a beer drinker. I didn't know how to make mixed drinks. It was embarrassing to have to call Sally over to show me every time a mixed drink was ordered.

So Sally bought me a book entitled *'How To Mix Drinks'* or something like that.

I felt like a real pro now!

Whenever I got repeat orders for my concoctions, my chest swelled with pride.

One night, I got an order for an intricate drink that I hadn't served before.

I smiled as I reached under the bar for "*How To Mix Drinks*" (or something like that).

I sent it out, and my chest swelled even more when, fifteen or so minutes later, I got an order for TWO more of my fantastic mixed drinks from the same table.

Another fifteen minutes and another two orders. Sally came over, and I bragged about my newfound prowess as a bartender!

She said, "Let me take a look at that recipe!" as she reached for my book... "*How To Mix Drinks*" (or something like that). She burst out laughing when she turned the page (I hadn't turned the page.) On the next page, in brackets, and I swear it was smaller print, it said... *serves four!*

Here I had been sending out drinks containing a LOT of mixed shots for the cost of a single. No wonder this drink was so popular at that table that night—but—the tips were GREAT. I never made that mistake again. From then on... I made sure that I always turned the page... and looked for the fine print!

One night, Sally came to the bar to give me an order and said, "Be extra generous with this."

I watched as she took it over to an easily recognizable gentleman dining alone that evening.

I watched as she served the drink that 'I' made to . . .

DONALD SUTHERLAND!

Neither of My Amazing Hands shook Donald Sutherland's hand that night. But it did mix the drink that he enjoyed with his supper. Does that count?

No? Oh, shucks!

1981

I knew I didn't want to be a bartender in a Chinese restaurant for the rest of my life, so I kept my eyes and ears open, and I heard that a company called Automatic Data Processing (ADP) was looking for a sales executive for Southwestern Ontario.

This company sold computer systems to automotive, truck, and farm dealerships.

They perused my qualifications, and I was hired. I was in charge of sales and follow-up visits in the region. This comprised a huge territory that went from an imaginary line between Collingwood and Hamilton and everything west of that line!

The company flew me to Portland, Oregon, all expenses paid, for a two-week course that taught me all about the two computer systems that they sold.

'All expenses paid'. I LOVE that term!

On the way there, we landed in Chicago.

We were told that the plane flying from there to Oregon was overbooked and as my flight wasn't first-class, I got bumped to the flight leaving early the next morning.

The airline provided accommodations in a local hotel overnight.

So . . . I can officially say that My Amazing Hands spent a night in Chicago . . . although all I saw was the inside of a shuttle bus and a hotel room. Still . . . I saw the Rocky Mountains for the first time.

Well—that's not *exactly* true. I actually saw the *tops* of the Rocky Mountains sticking up through the thick clouds as we flew over them. Beautiful!

I was still really impressed, though!

Because the airline bumped me, I arrived a day later than the other three or four new hires.

The week was uneventful . . . breakfast in the hotel, then across the street to a classroom in the ADP building there, repeated in the afternoon, then, after supper, escorted to local theatre and other entertainments.

On Friday, we were told that a car was provided for our use that weekend. The other guys in the class lived a short drive away in all directions and didn't need the car, so I had exclusive use of it.

Mount St Helens, only an hour's drive north of Portland in Washington State, had erupted just the previous year. While I wasn't really into geology, I thought it might be something interesting that would occupy my time on Saturday, so I headed to Washington to look.

Besides, in all my worldly travels, I had never been on a mountain.

As I ascended the mountain, I noticed a dry, warm stillness in the air and not much traffic. I stopped a couple of times where streams crossed under the road and saw hardened lava on both banks and a lot of gray ash in the water . . . and an absence of wildlife!

I ascended Mount St. Helens slowly for thirty minutes or so, and it was getting bleaker and bleaker.

I saw many areas that had burned and more and more hardened lava.

Finally, I had had enough— turned the car around— and drove back to Portland.

Enough adventure for My Amazing Hands for one day.

We finished our classroom education at ADP about mid-week, then I flew home.

On the way, I saw the tops of the Rockies again.

***

We were living in a high-rise in the then-notorious-for-crime Jane and Finch area of Toronto, so we decided to move to London, a much nicer city, in the centre of my sales area.

However, it meant that I couldn't get involved with music. I just made some appearances when it was Talent Night at various venues. Of course, my guitar and I also jammed with friends whenever possible.

Computers for business purposes were just starting to break on the scene.

The car, truck, and farm dealerships either had an in-house computer system or a 'pad' system, just for accounting and inventory control.

The pad system was pretty straightforward.

The daily activities in accounting (bought, sold, rented, or leased) and inventory (new and used vehicles and parts) would get tracked on large pads as they happened. Every Tuesday, they were picked up during the night and delivered to our offices in Toronto, where the information was then updated in ADP's monstrous computer system.

Then new 'pads' were generated with blank fields for all vehicle activity. A separate set went to the parts department. A third set tracked employees' income and generated paycheques. These blank pads were delivered on Thursday nights, ready to start Friday's business.

The in-house system consisted of a large room with printers and boxes of paper so that the lists could be printed on an as-needed basis. And inside this room was another glass-enclosed 'computer' room, where the actual computers did their thing—spinning spools and all.

It was kept as dust-free as possible—the operators wore special suits, and special units kept moisture and dust out of the room.

It was lit with special fluorescent lights.

At the time, I knew zero about these computers.

My job was to get a room full of management personnel together at a dealership and assist an 'expert' from our company to come to the meeting where we could extol the virtues of a computer system over the old hand-written card system.

Most of the brands (Ford, Freightliner, Allis-Chalmers, etc.) loved the new computer systems, and highly recommended us to their dealers, but it was still a hard sell to some of these old, change-resistant owners and managers.

That's where I came in.

All those years of performing in bars around the country had totally destroyed any fears that I might have had of facing the public. I could talk to a room-full of hard-noses with total confidence both in myself and our product, and I did well in this challenging market.

There was one of our in-house computers at a truck dealer in Kitchener, in my area, so I got the call when the computer stopped working correctly. Although there was not much that I could do, I rushed to the dealer, got a technician on the phone and tried the primary repair steps that he suggested.

It worked, the computer was repaired, and I was a hero. That was on Tuesday morning.

Next Tuesday, the same thing happened again.

So I rushed to the dealer, phoned the technician, fixed the computer, and left, not so much a hero.

The next Tuesday morning, again, a phone call. Again I fixed it. They were getting irate and looking at me angrily.

So, the following Monday, I decided to drive to Kitchener to spend the night in the outer section of the computer room to see if anything untoward occurred. Around two a.m., I heard a commotion in the outer hall, heard a key turn in the lock, and a cleaning lady came in with her cart of mops, brooms, etc. She cleaned the printer room area, and everything was fine.

However, when she entered the computer room, I could see sparks around the woman as she swept the floors, and suddenly the computers gave a whirring, zapping sound and quit working! A-HA!

This overweight cleaning lady was wearing a pair of nylons, tops rolled down, and the friction of her thighs rubbing together as she worked generated a LOT of electricity.

She was a big girl! I guess her rubber-soled shoes prevented her from feeling anything. But enough electricity was built up in her body, then released when she got near this super-sensitive equipment that the computers went wonky every Monday night!

By now, I knew what to do to reset the computer, then I drove back to London and finally got a good night's sleep.

I was a hero to the dealership once again. The owner shook one of My Amazing Hands!

The cleaning lady was happy—she didn't have to clean the printer or computer rooms (and she was more than a little bit afraid of the whirring machine, anyway).

ADP was happy enough to give me a raise and a day off to compensate for the night I worked.

Sally was happy—I took her shopping on my day off.

And I was happy. I got an excellent recommendation from the dealer. It paved the way for even more sales!

1982

In 1956, I promised to tell you how I quit smoking in 1982, and here we are.

Well . . . for years now, every night, the last thing one of My Amazing Hands would do after going to bed was to reach over and butt out the cigarette I'd been smoking.

And every morning, I'd wake up, and even before I swung my legs out of bed, I'd grope the nightstand until I found my pack of cigarettes, take up my lighter, take a big, long puff, then cough —and cough—and cough—until I hacked up a big gob of phlegm, then I'd make my way to the bathroom.

I'd cough some more, then spit out this big gob of green phlegm. One morning, July 22, 1982, to be exact, I spit out a big gob of RED phlegm.

My children were old enough to smoke.

Wasn't I setting a great example for them!!!

And that big gob of red phlegm bothered me all day long!

I didn't want to get throat or lung cancer. My family needed me alive and healthy.

So . . . .

My wife had gone shopping that evening, and the kids were out doing their thing.

So . . .

My Amazing Hands got a large black plastic garbage bag.

I had two unopened cartons of cigarettes . . .

They went into the garbage bag!

I had four unopened packages of cigarettes...

They joined the cartons in the garbage bag!

The rest of the opened package of cigarettes went in there!

Every ashtray in the house went in there!

Every lighter in the house went in there!

I covered them by dumping all the rest of the garbage in the house on top of them!

I knotted the garbage bag and placed it on the curb for pickup the next morning!

Then I went into the bathroom and got nose-to-note with myself in the mirror there—and I made a solemn vow... by myself... to myself... for myself ... that ...

NO TOBACCO OF ANY KIND WOULD EVER AGAIN TOUCH MY LIPS!!!

This **solemn vow** was made... by myself... to myself... for myself... !!!

And, do you know what?

No tobacco has touched these lips since seven p.m. on July 22, 1982!

This means that, as of the closing of the writing of this, my book—midnight, December 31, 2020—

It has been over **THIRTY-EIGHT YEARS, TWENTY-TWO DAYS, AND FIVE HOURS!** since any tobacco has touched these lips! That includes cigarettes, cigarette filters, pipes, cigars, chewing tobacco, cigarillos, or any other tobacco product!

Alas! — No more smoke rings, either. But I KNOW I am going to live MUCH longer without them!

As I was travelling around South-Western Ontario, showing the inventory control system to the various dealerships, I found myself in Leamington.

One of the managers at the dealership where I was making my presentation suggested that I might be interested in seeing ketchup being made at the local Heinz processing plant while I was there.

It was the perfect time of the year for them to make the great ketchup that Heinz is known for.

He knew somebody, made a phone call, and away we went.

Some history — H.J. Heinz started making ketchup back in 1892.

MY AMAZING HANDS

Looking for a logo, he took his lucky number, '5', and put it together with his wife's lucky number, '7', and the infamous '**HEINZ 57**' brand was born.

My buddy said, "I hope you like tomatoes!" as we put our gloves and coveralls on to protect our clothing from the tomato juice that was everywhere!

But the clothing didn't stop it from getting all over our faces and in our hair.

It took a few days of firm scrubbing to get back to normal.

My kids said I smelled like a sandwich.

The plant at Leamington closed in June 2014!

1983

Mom died in 1983.

This lovely lady was born in 1919. She only lived to age sixty-four.

She had heart issues.

A stroke paralyzed her left side, but she fought and fought and recovered so much that one day in the city of Woodstock (I used to take her window-shopping there), we crossed an intersection just as the light had turned orange.

I was ready to stop and go back to the curb, but she grabbed my hand, shouted, "Come on!" and the two of us RAN to the other side. Then we stopped!

And she LAUGHED!

Again and again!

An oh-so-joyful carefree laugh of a young-at-heart sixty-four-year-old GIRL!

My mom died a short time later from another stroke.

My Amazing Hands wiped away an ocean of tears that day.

***

I went to the Western Fair in London and stopped at a booth manned by 'Happy Jack' Summerfield.

He told me that he owned a variety store just outside Strathroy.

He had a display showing how metal detectors could locate coins and jewelry, sometimes quite valuable, and how to retrieve them from the ground.

MY AMAZING HANDS

He was the White's dealer and distributor in Ontario, and he invited me to his store to see some of his 'treasures.' So I drove over, chatted with Happy Jack, and purchased a metal detector and accessories.

I was anxious to get started with this new hobby.

He said that he would help me to form a club in London by giving me a list of his customers that I could contact, arrange a meeting, and perhaps form a metal-detecting club. He was sure that his competitors would do the same.

Many phone calls later, a group of like-minded men and women met in a donated room, and I chaired this meeting.

I asked for and received volunteers as assistants to help organize the club. We set a future club meeting date, and I met with the volunteers in the interim. We decided what officers we required and prepared a draft of club rules and regulations to present at the next meeting.

I was elected club president, and Al Gretzky was elected vice president.

I won't tell you all the details about the club . . . perhaps that can be a story for another time.

Just about Al Gretzky.

My Amazing Hands shook the hand of Wayne Gretzky's uncle Al. He was a nice guy, married, with one son, Tyler. The family lived on the outskirts of London.

Like myself, Al worked during the week, but we had our weekends free to go metal 'tecktin.

We would take turns picking each other up and would drive to some old site to dig up artifacts.

One day, driving down the highway on the way to a site in Sarnia, as we were half-listening to the radio, they announced that Wayne Gretzky had just achieved another milestone.

Al pumped his fist in the air and said, "Way to go, nephew!"

Not being a big hockey fan, this was the first time I associated Al's last name with The Great One.

Al told me that he was Walter Gretzky's brother. I guess everyone knows that Walter was Wayne's dad.

Sadly, Walter passed away on March 4, 2021, as I was still writing this book.

My Amazing Hands had the honour to meet him on a couple of occasions when he would drop in to visit, and sometimes pick up, his brother Al.

They would be on their way to Windsor to watch Wayne's brother, Keith, who would be playing that night. He played for the Windsor Spitfires at that time.

Al's wife, Marilyn, always had coffee for us whenever we visited.

On one occasion, the Gretzky family had an outdoor get-together at Al and Marilyn's house, and my wife and I were invited.

Wayne couldn't attend, but Walter was there.

One of My Amazing Hands shook the hand of Wayne Gretzky's sister, Kim. and also met Wayne's mother and Walter's wife—Phyllis Gretzky.

What a VERY nice, very gracious lady! No wonder Wayne is such a great guy with parents like his!

About that time, I purchased a 1979 O-Pee-Chee Wayne Gretzky Rookie Card.

It was inside a plastic sleeve, which in turn, was sandwiched between two sheets of hard, clear plastic held together with four screws in the corners. That did a great job of protecting the card.

My Amazing Hands showed it to Al, and he offered to take it with him the next time he went to Brantford to see his brother, who would ask Wayne to sign it for me. I was so pleased when Al gave it back to me, signed, shortly after that. But I was somewhat disappointed that Wayne didn't sign it on the card itself but on the plastic sleeve that held the card.

However, Al told me that Wayne told him that signing it on the card itself would devalue the card. So Wayne did the next best thing... he signed the sleeve.

The sleeve and card had been placed back between the plastic sheets and screwed back into place.

Thank you, Al! Thank you, Walter! Thank you, Wayne!

1984

Glenda and I divorced on August 14. 1984. We had been married for twenty-one years.

Al Gretzky and I became close friends and remained as vice president and president, respectively, of the Thames Valley Metal Detector Association for some time.

We would go metal detecting together or with other club members most weekends.

My Amazing Hands poked around old churches, old schools, old racetracks, and old, affluent-looking houses and turn-of-the-century parks—anywhere we thought people might have gathered in the old days when coins or rings, or other valuables may have been lost.

Over the years, these items would get covered and would work their way deeper into the ground, until they finally rested on a bed of firmer material. We would come along, sweeping our metal detector over the ground until 'beep-beep' we would discover it.

We would sweep the coil over the target. Where the sound was loudest was when the 'target' coin or ring would be in the exact centre of the coil. So we would stare at the ground at that spot, and remove the coil.

Then....

Using a six-inch heavy-duty knife, we would cut a horseshoe shape in the sod. If we carefully pried the sod up, we could loosen the dirt, carefully, with the knife—extract the coin or diamond ring—and fold the sod back over. That way, the sod didn't die, and no harm befell the environment.

Occasionally I got requests to search for lost valuables.

One such request was to come to the racing stables. A lady there had been practicing show jumping with her prize horse when she noticed a valuable ring was no longer on her finger.

One of the groomers at the racetrack had a friend who was in the Thames Valley Metal Detector Association, the group that I had formed.

The friend wasn't available, so they called me.

My metal detector was able to differentiate between various metals, so even though there were many horseshoe nails and other metallic junk around, I had a good chance of finding her gold ring.

I looked in the horse ring first, where she practiced her jumps, and, in fact, found a small wedding band there, along with a handful of assorted coins. But it wasn't *her* ring.

Then I looked in the stable, to no avail.

I tried by the stable door one last time, and suddenly, 'beep, beep.' There it was.

Just under the hay.

The lady was ecstatic, and supper was 'on her' that night.

1985

That spring, we discovered metal detecting in the water.

As people played in the water, throwing balls, Frisbees, beach balls, etc., a combination of water and suntan lotion meant that many rings slipped off many fingers. Coins, often wrapped in bills, got tucked into bathing suits, and with the twisting and turning as folks enjoyed the exercise, slipped out and away.

Then Al, Jack, or I came along with our waterproof metal detector.

Beep! Beep!

And My Amazing Hands now have found more money, or a lovely diamond, ruby or (as I found) a nice star sapphire, ring.

Or, sadly, someone's engagement ring . . . or gold wedding band.

We kept cool, got our exercise, had fun, and often found a few dollar's worth of valuables. We always had our regular metal-detecting equipment in the car, so we could spend some time searching the grounds of an old church or park on the way home. We never knew when My Amazing Hands might turn up something ancient.

One day I discovered an old square Chinese 'CASH', also called 'QIAN' coin, that was used from the fourth century B.C. until the twentieth century A.D. It was even more fun when I investigated the coin's origins and found out its value! As I also did with the precious stones in rings and other jewelry that I unearthed. That year I found enough treasure that I was able to put a down payment on a house.

A year or so later, I was able to use the accumulated equity to purchase the house next door, which had an apartment in the front and another apartment in the back. My Amazing Hands collected rental income, which paid the mortgages on both houses.

YA-HOO!

1986

Because I was travelling around Ontario selling computer 'pad' systems and in-house computer systems to the automotive, truck, and farm dealers, it wasn't easy to play my music regularly.

I would sit in with other groups on 'jam night,' but it just wasn't the same.

So I quit travelling and got a job selling used vehicles for Bryan's Auto Sales in London. It was a good-sized operation considering we just sold used vehicles. The business consisted of the owner, Bryan Watson, a fellow salesman, Paul Ryan, and myself.

I found out early that Bryan liked to take his three-car transport vehicle and visit with the dealer principals in all the dealerships in the area. He would leave Paul and me to run the store but would always return with three VERY sellable vehicles.

Paul was away a lot, took a battery of tests, passed them, and became a firefighter for the city.

So I quickly learned how to evaluate vehicles, do trade-in or purchase deals, ship cars out to be painted and/or repaired, and the myriad of other things involved in running a used car business. Other than 'lot boys' who would come after school to help me keep the vehicles and the dealership looking spiffy, I pretty much managed the dealership.

My Amazing Hands made a LOT of money for Bryan. And me!

When I sold a sporty little car to a gentleman for his daughter, who was about to go away to college, My Amazing Hands filled out 'Bob's' financing application. I discovered that Bob was one of the approximately 500 workers who worked at the Kellogg's Plant in London. This plant produced a LOT of boxes of various types of cereal, including Corn Flakes, Frosted Flakes, and All-Bran.

I took Bob up on his offer to take me on a personally guided tour of the plant.

I saw how they received the raw grain, processed it, packaged it, and shipped it.

From that day forward, whenever I had some delicious Kellogg's Corn Flakes or one of their other great products, I would remember how happy Bob's daughter was when she drove her new (to her) car off the lot that day.

However, for various reasons, Kellogg's closed its doors for good on December 23, 2014.

I still enjoy Kellogg's products, though they are made elsewhere.

As Tony the Tiger says... they are all still GR-R-R-REAT!

1987

In 1987, Bryan bought a couple of out-of-service mail trucks that were not dependable enough to deliver the mail any longer, and Canada Post had traded them in for current models.

The old trucks had been sold at the dealer's auction in Milton and purchased as part of a package deal by Bryan.

He didn't really want them, so I bought the best of the two at a VERY low price.

It was just plain fun refurbishing this old truck.

My Amazing Hands were put to work again, turning this mail delivery vehicle into . . .

TA-DUM!!

DRUM ROLL, PLEASE!

A CHIP WAGON!

My son, Jim Jr., operated the business, which was a great source of income. I took a small percentage to recoup part of my investment and 'keep my finger in the bowl.'

We called our chip wagon 'MY-T TAS-T CHIPS.'

Jim Jr. and I put it all together, buying deep fryers, and mounting large twin propane canisters on the back to fuel them, and installing a small refrigerator and a deep freezer.

We cut a hole to serve the customers and manufactured a metal roof that we could slide up the side poles to open and slide back down to close the service hole. A double-lock system protected it from intruders when we weren't open.

We were SO green when we first opened!

I noticed that a discount store here in London had a LOT of customers on the weekend. It was located in a good-sized warehouse with a HUGE parking lot at the front of the store. I spoke with the owner who operated this store that sold second-hand and discounted new, antique and hard-to-find items. We asked if we could set up on his premises, and after working out some details, he agreed.

The business was open seven days a week and was the perfect location for our chip wagon.

I went to a local vegetable wholesaler who serviced local restaurants and grocery stores and bought fifty-pound bags of potatoes wholesale and at a reasonable price. I didn't know how many we would need, so I guessed that ten bags would probably be enough for the Friday that we were to open.

We fired up the twin fryers, opened the chip boxes and little forked sticks, and had all the condiments on their shelf, but we hadn't opened the service door yet... thank goodness!

For when we unloaded these ten bags and opened the first one... licking our chops in anticipation of munching these super fresh, old-fashioned style, MY-T TAS-T CHIPS... we discovered the horrible truth... THE POTATOES HADN'T BEEN WASHED!

We had five hundred pounds of filthy, dirt-encrusted, totally unpalatable spuds.

My Amazing Hands quickly put the 'CLOSED' sign up and loaded the sacks of potatoes back in the pickup that I had 'borrowed' from Bryan's Auto Sales.

We went to my house and carried these fifty-pound sacks of spuds up a flight of stairs to get into the house, then up another flight of stairs to get upstairs, where the bathroom with the bathtub was. Then, back down to the kitchen to get some scrub brushes while the tub filled with water. We proceeded to dump the potatoes into the tub one sack at a time. The burlap sack itself had to be carried back downstairs and out the patio doors... to be beaten until we had as much dirt and dust out of the sack as possible.

Then the sack was taken back upstairs.

MY AMAZING HANDS

We conscripted neighbours and friends to help . . . gave each of them a towel, and scrubbed these five hundred pounds of potatoes until they were clean. Then we handed them to our friends, who had towels ready to dry them, and the kids helped by putting them back into the sack. They were carried back to the driveway, loaded into the pickup, and driven back to the MY-T TAS-T chip wagon.

We first tasted MY-T TAS-T CHIPS at 7:15 p.m. that evening. They were delicious!! But . . .

PHEW! We were tired out!

But we were open for business at eleven a.m. Saturday morning.

And we ran out of potatoes at 12:45 p.m. Saturday afternoon.

So . . . .

The wholesaler wasn't open on Saturday.

People were yelling for more fries!

But J.J. and I were calm, cool, and collected. We knew what to do. We went to at least four retail vegetable stores AND BOUGHT ALL THEY HAD. Then . . . back to our house to quickly phone the neighbours, unload, carry upstairs, wash in the tub, clean the container, reload the potatoes, carry them back down to the pickup, and rush back to the MY-T TAS-T CHIPS truck and get cooking!

We decided not to open on Sunday!

Instead, My Amazing Hands spent a good deal of the day running a snake down my drain pipes, because all that dirt off the potatoes turned to mud in our pipes and clogged up the system.

There had to be a better way!

I went to church on Sunday morning and prayed for God's help and advice. Now I don't remember exactly how I worded that prayer. And I don't know exactly how I found it . . . maybe I read it in the paper, or perhaps somebody told me. Computers weren't invented for general use yet, so I KNOW we didn't Google it!

But J.J. and I went for a drive south of London and found a farm that specialized in growing potatoes.

When we asked about buying them washed—the farmer told us that he washed ALL of his potatoes before being delivered. He showed us the washing shed, and everything was spotlessly clean.

Most importantly . . . the potatoes were perfect for our needs. They were absolutely clean, and they came in fifty-pound mesh sacks. And they were just pennies more than the ones we were struggling with.

And the farmer was even willing to drop them off RIGHT AT THE CHIP WAGON a couple of times a week for us. No additional charge.

And the discount store owner had a small shed nearby where we could store them.

So we purchased our potatoes from a local farmer, washed and bagged . . . ready to be hand-cut in our wall-mounted chipper.

Do *YOU* believe in the power of prayer? Let me tell you—Jim Jr., I, and our neighbours CERTAINLY do! From the first order that we cooked up, our fries were DELICIOUS!

To add to the 'flavour' of the business, we said that the fries were prepared 'OLD FASHIONED STYLE,' and our portions were generous and reasonably priced.

Eventually, we added gravy, battered shrimp, onion rings, and battered mushrooms to the menu.

Of course, we also had a small assortment of soft drinks, and coffee; and a condiment table with the usual serviette dispenser, vinegar, salt, ketchup, mustard, etc.

My Amazing Hands kept it well stocked.

We purchased a couple of used picnic tables, which served us well after they were painted the red, white and blue colours of the ex-post office delivery trucks. They became our theme colours! JJ and I agreed that we would have chosen those exact same colours if we had painted the tables BEFORE we bought the truck. (Yeah . . . right!)

Not only was the discount store open seven days a week, but it was located in the heart of London's industrial area. Lots of factories meant lots of people . . . HUNGRY people!

So My-T TAS-T CHIPS became a seven-day business, and my son had a full-time job! A HUGE success all around!

Man . . . we were green . . . but it became the green shade of money when we finally got it right!

1988

Jim McCarthy married Sally Marcroft on March 18, 1988, in a cute little vine-covered church in Byron near London, Ontario. It was a small ceremony—just immediate family and friends.

After the ceremony, we went to Al Gretzky's house—he lived nearby—where we danced and dined.

Al and his wife provided lunch, and everyone had a great time.

A few weeks later, Sally and I were invited to join her son, Simon, and his wife for supper at a restaurant in northern Toronto. Simon was completing his education at York University.

I don't know his proper title, but basically, Simon was involved in the film industry. I believe he was training to be a film editor. Consequently, he knew a LOT of people in all aspects of making movies.

The meal was served buffet style in this quaint old restaurant in old Toronto. Apparently, it was home to a lot of movie people. After we were seated, ordered drinks, and were waiting for them to be served, Simon struck up a conversation with the gentleman sitting across the table from us. I was introduced to him, and one of MY AMAZING HANDS shook his, then we chatted.

I told him I was a musician, just getting involved in amateur theatre. Just small talk.

He told me that he was an actor and was currently making a Christmas movie called *Prancer*, which was scheduled to be released in 1989. He said he plays the father of the family.

Some years later, after computers were in every home, I remembered the dinner and meeting this gentleman, and the name of the film . . . *Prancer*! So I looked it up on Google!

That's when I discovered that MY AMAZING HAND had shaken hands with, chatted with, and had lunch with yet another hugely popular celebrity . . . Sam Elliott!

1989

My dad, Earl Corrie D'Alton McCarthy, passed away in 1989 at seventy-one years of age.

He got out of bed one morning and fell.

His legs wouldn't work.

My dad was a heavy smoker.

He learned that he had lung cancer in 1988.

The doctors said he only had a couple of years to live.

The cancer grew from his lungs to his spine and destroyed the nerves leading to his legs.

They operated on him in Toronto and then sent him to a rehabilitation clinic in Owen Sound to help him to get walking once again.

My Amazing Hands visited him there, and he was in high spirits and determined to overcome this disability.

That was Dad . . . a fighter!

He lived alone since my mom, Dorothy McCarthy, died in 1983.

My brother, Ken, drove our dad back to Wasaga Beach on his birthday, February sixth. The whole family gathered for what we correctly assumed was his last birthday. We have the party on film.

I think he just knew that it would probably be the last family get-together.

He had healed enough to take a few steps when the family was called one Friday a short time later.

We were told that they didn't expect him to last the weekend.

They had previously told us that he might live a couple of years.

But he only lived a couple of months.

My dad was a very nice, very kind, and very gentle man. A true GENTLEMAN!!

He loved Jesus!

He's with Him in Heaven now As is his wife, Dorothy Isobel McCarthy . . . our mother!

He was an amazing Dad!

He's missed.

***

I sold the two houses in London, saved some money, and had a small inheritance, so we bought a house and moved to Wasaga Beach to be near Dad in early 1989.

As I knew the business exceptionally well, thanks to my experiences with Bryan's Auto Sales and a number of prior years of selling assorted vehicles, I became a licensed dealer and opened up a used car lot, which I named 'Country Motor Sales,' on Hwy 26 near Wasaga Beach.

I had a staff of four, plus me and a guard dog.

There was a lady who managed the finances for the dealership, who also was my counter clerk in the variety store that I soon opened—a bookkeeper, cashier, and sweep-up person all-in-one.

I hired another licensed salesman besides me.

Also, a licensed mechanic who did repairs both on my inventory and on customers' vehicles.

And a 'lot man' who took care of the never-ending myriad of odd jobs.

I also had a guard dog that protected the premises at night.

My Amazing Hands would take a couple of 'drivers' with me and attend the 'dealers only' auctions in Milton, Toronto, and Barrie.

I would bid on vehicles that I thought were 'sell-able,' stick yellow dealer plates on them, and the drivers and I would drive them back to the car lot.

Yes, I had a Dealer's License. I often went to the Dealer's Auction in Milton or Barrie to obtain stock. I was only licensed to sell used vehicles, not new ones. That was okay with me!

Al came to visit and had a special surprise for me!

He handed me a package that contained one of Wayne's personal pictures.

It was a split picture that showed Wayne skating to a stop on the ice on one side, and a head and shoulders of Wayne in a suit and tie on the other.

The inscription read, 'Good Luck with Country Motor Sales,' and was signed 'Wayne Gretzky.' That picture proudly hung in my office until the very last day I was open.

When I worked at the car dealerships, I held a Salesman's License. I could sell ANYTHING!

We purchased vehicles at dealer auctions in Barrie, Milton, and Oshawa, and drivers brought them back to the dealership. The business owned a tow truck and would bring another car or pickup back on 'the hook.'

At Country Motor Sales, we had a variety of unique vehicles, and folks would come from Toronto to North Bay to see and buy them. The dealership, at various times, sold: a red Porsche convertible, a black 1983 Cadillac Fleetwood, a 1975 stretch Limousine, a 1927 Bugatti 'kit' car, which was a fibreglass Bugatti body on a Chrysler K-car frame, a 1957 Ford Ranchero and 1960 Dodge D100 ½ ton pickup, to name but a few.

My Amazing Hands <u>loved</u> driving the Porsche convertible!

But my personal favourite was a 1965 Pontiac Parisienne Custom Sport—red with black leather guts and tons of chrome everywhere. This is the car that starred in the movie 'Wasaga' (see 1993).

I also sold lots of motorcycles, including my personal ride, a 1200cc Honda Gold Wing—a big, heavy touring bike.

I got that 'M' stamped on my license back in 1958, remember?

And Country Motor Sales sold a variety of trucks and vans, from pickups to stake trucks: a 'touring' recreational vehicle, and many snowmobiles of all makes.

And boats, boats, and more boats of all shapes and sizes, from a small sailboat to a twenty-four foot yacht!

There was an empty store on the premises when I first leased it.

I had experience both managing a Becker's store in Belleville and owning a variety store and aviary in Clinton. I knew what I needed and how to arrange this variety store to maximize sales.

So My Amazing Hands obtained some stock and opened the store.

I renamed it 'Country Motor Sales & Variety'!

This is the store that, years before, used to be Mary Lou's Truck Stop. Ken and I would go there when we visited his family, and play 'Space Invaders'. We called it the 'Goosh-Goosh' machine, because that was the sound the guns made whenever we played the game.

Wasaga Beach has twenty-five miles of sandy beach—the largest freshwater beach in the world, so we would get lots and lots of visitors of all ages in the summer for the vehicles and the variety store.

Blue Mountain at Collingwood is only 15 minutes away. Known for excellent winter skiing. And we are on Georgian Bay with superb salmon, steelhead, and pickerel fishing during the spring and fall.

This made my two businesses, the car lot and the variety store, really busy with tourists year-round. We sold a lot of cigarettes, soft drinks, and confectionery items, as well as canned goods, pet food, and barbeque items.

And Country Motor Sales and Convenience was located right on Hwy 26, halfway between Wasaga Beach and Collingwood.

My Amazing Hands were VERY busy all day, every day.

I thought these two-in-one businesses would be a good investment. And for a while, for three years—I made good money. And had a heck of a lot of fun!

However, a HUGE recession hit in the early nineties, and my investment went rapidly downhill.

Oh, well—I did everything right!

Business got worse until, in 1995, I dismissed the staff, sold the stock, and closed the doors!

I was out of the car business, never to return!

***

Ken had been playing as part of a trio with Peter and Betty Johnson in bars and dance halls around the area. Peter was the drummer, Betty was on the organ, and Ken played guitar.

All three sang.

Ken was the frontman and did most of the vocals. The group was called 'Misty Blue.'

Peter used to play barefoot. I'm not sure why, but it was the way he preferred to do it. I used to sit in with the band when we drove up to visit Mom, Dad, and bro . . . great fun!

MY AMAZING HANDS

When we moved to Wasaga Beach, they asked me to join them full-time. I was thrilled to be playing in a band with my brother, Ken, once again.

My Amazing Hands got to play pretty well every weekend.

Eventually, Misty Blue ended, and I joined Clive Prentiss and Timberline. He needed a drummer and backup singer, and I still had my drum kit.

Just like what I did back in Goderich with The Country Boys, I would switch places with Clive . . . then he'd drum, and I'd sing lead while using his guitar.

It showed the band's versatility, and we were in high demand.

Rael Loiselle, the lead guitar player, left the group, and Ken took his place. Ken is a great singer and a fantastic guitar player, so he was a terrific asset to the group.

Now we had three singers that could sing either lead or backup. We had some excellent three-part harmony. It was fun.

Timberline played as far away as Manitoulin Island (cabins and a rowboat for fishing were provided), and we shared the stage with some travelling comedians from Yuk-Yuks.

It was a huge event that took place in a large arena.

My Amazing Hands even played drums when Timberline performed as the stage band on the radio during a Lions Club radio auction to benefit the Salvation Army in Collingwood. They asked me to sing a couple of songs solo. I accompanied myself on guitar. I still have a picture from the newspaper of My Amazing Hands performing on the radio! Clive was co-host along with the regular radio host and gave my business, Country Motor Sales, which I still had at that time, lots of free plugs on the air that day.

Thank you, my friend.

You are remembered!

A couple of years later, the band 'disbanded.'

1990

Mardi Gras was celebrated on Shrove Tuesday—February 27, 1990.

Sally and I went to New Orleans the week after Mardi Gras. You see, Sally and I owned a timeshare unit.

I bought it back in affluent times so we could get guaranteed, inexpensive accommodation for a vacation wherever another timeshare became available anywhere in the world.

A week was available in Gulf Shores, Alabama, and it had sleeping accommodations for four, so we invited Ken, and his wife, Sharon, to vacation with us. We drove to Windsor, crossed into Detroit, then flew to Biloxi, Mississippi. There we rented a car and drove west to Gulf Shores. Except for a fun day in Mobile, we pretty much laid around the beautiful Gulf Shores beaches, drinking drinks with umbrellas in them and soaking up that glorious sun.

Not only my feet, (remember my *thing* was to put my feet in famous bodies of water in my lifetime travels. See the EPILOG at the end of the book) but my entire body was in the Gulf of Mexico when we took a swim.

What does that have to do with My Amazing Hands? Well... we were doing a bit of exploring, and none of us had ever been to nearby Florida. So we drove to Tallahassee. Just on the outskirts, we decided to stop for a bite to eat and a couple of beers at this quaint little bar along the way. There was a small stage with a guy playing his guitar and singing a country tune.

We introduced ourselves when he took a break, and we bought him a beer.

MY AMAZING HANDS

As we chatted, we told him that we were also musicians. So he invited us to use his guitar and do a couple of songs. So . . . we performed on stage in Florida. My Amazing Hands played his guitar as we sang.

At the end of the week, we meandered across southern Louisiana, stopping only once to check out an old Civil War fort to get a feel for how life must have been back in those days.

As we drove across southern Louisiana, I noticed my brother, Ken (who was in the front seat with me), flicking with his fingernail at something on his right hand. I'm not sure exactly why I noticed, but later this little act led to drama.

On the outskirts of New Orleans, we booked a motel room for the night, then headed into the city.

We parked near what looked like the town hall, then took a walk along the banks of the mighty Mississippi River . . . taking in too many sights to even begin to tell you in a mere book.

However, as was my wont, I took off my shoes and socks and dangled my feet in yet another famous water, the mighty Mississippi. Along with the Seine in Paris, the Detroit River, the St. Clair River, and later you'll read about the Thames in London, England.

I didn't know it yet, but there was more foot-dangling in famous rivers to come, in later years. Fast forward to the EPILOG at the end of the book for more!

We meandered into the French Quarter. One of My Amazing Hands tipped the street performers on Royal and Bourbon Streets, and we all had drinks at The Spotted Cat on Frenchmen Street. Though Mardi Gras had been over for a week, there were still a lot of sights to see and souvenirs of Mardi Gras to get a deal on.

Being musicians, Ken and I took the ladies to see Preservation Hall, where old-time negro and white players have been performing traditional New Orleans jazz since 1961. We entered through the double doors at the front right, past the bins full of old 78 rpm records, and into the rear of the hall where the musicians were performing. The crowd slowly made its way forward until we were immediately there—these amazing jazz musicians were performing on the floor RIGHT IN FRONT OF US.

Then we made our way through the left doors and onto the street.

While there never was an actual streetcar named 'Desire,' there were streetcars on an actual streetcar line named for its endpoint on Desire Street. One of these streetcars was restored in 1967 and became quite a tourist attraction. It sat on a pedestal on tracks of its own, and, yes, My Amazing Hands rested on the brake handle that controls the air that goes to the brakes to make the stops nice and smooth.

We had a traditional southern meal in one of the many Cajun restaurants in the area and headed back to our motel.

Tuckered out from all that drivin' and walkin', we couldn't wait to hit the sack.

We drove back to Biloxi to return the rental car and catch the plane back to Detroit the next day.

As we drove through downtown Detroit, we passed the famous 'Fist,' a memorial at Hart Plaza dedicated to boxer Joe Louis. Then we were back in Canada after a short tunnel ride under the Detroit River. A couple of hours later, we were home.

As an aside . . . I had put my feet in both the Detroit River and St. Clair River when I was living in Chatham and Dad had taken me there to catch fish in the spring and fall runs.

Back to my story . . .

The 'thing' on Ken's hand that he had flicked off on the way to New Orleans became infected. Red lines had appeared and were going up his arm. We took him to the hospital, and while we were sitting in the emergency room, a doctor going by stopped, then came back to talk to Ken and me.

He told us that he had just gotten back to Canada after working down south, and it looked as if Ken was possibly bitten by a Black Widow or Brown Recluse spider. The doctor ordered some special venom antidote, which he administered a couple of hours later when it arrived by a special courier.

He guessed Ken had gotten the spider bite at that old Civil War fort we explored.

The doctor said it could have killed him if the red veins had made it to Ken's heart.

***

In the early nineties, I volunteered to serve with St. John Ambulance.

I guess the death of my parents got me thinking . . . would I know what to do if someone, especially a loved one, had a medical emergency?

So I joined St. Johns Ambulance in Collingwood.

As a result, if someone passes out, stops breathing, or any of the other things this flesh is heir to (Shakespeare's Hamlet Act 3, Scene 1), My Amazing Hands will be able to help . . . maybe even save someone's life.

We were given a uniform, a personal first aid kit, and LOTS of training. We sometimes used our unit ambulance, which had even more equipment.

After receiving intensive first-aid training, I passed the certification test and was qualified to give first-aid assistance for three years before requiring recertification.

St John Ambulance provided our uniforms, bandages, and some common medication. There was no charge for our services or the ambulance to medical facilities if required. We attended many indoor and outdoor events and helped anyone who needed us.

Some got heat stroke from the sun. We treated it.

Some got frostbite from the cold. And we treated that, too.

There were broken bones and stomach aches. Everyone got treated to the best of our abilities.

It had its moments, however!

For example, I attended a ladies' softball tournament in Collingwood – young ladies in the eighteen to twenty-four age range. There I was, seated in the stands, in my uniform, with my first aid kit— enjoying the game—enjoying the sunny day. Suddenly there was a flurry of excitement at home plate! The batter had hit a pop-up.

The batter took off for first base, then changed her mind and headed back to home plate. The catcher and the umpire tossed off their face masks and looked up at the ball. The player who was on third– who, incidentally, I thought was the prettiest girl on the team, squealed off third base and raced for home.

(Most female ballplayers actually DO squeal with delight).

There quickly was a kerfuffle at home plate when these three young and pretty players collided, together with the umpire. Only two of them and the umpire got up.

The player, the pretty one, who had been on third base, was sitting there holding her leg in both hands.

After a moment or two, the other two players, with a display of true sportsmanship, helped her to her feet and off the field as she continued to hold her leg, which was bleeding profusely. I leaped off the bleachers where I had been sitting and raced to the bench where this poor girl was trying to staunch the flowing blood with her hands. Players standing in the way got abruptly moved aside as I elbowed my way through!

When I reached her, I calmed her down, then examined the gash on her leg.

I directed someone to call an ambulance, and My Amazing Hands applied a bandage to the wound and a tourniquet to her upper leg to slow the blood flow. She was going into shock, so I had the spectators make way so she could lie on the bench.

After a few minutes, colour was slowly coming back into her cheeks.

I asked someone to get some water, and I took a washcloth to wash some of the blood and dirt from her leg.

Then, after it stopped bleeding, I left the tourniquet in place but put a clean dressing on the open wound.

Shortly after, the ambulance arrived and took her to be treated. I was pleasantly surprised when I got a round of applause from the players and spectators when I returned to my seat.

Suddenly, one of the other players, another pretty girl, came and kissed me on the cheek.

Someone whispered to me that she was the injured girl's sister.

However, I already had my reward—she was safely treated with no ill effects, and...

HER TEAM WON THE GAME!

My AMAZING HANDS helped again!

***

Once a week, I bowled!

By now, I had learned how to bowl ten-pin. I already knew five-pin bowling from my younger days setting pins at the Little Bowl when I was still in high school.

Over the years, I belonged to many leagues, and I was a pretty good bowler.

My Amazing Hands achieved perfect games in both the five-pin and ten-pin leagues. I think my boys have my trophies. I found one old trophy photo.

My Amazing Hands also used to play a LOT of darts in leagues ever since I lived in London. I think I got five 180s in my lifetime... hey, not bad for a guitar picker with no physique!

1991

In 1991, the Canada Cup tryouts were held in Collingwood, Ontario.

As I said, I was a volunteer with St John Ambulance. I was assigned duty at the Collingwood Arena to look after anyone injured.

St John had use of the first aid room in the bowels of the arena ... right across from the coach's room and just down from the players' dressing rooms.

My Amazing Hands could use it for treating anyone—staff and patrons of the arena, management, security ... anyone who required medical attention.

The players and supporting staff had their own medical personnel.

When I arrived at the arena for the first time, dressed in my St. John uniform, I got in line to enter. I was spotted by Alan Eagleson, the lawyer that negotiated contracts for hockey players. He took me out of this line and ushered me into the arena through a special entrance for notable persons. He took me upstairs to his office and had his people get me a pass allowing me to go anywhere in the arena at any time.

While waiting for this pass, I was seated at Alan's desk, which was right beside Roger Neilson's desk.

Roger was a Canadian professional hockey coach.

I overheard him negotiating with someone on the phone for television coverage in Europe for the Canada Cup series.

Hundreds of thousands of dollars were being discussed! WOW!

Then I was introduced to him! Yes, one of My Amazing Hands shook Roger Neilson's hand. Pretty cool! They say that Alan Eagleson did things that were frowned upon by the hockey world, but I've got to say, he was VERY friendly and treated me with a ton of respect.

I received the pass and used it to go into the coach's room, where I met and chatted with <u>all</u> of the coaches—Mike Keenan, Pat Burns, Brian Sutter, Tom Webster and Tom Watt.

My pass also got me into the player's dressing room, where I met a lot of the superstars from Canada's Olympic team and equally famous sportswriters who were interviewing the players.

The fact that a lot of players were naked—in and out of the open showers—didn't distract these professionals one bit.

I got an autographed hockey stick from Steve Smith. It was a left-handed stick, and I was right-handed, so I gave it to my son, Jim Jr. My picture was also taken with Brendan Shanahan, Wendel Clark, Al MacInnis, and others.

I went to the room where all the exercise equipment was available to the hockey players. Wayne Gretzky was finishing up a workout. One of My Amazing Hands shook his Amazing Hand, and he put his arm around my shoulders. I mentioned his uncle and my friend, Al Gretzky, and we exchanged chit-chat about his family.

After thanking him for the autographed picture Al had given to me and for signing the rookie card's plastic sleeve, My Amazing Hands had their photo taken shaking hands with The Great One!

How KOOL is THAT!!

***

A few years later, after marrying Sally and moving to Wasaga Beach, I discovered that she was also interested in amateur theatre. When we found that some folks here in town were going to form an amateur theatre group called Wasaga Community Theatre, Sally was at the inaugural meeting.

The first play performed by the group was called *Exit The Body*. It was a comedy that revolved around a body that kept appearing and disappearing.

Besides doing sound and lighting . . . I played the husband. I didn't appear until the third act. I stood behind my 'wife' when she opened a closet door near the end of the play, saw the body there, and fainted back into my arms.

I easily caught her during rehearsals, but everyone was in costume during the 'dress' rehearsal. She wore a silk nightgown when she fainted and fell back into my arms. I put my arms around her to catch her, but the nightgown was slippery, and she slipped right down. Not wanting to let her fall, I tightened my 'bear hug' and (you *know* what's next) . . . yup, I prevented her from falling by grabbing her ample breasts . . . one in each hand.

As she was still slipping and falling, I grabbed her even tighter.

All I can say is . . . it's a good thing My Amazing Hands did their job . . . she could have had a nasty fall, and then what would we do for a leading lady?

So, My Amazing Hands saved the day . . . AND the play!

You know, she didn't even miss any lines! What a trooper!

We practiced with her nightgown on, devising a way that she could fall sideways so she would be safe and still be able to speak her lines . . . without embarrassment!

For the next few years, we were involved in many plays locally, both with Wasaga Community Theatre, and Collingwood Pretty River Players.

My Amazing Hands provided most of the sound and lighting effects for both groups.

I actually *directed* two plays in Collingwood and one in Wasaga Beach.

I acted in many plays . . . most notably, I played Mr. Bumble in the musical version of *Oliver* and played a tuxedoed drunk singing *Brother, Can You Spare A Dime* in *Roaring In The 20's*.

I was 'Grandpa' in *You Can't Take It With You* and a cop in *Our Town*.

I also did some open-air acting with the Collingwood Pretty River Players theatre troupe.

So, if the local theatre troupe gets rolling again, after this Covid thing . . . I'm ready.

My Amazing Hands are also ready to take another run at the husband in *Exit the Body*.

I know . . . it's a tricky part . . . but *somebody* has to do it!

1992

I remained interested in amateur theatre, and though I wasn't on stage—Sally was. I was more involved in lighting and sound.

Sally and I donated money to Stratford Shakespearean Theatre, and My Amazing Hands became a 'Friend' of the theatre.

One day in the spring, we received an invitation to have a personally guided theatre tour, including the director's seat, backstage, and under-stage.

WOW!

The Stratford Shakespearean Festival started in a tent back in the fifties, but a huge, amazing building had been erected as a permanent home for the Festival but made to resemble a tent, completed in 1957.

When I phoned to schedule a day to visit, the lady who answered and I chatted for a few minutes. I proudly told the theatre person that I was born in Stratford, Ontario, and that my ancestors were among the first settlers. My great-great-grandfather was the first white baby born in Perth County. And that there even is a street... McCarthy Road in Stratford... named after my family.

I told her that my mother had worked at the theatre as a 'dresser' in the seventies and that my wife and I are involved in theatre... amateur theatre.

I told her about my grandparents boarding **William Hutt** in the early days of the Stratford Shakespearean Festival, and how I had shaken his hand when I was just a very young lad.

MY AMAZING HANDS

I mentioned that I had directed three plays, acted in many plays, and was the lighting and sound director for many others. She told me she was on the theatre's executive and would meet my wife and me at the stage door and give us a personal tour of the theatre.

My Amazing Hands met this wonderful lady on the appointed day at the stage entrance.

We were expected!

As rehearsals were in full swing for the live theatre production of *Gypsy*, a musical about 1957 memoirs of striptease artist Gypsy Rose Lee, we were silenced with a 'finger-over-the-lips,' and seated a dozen or so rows back while the actors and musicians did a 'cue-to-cue' rehearsal.

How exciting is that—watching these professionals getting stage direction from more professionals.

When everyone stopped for a fifteen-minute break, we were told, "Come with me!" and taken to a small elevator in a back hallway.

After a short elevator ride, we exited to find ourselves at the very top of the gigantic tent-like building.

Huge potlights and spotlights and speakers were everywhere, joined by a maze of screened walkways.

One of these walkways ended in a small room at the centre. It had just one chair, surrounded by microphones, lights, headphones, control panels, and assorted technical 'stuff.'

I was invited to sit in this, the 'Director's Chair.' It was way, way above the stage. From here, the director could see everything below and direct whatever he wanted.

My Amazing Hands sat in the Director's Chair at Stratford Shakespearean Festival.

How GREAT was THAT!

Then we took the elevator back down, continuing to the basement. Our lady guide showed us the 'costume' area . . . lots of sewing machines and rack after rack of actor's costumes. These were hand-sewn right here for each of the actors for each play.

We were shown the stars' dressing rooms and the general room for the rest of the troupe. Another fenced-off area was for sword-fighting lessons and practice for the plays that required it.

At each end of this huge room, there was a ramp. We were invited to walk up it, and the lady guide told me that it was here that my mother would work when the players were on stage. As the play progressed, the actors would show the passing of time by changing clothes with the assistance of a 'dresser,' like my mother.

For example, if it were a sword-fighting sequence, the hero would be on-stage with shiny armour. As the sword-fighting progressed, he would work his way off-stage, where he would remove the outer armour and don somewhat scuffed-up armour. Then, after more fighting on stage, he would work his way off-stage, now donning more banged-up armour. etc., to show time elapsing until his death scene!

Also, the actors could use a 'stage centre' elevator if they needed to suddenly 'appear' onstage.

My Amazing Hands rode me up that central elevator, and I found myself alone on centre stage in the Stratford Shakespearian Festival tent, where thousands of friends and fans of William Shakespeare's brilliant work witnessed the performances that dozens of professionals had performed over the years.

It took me a minute to realize and appreciate where I was standing...then....My Amazing Hands came together as I bowed my head in reverence!

1993

One day the phone rang. One of My Amazing Hands answered.

A woman introduced herself as Judith Doyle. She said that she was a movie director making a full-length feature film that would be called *Wasaga*. She heard I was involved with amateur theatre in both Wasaga Beach and Collingwood.

She wanted to use local talent in the movie as much as possible and thought that I could help her to connect with local thespians.

She was also interested in one of my cars . . . not to buy, but to lease—to be used in the movie. The vehicle she was referring to was a 1965 Pontiac Parisienne Custom Sport 2-Door Coupe. Fire engine red with a black leather interior and chrome everywhere!

We all called him . . . '*Big Red*!'

One of the really nice things about owning a car dealership is that I could drive anything on the lot anytime I wanted, anywhere I wanted! The 'flavour of the week' I chose for myself was this eye-catching red beauty.

I invited Judith to my dealership, and she arrived shortly afterward.

After introductions, we talked about possible local actors, and I gave her some names and phone numbers of fellow thespians with whom I have shared a stage for local amateur productions. She offered me a small part in the film, which I, of course, accepted.

Wouldn't you?

Then I let her take Big Red for a drive to ensure it would be movie material.

She returned shortly, just gushing about how Big Red will be just perfect in her film.

We took care of the business details back in the office, and then we both signed an agreement that My Amazing Hands typed up detailing who is responsible in case of blah... blah... blah....

And how much my acting skills are worth (I was glad I didn't get paid by the lines spoken), and most importantly... how much money I will get to let them use Big Red for this epic.

I was delighted when I saw the finished movie and saw that they used local talent as much as possible.

Filming commenced immediately. However, it was the next day before they were ready for MY speaking part as the Drive-In Theatre owner.

As you could see (if you found a copy of *Wasaga* and fast-forwarded to 45:50), my speaking part was close to perfection and one of the highlights of the film (tongue firmly in cheek).

I got a phone call from the movie company one day informing me that *Wasaga* was one of the Canadian films selected for the 1994 Toronto International Film Festival, and would I like tickets?

Heck, YEAH!

So my wife and I saw *Wasaga* for the very first time on the big screen in Toronto.

There I was! My Amazing Hands were in the movie!

And in the credits!

My name was front and centre as the credits went scrolling by. There it is... Drive-In Theatre Owner – Jim McCarthy (at 1:23:04 of the movie).

Wasaga was often shown on television, usually on the really late, late-late shows.

And when the film was over, and the audience was congratulating everybody, and we were exiting the theatre, I was approached by this breathless young lady who said, "I just saw you on the big screen inside, didn't I? Weren't you the owner of the drive-in theatre in the film?"

When I confirmed that, indeed, it was I, she pulled a booklet out of her purse and asked me for my autograph.

Because I doubt that the movie generated enough profit in such a short time to afford to hire people just to make insignificant extras feel good, I have to assume she was the real thing!

She certainly did the job, though!

It felt GREAT to be asked for my autograph! Could this have been the humble beginning of a fabulous new career?

Was I going to be a movie star?

H-m-m-m? NAH!

But . . . My Amazing Hands can list among my many accomplishments—MOVIE ACTOR!!

My Amazing Right Hand went on to bigger, better theatrical things.

Be sure to check out what happened in 1994!

1994

One evening, My Amazing Hands got an excited phone call from my friend Cecil Brady.

He told me that a movie was being made in Collingwood, and they were looking for extras, preferably, but not exclusively, with some acting experience.

I picked up Cecil the following evening, and we both signed up for an experience of a lifetime.

My Amazing Hands were going to be on-screen in a Hollywood movie. The film was called *The Long Kiss Goodnight* and starred Geena Davis and Samuel L. Jackson.

It would be co-produced and directed by Geena's then-husband, Renny Harlin.

It would be partially shot in Collingwood, and as this was late February, there was still lots of snow on the ground. A necessity, as many scenes occur on Christmas Eve. The movie company 'took over' the main street of Collingwood from about ten every evening until about four o'clock each morning.

The town was resplendent with Christmas decorations everywhere. That generated the holiday atmosphere that permeated the town.

The Collingwood High School marching band, dressed in Santa suits and marching in formation, played Christmas music in the film.

It was VERY cold every night that the movie was being filmed. The movie company had anticipated that, though, and had three locations where the movie people, including we extras, could keep warm and enjoy complimentary hot coffee or cocoa, sandwiches and chips while the crew set up for the next scene.

During one of our breaks, on the second or third night of filming, I noticed a couple of children approach the gentleman sitting across from Cecil and me.

They asked him for his autograph. After this was repeated a second, then a third time, I asked one of the kids why.

He told me that the man was famous! He was right!

That's how I met . . . **CAPTAIN HIGHLINER!**

My Amazing Hands shook the hand of yet another celebrity when I said hello to this very pleasant gentleman!

We returned to the 'set' and, while the crew was getting things ready for the next 'shoot,' I stood near Santa's sleigh—parked in front of the Gayety Theatre.

If you pause the film and look carefully, you can see the Gayety close to the main corner, behind the crowd. I was standing just a few feet from a couple of superstars!

Santa Claus and Geena Davis!

My Amazing Hands waved at them.

Santa was busy, on the phone to the North Pole, but . . .

Geena waved back!

How great was THAT!

Cecil and I continued to the corner and waited for the next scene's filming to start.

In the previous scene, a car had flipped over, and a couple of cops were trapped inside (supposedly).

Suddenly, we were being spoken to by this man with a bullhorn who told us to move down off of the sidewalk and come over to him. He asked us if we wanted to be more involved in the movie. DUH!

He wanted us to return to where we were standing, then, when cued, to rush down onto the street, have My Amazing Hands check out the status of the two guys in this burning car, then act excited and try to get the attention of the guy playing the cop!

The fire was very much controlled . . . just a pipe with holes along its length, connected by a hose to a propane tank. When ignited, it looked like the car was on fire, but with no danger to anyone. The 'men' in the car were fireproof dummies.

I recognized the man with the bullhorn . . . Renny Harlin, co-producer and director of the film.

One of My Amazing Hands shook his and wished him success with the movie. Another celebrity who met My Amazing Hands!

So where are Cecil and I in the movie, you ask?

Well . . . we ended up on the cutting room floor, unfortunately.

I guess Hollywood and stardom weren't ready for My Amazing Hands—yet!

1995

By 1995, I was broke.

We lost our entire investment in Country Motor Sales and Variety, plus everything we had saved.

During the last six months, my wife had to work, and I had to play as much music as possible on the side to keep ahead of the bills at the used car business, the variety store, and our home, which we purchased.

A 'blankety-blank' RECESSION WIPED us OUT!

COUNTRY MOTOR SALES AND VARIETY CLOSED ITS DOORS in 1995!

I take pride that I just closed the doors—I left the premises not owing a cent. But I lost the money I had invested when I sold the two houses in London, my small inheritance from my mom and dad, and all of my savings.

So . . . it was time to start over and get back on top again!

I took stock of myself!

Sally was a good wife. My mortgage on my house was current—so I had some equity there. I was in excellent health, reasonably intelligent, and had a car . . . I kept the best and sold the others at auction.

My heart ached when My Amazing Hands handed over the keys to Big Red! He was an old friend and a big part of the family!

Then, one day, while collecting the mail, I met a neighbour at the mailbox. She commented that she saw Country Motor Sales had closed and asked me if

I had plans. When I told her I was looking for something else, she suggested I might make a few dollars working for her, dealing cards weekends at the local charity casinos, until some full-time employment came available.

I knew she and a partner ran the local bingo hall open afternoons and evenings.

She suggested I meet with her the next afternoon to discuss her proposal.

She had a blackjack table set up at the back of the bingo hall and asked if I knew the game. I told her I had played it a few times when the guys had a 'poker night,' but that was all.

She proceeded to give me a couple of hours of instruction, then asked me to come out to the next charity casino being held at the local legion that coming Saturday. She gave me a bow tie and asked me to wear dark pants and a white shirt.

The only difference between a charity casino and the real thing was that the bets were only a quarter, with a fifty-cent maximum raise. It was more of a fun, community thing. The local charity, in this case, the Legion, got the receipts after all fees and salaries had been paid.

I became a CROUPIER!

My Amazing Hands were dealing Blackjack that night, and again and again . . . and I loved it.

***

I love music. I love listening to it, and I love performing it. And I especially love making money when I am performing it. But . . . it was tough to find musicians to put together a group, practice, and play gigs.

So, it seemed like a natural thing to do to control ALL the music that I played instead of organizing musicians. As time went by, the internet happened, and I discovered sites where I could get songs—free.

Lots of them. All genres.

I already had the electronic gear I used to perform with my guitar.

So, I filled my computer with music, designed and had some business cards printed, phoned some musical establishments for gigs, and now My Amazing Hands belonged to a DJ.

I came up with the name BLACK VELVET DISC JOCKEY SERVICES and the logo:

MY AMAZING HANDS

'THE DJ WITH CLASS.'

Because I had a top hat and walking stick (that I used in my theatrical career), a tux vest, and a black bow tie, I thought it would be a good 'costume' to wear while DJ'ing formal events (that paid better than beer parlours).

Events like weddings (including the ceremony in the church itself . . . I had the Wedding March, etc., in my repertoire), Buck 'n Does, proms, private parties, company events, etc. So I paid for a booth at local Wedding Shows, where people who supply wedding 'things' like dresses and tuxedos, flowers, food caterers, etc., have them on display.

I occasionally saw other DJs there, but they usually wore jeans with ripped knees and T-shirts.

No competition at all for me, with my top hat and walking stick. I was, indeed,

'THE DJ WITH CLASS!'

To REALLY put the icing on the cake (so to speak), I would hire a couple of beautiful hostesses dressed in white shirts with bow ties, nylons, high heels, and black mini-skirts. First-class all the way for My Amazing Hands!

The bride-to-be received a white corsage, and the mother of the bride received a pink corsage when they first entered the bridal show. These were significant events with many booths, usually in an arena or recreation area. The corsages made it easy to spot the ladies who could be our customers.

The girls would approach the brides and mothers, and if they didn't have their wedding music arranged yet, they would bring the ladies to our booth, to my table, where I would take over.

They often would have already arranged the wedding music but forgot about the Buck 'n Doe. I filled my calendar for the year pretty quickly. And I found the ladies were willing to pay extra for the best.

I used a laptop computer to play the music, amplified through a mixer. And a couple of manageable speakers that were mounted on stands. I used a Shure microphone, and it sounded great. I would let the patrons use it to make announcements when apropos.

I also kept a spray bottle of alcohol and tissues to keep it sanitary, as often, it would be used to make speeches. Later, I purchased a portable microphone for the speeches.

My Amazing Hands designed a poster that would cover the front of the table that held the laptop computer, control panel, etc. An online printing company supplied it with our name in big black letters. This let everyone know that I was BLACK VELVET DISC JOCKEY SERVICES, and, as I performed on a stage at many venues, it hid our legs and the myriad of wires that ran under the table.

I bought a white tablecloth and some Velcro at the local dollar store and had a seamstress attach them.

So the tablecloth was on the top, and the poster hung down the front, joined by the Velcro.

I designed the business cards and had them printed by Vistaprint.

I designed songbooks that listed about 2,500 songs and put copies on half a dozen tables, with request slips, pens, and business cards so the folks could request their personal favourites. The songs were sorted into SONG TITLES and ARTISTS, and every page had appropriate graphics.

Again . . . My Amazing Hands designed them.

Of course, on my personal computer in my office at home, I had thousands of songs . . . I just picked a couple of thousand, that I thought might be appropriate to the occasion, to take on the job with me, pre-loaded into the laptop.

I had songs for special occasions—like Hallowe'en, Christmas, St. Patrick's Day, New Year's Eve, Italian tunes, Irish jigs, hymns, down east music, etc. I had the music to fit any occasion.

People loved it!

If I had a request for a particular song, I would always say: 'If I don't have it, I can get it.'

And I usually could!

I would let 'Uncle Joe' use my top hat and walking stick at the events. (There's always an 'Uncle Joe' at family events).

I would get all the ladies on the floor for a long kick line in *New York, New York*, with 'Uncle Joe' in the middle of the line.

Or we would perform some line dancing to *Chattahoochee* or *Achy, Breaky, Heart*, or perhaps some Italian folk dancing.

Folks loved the 'special-ness' of BLACK VELVET DISC JOCKEY SERVICES.

We all had a great time.

***

MY AMAZING HANDS

The Chippewas of Rama Mnjikaning First Nation were selected to open a casino in Ontario.

At one of the wedding shows, Chief Ted W. had a model showing what Casino Rama would look like when it was completed.

While the models displayed the latest wedding fashions, I wandered over to say hello.

While we chatted, I told the chief that I was a croupier, licensed to deal at Charity Casinos.

He suggested I might be interested in applying to Casino Rama. He took my name and address, and promised to pass it on to their Human Resources department.

To tell you the truth, I forgot about it.

Then I heard on the news that 30,000 people were lining up around the block in Toronto JUST TO GET AN APPLICATION. There were just under 3,000 jobs available.

I spoke to a friend who said he was applying to work there as a slot attendant. He said the starting pay was an unheard-of eighteen dollars an hour. The minimum wage was 'frozen' at $6.85 an hour from 1995 to 2003.

I wished him well (but thought he was 'stringing me a line').

I didn't think I had a hope of getting a dealer's job with my meagre casino knowledge.

Heck... I had never even SEEN a real casino.

BUT...

A couple of days later, I was stunned to find a large brown envelope in my mailbox.

It was an application for employment at Casino Rama. The attached letter gave me a date and time to come for an interview.

Chief Ted W had. made good on his promise.

At the interview, I was told I should have a couple more games to ensure a job.

So I attended the local college where they had added courses about how to deal roulette, and baccarat.

I also took blackjack to learn the 'casino' way of dealing the game.

The college charged five hundred dollars per 'game,' and I thought I would have to put a second mortgage on our home when, out of nowhere, my son, Peter, won a draw for a new car, but took the money instead.

He loaned it to me to take these courses. I repaid him, with interest, within a year.

And My Amazing Hands passed the requirements to be credited with these courses with flying colours.

Thank you so much, again, Peter!

So... did I get hired as a croupier at Casino Rama?

Sorry... you'll have to wait until 1996 to find out!

1996

As I completed each course, I dropped into HR to show them the paperwork confirming that I 'had' the game.

One day, I got a VERY thick package in the mail from Casino Rama, the contents of which they sent out to only those applicants WHO GOT THE JOB!

YA-HOO!

I was now a licensed croupier, licensed in Ontario. Now I can deal at Casino Rama.

A large hall had been leased for the month prior to the casino's grand opening, and they held what they called a 'mock casino' to get everyone at ease with their new job—and to check US out. I was initially hired as a part-time dealer, but, as I had obtained the other games, they promoted me to full-time at the mock casino.

Opening night, July 31, 1996, fell on my scheduled day off, but I went anyway, just to check it out.

My Amazing Hands belonged to a full-fledged croupier, and the next night, I proved it! I stood there in the pit, dressed in my gold vest, white shirt, bolo tie, and dealt blackjack!

Some nights I dealt baccarat—some nights— roulette!

I learned how to deal additional games, including mini-baccarat, Casino War, Texas hold 'em, Sic Bo, pai gow, and Caribbean stud. Also, to spin the big 'Wheel of Fortune'. Three months later, I was promoted to a dual-rate position—supervisor, except when they scheduled me as a dealer. A year later, I was promoted to full-time supervisor. I stood in the pit in my suit and tie and controlled the dealers and the play of up to four tables.

I was given a box of my very own Business Cards. With my name imprinted on them. Kewl!

The following year My Amazing Hands were supervising in the V.I.P. lounge.

Each promotion meant even more money.

Yes, they paid me well—but more importantly...

IT WAS GREAT FUN!

BLACK VELVET DISC JOCKEY SERVICES was still booking a LOT of weddings.

Fortunately, my days off were weekends at Casino Rama, so that wasn't a problem.

And I could STILL make music while having lots of fun jammin' with my brother Ken, and his wife's brother, Jimmer, during the day on the weekends. All three of us could sing and play drums and guitars, so, musically, we mixed it up pretty well.

We not only played at local bars and Legion halls, but often played for the seniors at the old folks' homes. Of course, we didn't charge anything and had a LOT of fun.

We were paid well—just not in money!

That suited us just fine!

1997

After the casino was open for a couple of years, someone in management decided that it would be a great idea for Casino Rama to join the entertainment circuit.

Superstars in the entertainment industry would be booked at various venues across the United States and Canada, as I'm sure you all know.

It wasn't long before this new casino—Casino Rama—became one of Ontario's premier entertainment destinations.

A giant marquis tent was erected in the corner of the parking lot. It had bleachers that would seat up to 2-3,000 people. Also included was a vast stage, confectionery booths, washrooms, and a big backstage area with dressing rooms.

They hired staff as required, and we employees were allowed to work there on our days off. We were allowed to make an additional income, so I jumped at the chance to apply as a security guard.

As a supervisor, I was in charge of the security guards on one side of this enormous tent. Of course, I was paid extra as a security supervisor.

There were six emergency exit doors on the sides, as well as the entrance-way doors, and there were also entrances to the backstage area in front and the sides of the seating area. All entries required guarding, so my job included allotting a security guard to each entrance. I rotated the guards every fifteen minutes, so we could all enjoy the added perk of seeing the shows for free. And we were paid!

I also stood in for them when they needed bathroom breaks.

And in between, I would sit on the bleacher stairs and take in the show.

And I got paid for that, too.

It was great fun ... and ... did I mention—I GOT **PAID** FOR IT! YAY!!

After three seasons of success with the giant tent in the parking lot, casino management decided that it would be a brilliant idea to build a permanent entertainment centre attached to the casino itself.

A top-of-the-line hotel had recently been built.

{Little known fact} While country superstar Faith Hill was the first to perform on the Entertainment Stage before a sold-out audience, the first superstar actually ON the stage was Beatle Ringo Starr.

He used it to rehearse before starting his All-Starr Tour.

However, that meant I no longer had my cushy security guard supervisor job ... Aw-w-w!

BUT ....

In chapter 1999, you'll read about My Amazing Hands performing live on Rama's Entertainment Stage at Rama's new ENTERTAINMENT CENTRE!

1998

One evening I was on my way to work at Casino Rama, around five-thirty or so.

I was driving through a little one-horse town in the middle of nowhere.

I knew the speed limit was sixty kilometres an hour, but I was running a little late, so I was moving right along at about eighty.

It was twilight-y.

Up ahead, I saw a car on the shoulder of the road.

Suddenly, I realized that it had been stopped—**by the police.**

Of course, I hit the binders to slow down and kept my fingers crossed that I was going slow enough that the officer wouldn't be interested in me. Perhaps he hadn't finished with the guy he had pulled over yet!

I left them both in the rear-view mirror, and My Amazing Hands carried on . . . at the speed limit!

Now I don't know how it is where YOU live, but where I live, it's courteous to assist your fellow drivers. Especially since, with the rapidly approaching dark, drivers approaching you on the other side of the road wouldn't see the policeman until they were right on him.

So, practicing good highway etiquette, My Amazing Hands flashed my high beams to the oncoming traffic.

Suddenly, OH—OH!

One of the approaching vehicles suddenly put on its flashing red and blue light bar on its roof, 'pulled a u-ey' and speeded up behind me.

"OH! NO!"

So, as a good law-abiding (most of the time) driver, I pulled over.

I was pretty sure I was doomed and was getting my wallet ready when a lady constable got out of her police car and approached my window.

"Why were you flashing your lights, sir?" she asked.

"So I could get your attention!" I replied, "I wanted you to stop!"

"It wasn't to warn other drivers about the police stop just ahead?" she asked, smiling at me.

I replied, "Heck no! A big dog ran into the side of my car. I will be late for work if I go back to see if it's all right. Then I saw you coming and flashed my lights to get your attention so you would take a look and take whatever action is necessary!"

It's now rapidly becoming nighttime, so the lady constable turned on her flashlight, and we went around to the passenger side of my car.

And there it was!

Right in the middle of my dust-covered rear passenger door!

A rather large area that could only indicate that something furry had, indeed, hit the door!

One of My Amazing Hands pointed.

The constable let me go with, "I'll look after things from here! Have a nice evening!" as she got in her car.

I could see her taillights heading on down the road as I hurriedly drove away in the other direction.

... Here's the story behind the story ...

Earlier that day, I pulled into a parking space at the pet store. I needed food for my cat.

A car pulled in beside me.

A lady got out, then opened her rear car door to let out her pet—a huge St. Bernard.

I asked if he was friendly and if I could pet him, as I just love the breed.

She answered in the affirmative, and, as My Amazing Hands were patting him between those big soulful eyes, his tail started furiously wagging his delight ... all over my dusty rear passenger door!

I noticed!

'Nuff said?

1999

My Amazing Hands are so proud to tell you that a few generations ago, in 1845 to be precise, a HERO was born in our family!

His name was John Augustus McCarthy Jr.

He was the second chief of police in Stratford, Ontario since it became a city. His father was the first!

In 1913, the steeple of the Knox Presbyterian Church in Stratford was hit by lightning. The fire that it caused spread quickly, destroying the sanctuary and engulfing the roof and steeple.

Four men were positioning a ladder when the steeple came crashing down, killing Police Chief John McCarthy Jr., Fire Chief Hugh Durkin, and Constable Matthew Hamilton. Firefighter Syd Vanstone was badly injured.

Chief McCarthy was sixty-seven years of age when he died.

He is buried at Avondale Cemetery in Stratford, Ontario.

In 1999, a memorial to all the fallen police officers was erected in Toronto at Queens Park, and the family was invited to attend.

Sally and I attended the ceremony. Also, my sister, Cheryl, my brother, Ken, and his daughter, Teresa.

CHIEF JOHN AUGUSTUS MCCARTHY JR. IS THE ONLY POLICE CHIEF <u>EVER</u> WHO DIED WHILE ON DUTY IN ONTARIO!

We are SO proud of our ancestor!

This was the first year that My Amazing Hands performed at the 5036-seat Casino Rama Resort Entertainment Centre!
 I WENT ON TO PERFORM THERE SIX YEARS IN A ROW!!!!
 Yes, I did!
 Before an audience of over 2,500 people each year.
 Here's the whole story . . . .
 Superstars rotated through various casinos across the United States and Canada, putting on shows. Casino Rama was part of this rotation. The season started in late summer and continued weekly through the winter until late spring.
 The equipment for lighting, television, jumbo viewing screens, and, of course, sound, had to be in tip-top shape, ready to be used when the first superstar act performed.
 However, there was . . . a problem!
 They didn't have live performers to test the equipment—or did they? Someone had the great idea of utilizing the multi-talented staff at Casino Rama.
 C.R.E.W. NITE LIVE was invented!
 Any 'C.R.E.W.' (Casino Rama Employee Workgroup) member who wanted to perform was given a one-night-stand engagement the week before the first superstar act. No pay, but . . . it was a chance to perform on Casino Rama's stage, with full lights and a professional sound system.
 With the Jumbo viewing screen.
 And receive a free video cassette of the entire C.R.E.W. show.
 And have a professional photographer give us an 'in costume' eight by ten glossy.
 And we utilized the catering truck . . . no charge.
 And the makeup tent.
 . . . yes, they treated us like SUPERSTARS!
 My Amazing Hands—SUPERSTARS? . . . YOU BET!!
 Yet we were merely CREW members that had regular jobs in the casino: dealers, supervisors, slot attendants, restaurant workers, cocktail waitresses, janitorial staff . . . even some management guys and gals, and those employees operating the 'eye-in-the-sky' cameras.
 The latter had to perform wearing masks for security reasons . . . but they did it!

MY AMAZING HANDS

And there was no 'trying out.' If you wanted to perform . . . you performed! Great fun for everyone!

And, they opened it up to the public, charging a very nominal fee of just a couple of bucks that was, in turn, donated to charity.

2,500 of the public showed up, to our great delight!

We had Filipino folk dancers and singers, down-east singers and guitar players, a girl playing conga drums, comedians, a three-piece rock band, an Austin Powers look-alike, a chorus line of burlesque dancers, a trumpet player, and so on.

In the break room, I chatted with three friends, and we arranged to get together for a rehearsal.

We didn't sound too bad, so we formed the 'Rama Ramblers' and put in our names for C.R.E.W. NITE.

My Amazing Hands played guitar as I sang backup harmony behind Trish and Suzanne while Frank blew some mean licks on his trumpet.

Trish played her bass—and we all sang.

Later in the show, I *faked* playing saxophone behind another performer/dealer who mimed James Brown's *'I Got You!'*

Should I count that as one of the instruments I can play?

Nah! I'm too honest.

I WILL, however, count it as the only instrument My Amazing Hands can FAKE play . . . to 2,500 screaming fans!

The audience absolutely loved it! And it was one heck of a lot of fun!

And the equipment all got tested and tweaked with live performers!

It was so successful that the casino decided to use the Rama employees to help prepare for other superstars again the following year.

So, of course, I did it again the following year, too.

And the year after that . . . .

And the year after that . . . .

In all—for SIX CONSECUTIVE YEARS, I APPEARED ON THE CASINO RAMA STAGE!

YIPPEE!

2000

My Amazing Hands did a comedy routine at C.R.E.W. NITE LIVE 2000!

A couple of female dealers, Josie and Linda, joined me, and we put together a complicated ventriloquist routine that was great fun!

Josie had long blonde hair. She coloured it bright red and braided it with a couple of bright white bows on the ends—just for the show. Then she made her face snow white, with big red freckles all over. And a b-i-g lipstick smile! Black lines going down at the sides of her mouth made her into a human dummy.

She was wearing a dealer's vest with a white shirt and bolo tie, the dealers' uniform at Casino Rama.

But her arms went under the shirt and vest and down her side. Hidden.

I had stuffed a pair of black pants, then attached lightweight socks and foam shoes so they looked like the dummy's legs. They were attached to sticks so Josie could manipulate them. She could kick with them, cross them, or throw them over her head!

She was sitting on a stool.

Linda put on a white shirt, then stood behind Josie. She had a black cloth bag over her entire body, with holes cut for her arms to go through. She wrapped her arms around Josie—they looked like Josie's arms.

And, VOILA! . . . I had a puppet!

We called her 'Debbie, The Dealer.'

As the puppet master, I put my arm behind her and pretended to make her talk. I had on a dressy black suit and tie.

When the curtains opened, there we were . . . set to have fun!

I did both voices . . . my own and Debbie's. I would turn my head, so I was facing the audience and speak in my own voice . . . slowly . . . so the audience could understand what I was saying.

Then I would talk in a high 'little girl' falsetto when Debbie talked.

I told six or eight jokes.

With my own voice, I was the straight man, and (in falsetto) 'Debbie' said the punch lines.

Then 'Debbie' asked about the guitar on stage and asked me to play her a song. When I let go of her, she collapsed as a puppet would do.

Josie and Linda were brilliant!

I picked up my guitar and sang *'Two Out Of Three Ain't Bad,'* which was the punchline of the last joke that we told. The music brought 'Debbie' back to life, and she clapped with delight.

It was so much fun.

And . . . I performed once more on Casino Rama's stage, with its fantastic sound system.

The entertainment centre seated 5.036 people.

Unfortunately—the lighting guy wasn't so good on the night of the performance. He just didn't 'get' it.

He put a couple of bright spotlights on us, which meant you could see Linda through the black cloth bag, standing behind Josie.

Oh, well . . . everybody seemed to like our jokes!

In fact—I even got contacted by a guy who wanted us to perform somewhere in Toronto.

He understood the spotlights issue. . . but I couldn't make it, as I was already entertaining elsewhere on the weekends.

Also, in 2000 I was still supervising table games at Casino Rama.

In April, I was asked if I would be willing to learn how to deal and supervise the soon-to-open (June 2000) twelve-table poker room.

My Amazing Hands gave a big 'thumbs up' as I, of course, said, "Yes!"

***

Superstars would often come to the casino to gamble.

One evening, I went to take my break in the employee lounge. I took a short-cut through the slot machines area. It was crowded, so I could only move slowly through the folks playing the slots.

Suddenly, I felt a tug on the sleeve of my suit jacket. I looked down, and this sweet old lady was sitting in her wheelchair. She had noticed the identification tag on my lapel.

She asked, "Excuse me, sonny! Can you please ask that gentleman to come over and see me?"

I looked where she was pointing, and there was a world-famous country and western superstar –

Vince Gill!

He had headlined on the Rama stage that night and decided to mingle with his fans and put some money in the slot machines they were playing, just for fun, after his stage show was over.

I went to him, caught his attention, and I SHOOK HIS HAND!

Yes, My Amazing Hands shook Vince Gill's Amazing Hand! HOW GREAT IS THAT!

"Excuse me, Mr. Gill, do you mind saying hello to the lady in the wheelchair?"

He replied, "I'd love to, but please call me Vince!"

They spoke for a few minutes . . . Vince kissed her cheek and put a dollar in the slot machine she was playing.

And I continued on my break.

I wonder —how long was it before she washed *that* cheek?

2001

At C.R.E.W NITE LIVE 2001, I performed solo.

I walked out in front of the curtain while the backstage folks set up another act.

Just My Amazing Hands, my guitar... and around 2,500 people.

I sang my all-time favourite song, '*The Auctioneer*'... however...

I SCREWED UP!

I learned this song in 1958 when Leroy Van Dyke first brought it out.

I sat in my bedroom when I was sixteen and played it over and over on my 45 rpm player. I put my thumb on it to get the exact sound that Leroy did, and I have been singing it pretty close to perfect all these years.

But when I got on the Casino Rama stage... in front of so many people...

I got the introductory auctioneer's rattle off just fine, but...

I FORGOT THE WORDS TO THE FIRST VERSE!

A singer's worst nightmare!

I stopped, apologized to the crowd, and started again... but... but...

I ***STILL*** FORGOT THE WORDS TO THE FIRST VERSE!

It just WOULDN'T pop into my brain!

My brother, Ken, was there that night, front and centre in the first row, with his wife, and he saw I was in trouble, so he stood up and shouted the first few words of the first verse up at me. I have never felt such a rush of thankfulness in my life as I did that night. He is a SAINT!

Thanks again, Ken. I LOVE YOU, bro!

Okay... I screwed up...

BUT, HEY... I DID WHAT DOZENS OF MUSICIANS WOULD DIE FOR MY AMAZING HANDS PERFORMED FOR OVER 2,500 PEOPLE ON THE ENTERTAINMENT STAGE AT CASINO RAMA! YAY!

***

Later that year, I had a mishap!

I had been using my radial arm saw to make some forty-five-degree cuts in some lumber in my Workshop—stupid me—I forgot to readjust the saw blade back to ninety degrees.

And when I went to make a precise-on-the-line cut for a different project, I accidentally drew the blade into my left hand.

It was so fortunate that I was making precision cuts that necessitated drawing the blade slowly into the wood, instead of quickly drawing it across like I would have done for a regular cut!

My eyes were on the blade when I simultaneously noticed that it wasn't in its correct position, and that there was a red line, getting thicker, being painted on the wall behind the saw.

A lady friend, Joyce, was visiting that day. I quickly shut the saw down and grabbed a nearby towel, and Joyce drove me to the hospital.

This was on Friday evening of a long weekend, and there wasn't anyone available until Tuesday.

So the medical staff in the emergency department stopped the bleeding, immobilized my hand, and made a Tuesday appointment for me with a local plastic surgeon well known for his expertise.

My bad hand was in good hands!

I was SURE that I would never be able to finger the neck of my guitar again. However...

To make a long story short... the surgery was a huge success.

After a few weeks of therapy, I had *almost* full use of the cut fingers.

Actually, it turned out to be a blessing! Because...

MY AMAZING HANDS

Over the many years that I had been playing, I never was a real good guitar player, as I only knew a handful of chords, and they were at the very bottom of the neck.

I just knew enough to accompany my vocals.

I faked it when there was a chord that I didn't know.

Now, however, my first two fingers wouldn't bend enough to allow me to play some of the songs that I used to play.

The only way I would be able to play the way I wanted to was to learn barre chords!

I took a run at learning them in the past, but because I could manage without them, I didn't take a serious run at learning them. Now I HAD to!

It turned out that there were only two prominent chord positions that I had to learn.

I learned them, and now, I can play thousands of songs – correctly!

They made playing more fun, and the music I could make... SO much better!

Would I do it all again if I knew the outcome?

HELL NO! ARE YOU NUTS?

I WOULD HAVE LEARNED ABOUT BARRE CHORDS RIGHT FROM THE START!

2002

For C.R.E.W. NITE LIVE 2002, I decided to do something different, so I got together with a couple of co-workers, and we all dressed up in hillbilly clothing. I wore overalls with one strap undone... the legs rolled up some—and a string mop for a beard. My Amazing Hands blackened one of my front teeth (electrical tape), and I wore work boots and a floppy black hat.

The younger girls (a dealer and a pit boss) freckled their faces, pigtailed their hair, and wore short skirts and boots. They looked like 'Daisy Mae' characters right out of the comic strip *Li'l Abner*.

The older woman, also a dealer, wore 'Mammy Yokum' clothes, complete with corncob pipe and bonnet. Of course, her slip was showing.

I played my acoustic guitar as I sang *"I Am a Man of Constant Sorrow"*.

The girls linked arms and danced in a circle, just like in the movie *O Brother, Where Art Thou*.

And 'Mammy Yokum' danced across the stage, kickin' up her legs, tuggin' on her slip, and jabbin' her corn-cob pipe at the audience with an angry look on her face. It was priceless!

***

I purchased a small lathe and the tools required to 'turn' pens (chisels, sandpaper, etc.), as well as exotic wood pen blanks from around the world, and My Amazing Hands had fun making my own beautiful pens!

To give you a little information about pen making... the pen blanks are purchased six inches by one inch by one inch and are wood blanks or kool colours made from acrylic acetate.

I have a drawer full of 100 or so blanks of assorted woods and colours.

Some of my woods are: Coyote (Panama Rosewood), Ancient Bog Oak (from wood that has been submerged in bogs in England for thousands of years), Teak (Florida), Imbuya (Brazil), Peruvian Walnut (Peru), Pau Ferro (Bolivia), Western Red Oak (USA & Canada), Bubinga (Western Africa, Gabon, Congo & Angola), Padauk (India, West Africa) and Leopardwood (Central America).

And dozens of more woods are available to make lovely pens and things.

The acrylic acetate pen blanks are unlimited in colours. Some of mine are Blue/Gold Swirl, White Marble, Pink Marble, Chocolate Pistachio, etc., etc. You get the idea.

You can buy pen blanks with various themes as well... about a country, for example.

Or music (treble clef, guitars, violins, etc.). Or many, many other themes.

Once a year, they also prune olive trees and sell the trimmings. These olive trees are exceptional... they are from the Holy Land—specifically—Bethlehem!!

And some of them (you can tell which by the dark-coloured veins in the wood) date back over two thousand years to the time of Jesus.

I provide a Certificate of Authenticity with each pen made with a Bethlehem wood blank which reads:

CERTIFICATE OF AUTHENTICITY

Your purchase is a product made from authentic Bethlehem Holy Land Olivewood. Some of these trees have been bearing fruit since before the time of Jesus. Older trees have a darker grain. The tree ranges in height from three to eight meters (ten to twenty-seven feet) or more. The trees are pruned in October, and the wood is sold to craftsmen who create different crafts. No trees were damaged in the pruning process.

www.behlehemolivewood.net

Imagine making a pen from a tree that perhaps Jesus walked under—or touched! WOW!

You can purchase many different pen kits to complete the pen you just turned. For example, you can get kits with a cross for the pocket clip part of the pen, or a medical insignia, deer head, fish, etc.

Not only pens, but I also turned beautiful sets of darts.

Incidentally . . . the darts work VERY well. Just ask my dart league opponents. <grin>

Other things can be turned as well—ballpoint pens, fountain pens, stylus markers, etc., etc.

And you can purchase gift boxes of plastic, cardboard, or even leather for when you sell them.

For example, a lovely fountain pen that My Amazing Hands turned is in a leather gift box.

There was a fall craft show at our recreation centre, so I rented a booth and set up a display.

A few pens were sold, I had fun, and the show was a big success.

2003

At C.R.E.W. NITE LIVE 2003, we were limited in how much time we had to perform as there were so many crew members wanting to experience the thrill of performing on the Casino Rama stage.

And with my karaoke business going full tilt, I was really busy and didn't have time to put a 'show' together. So I dressed 'western' and sang another snappy country tune..."*SOLD, The Grundy County Auction Incident!*"

Except I changed it to "*The Simcoe County Auction!*"

Made it somehow—I don't know—*homier*!

***

This year, Sally and I decided to go to England.

A few years ago, I purchased a time-share unit, which meant that I purchased a week's use of a vacation unit in Collingwood.

Of course, I could stay that week in my own timeshare at the resort in Collingwood, but I could also make it available in a 'pool.' Anyone else throughout the world could swap with me . . . I go to *their* timeshare . . . they come to mine! Sally and I, in this case . . . traded our week for a week at an old renovated castle in Lancaster!

Sally was born in England, in Nottingham, and wanted to visit her old neighbourhood.

So when holiday time rolled around, we booked our flight, and off we went to England, getting our passports stamped in Birmingham at about five a.m. local time. Although we had reserved a car, the leasing company didn't open until eight a.m.

So, at that time, we completed the paperwork, were handed the keys, and were wished *'appy motoring, mate!'* We asked about travel maps but were told there weren't any available.

I climbed in the driver's seat, My Amazing Hands grabbed the wheel, and we were off.

In early-morning rush hour traffic!

On the wrong side of a strange car!

On the wrong side of a strange road!

And the first thing I encountered was a strange roundabout!

I had never seen one before—we didn't have them in Ontario at that time. We do now!

Sally wasn't any help—she had moved with her parents to Canada before she could drive.

My stress level would have blown out of the top of any device used to measure it. I have NEVER felt pressure like that before or since! My Amazing Hands wiped a LOT of sweat off my brow! But I stayed calm.

I went to the middle and drove around and around six or eight times until I felt confident that My Amazing Hands could control where we were going. As I drove around, I noticed that the other vehicles would work their way to the outside, so they could ease into the lane where they wished to exit.

I had no idea where I was going, but I spotted a friendly sign . . . it said 'Stratford-upon-Avon' with a big black arrow indicating the way. If you remember, I was born, went to high school, lived in Stratford, Ontario, and watched the boats and birds on the Avon River.

Believe it or not . . . I could feel my stress dissipate rapidly with this 'touch of home,' even if it was just a name.

I eased my way to the outside on the next rotation and exited.

They tell me that the man who invented round-a-bouts also invented Cat's eyes . . . white reflectors in the middle of British roads. The guy said that if the cat was going the other way, he would have invented the pencil sharpener! <grin>

A few minutes later, we reached the city limits of Birmingham.

MY AMAZING HANDS

As we exited this super-busy metropolis, Sally said, "I didn't know we were going to visit Stratford." I tersely replied, "we weren't—but we are now!"

Actually, all I wanted to do was get the heck out of that bustling city's morning rush hour, find some maps, get my bearings, and figure out how the heck to navigate to our destination. A 'petrol station' along the way provided the maps and a *much*-appreciated cup of coffee!

However, since we were so close, we decided to take a quick drive to Stratford-upon-Avon after all. I thought it would be cool to visit the sister city of my birth city.

It was pretty darn cool!

I guess everyone knows that it's where William Shakespeare lived in the late sixteenth century, so it was great to visit Stratford, even for such a short time. Then we were on our way north to Sally's birthplace, Nottingham.

We took a room there and did a bit of sightseeing.

During the day, we went to Lace Market and bought some Nottingham lace curtains. Sally had measured the windows in our kitchen and bathroom, knowing she would be going there.

Not far away was the school she attended. When we chatted with a passerby, we were told it would be demolished in a couple of years.

Back to Nottingham.

We took a trip to Sherwood Forest and saw the Major Oak where Robin Hood and his Merry Men slept. It's HUGE! Its weight has been estimated to be twenty-three TONS – its age is 800-1000 years My Amazing Hands picked up a leaf from the ground.

I just can't remember which book it got placed into for safekeeping.

Maybe we should go back there once again so My Amazing Hands can get another leaf.

We stopped back at our room for fresh, warmer clothing and had supper while there, then off to Nottingham to drink at 'YE OLDE TRIP TO JERUSALEM,' the 'oldest inn in England.'

This ancient pub is on the left side, on ground level, of the walls of Nottingham Castle.

1189AD is painted on the outside of the building, just below the name. I assume it's the date that the pub was completed. As of 2003, *that makes it 814 years old*... HOLY SMOKE!

Before long, all that ale I was drinking meant a trip to the 'little knight's room.' WOW! Was *THAT* ever an experience....

....you enter the room at one end.

A long stone trough runs the length of the facing wall.

Water enters from an ancient pipe at one end, runs the length of the stone trough, and out the other end.

You pick a spot among the men already there and say hello to the gents on either side.

Then one of My Amazing Hands takes ahold of the situation, faces the wall, and lets 'er go.

I'VE JUST PISSED IN THE OLDEST INN IN ENGLAND!

I have no idea how the ladies manage... something about bidets!

It's hard not to notice Nottingham Castle. The inn is to the left and down on the ground level.

Nottingham has numerous caves beneath the city. Most are believed to be haunted.

After sundown, there is a group 'haunted' tour of the pubs, the cellars under the pubs and the caves under the city. A tour leader tells gruesome stories about killer knights, ghosts, etc.

Our trip to England continued the next day when we travelled through Manchester, past the famous Manchester United's Old Trafford, to Lancaster.

Here was my timeshare trade—a medieval castle— with walls four feet thick—of solid stone.

How great was that!

We spent that day relaxing, drinking beer, and chatting with all and sundry.

We listened to tales of the castle and how there is a secret passageway behind the massive fireplace in the reception area that leads to the stables.

Apparently, it was for the use of the clergy in the days when they were persecuted.

We spent the night in this ancient, musty-smelling, four-poster bed—had a robust breakfast late the next morning—then headed off to my nana's hometown... Barrow-in-Furness, which was in England's coal mining belt.

This was also the home of Sally's son Simon's favourite football team, the Barrow Association Football Club, otherwise known as the Bluebirds.

After explaining who we were and where we were from, Sally and I went to the club office and received gifts from this generous club—a jersey, pennants, flags, and two complimentary tickets to the next game. Even after we explained that we would be back in Canada by then. Simon loved the gifts!

Then they opened the gates and let Sally and I out into the pitch itself and up into the stands.

I took pictures of Sally in the middle of the pitch from the stands to give to her son.

Nice folks!

We travelled across the famous Yorkshire Moors, stopping once at The King's Arms in Askrigg.

This was the pub made famous as James Herriot's drinking spot in the TV series 'All Creatures Great and Small'.

We continued across the Moors to the ancestral home of MY forefathers.

A quick history lesson, okay? (I'll keep it as brief as I can)

First of all . . . my last name is now McCarthy, but it used to be Scottowe. It has also been spelled Skottowe, Skottow or Scotto. I don't know which is correct. I guess it wasn't important in the 1600s.

The Skottowe family was granted its own coat–of-arms.

For any person to have a right to bear a coat of arms, they must either have had it granted to them or be descended in the legitimate male line from a person to whom arms were granted or confirmed in the past.

Richard Skottowe, who died in 1618, had a son Augustine Skottowe, who died in 1636.

Augustine Skottowe had a son, Augustine Skottowe Jr. He died in 1683.

Augustine Skottowe Jr., in turn, had a son—Thomas Skottowe. He died in 1756.

And Thomas Skottowe had a son, Thomas Skottowe Jr., who died in 1771. I want to talk about him.

He was a Lord.

Born at Little Melton manor house, he bought then lived at Great Ayton Manor in 1718.

His son, Thomas Skottowe III, was born in 1732.

Captain James Cook, who discovered New Zealand, moved to Great Ayton with his family when his father, a farmer, was hired by Thomas Skottowe Jr. It was 1736, and James Cook was eight.

Thomas Scottowe III was four.

A travelling tutor moved into the Great Ayton Manor to teach Lord Skottowe's children, but James was such a bright boy that he was also tutored in the manor along with them. He had his own room.

James Cook left the manor in 1741 when he was thirteen.

Thomas III took a post in the then-British province of South Carolina in 1762 and married in 1766.

Thomas IV was born in South Carolina the following year, 1767.

Captain James Cook, as you know, discovered Australia, New Zealand, Hawaii, and other lands nearby.

He asked the king of England for English settlers, but he would only give him Irish convicts.

James Cook was killed in Hawaii on February 14, 1779.

The Irish convicts had built a mansion for Thomas IV in New Zealand, so he sent to England for his family. A storm at sea did considerable damage to their ship on the return voyage off the island of what is now called Sri Lanka. The Kingdom of Kandy was a monarchy on the island.

Thomas IV's son, Thomas V, was on board with his mother and the rest of the family.

Although he had seen many white sailors, the king of Kandy had never seen a white boy before.

So, after repairs to the ship, when they left to continue their journey to New Zealand, he gave young Thomas an albino elephant as a parting gift. This was the first elephant in the country.

Thomas V grew up, joined the military with the rank of lieutenant, and married Mary Ann McCarthy.

However....

His family was distraught that he would court an Irish convict's daughter... away beneath his station in society. His father said that if he married the girl, he would forfeit the Skottowe name, all the Skottowe titles and claims to any lands owned by the Skottowe family.

He said something like, "The heck with you and the rest of the family, dad! I'm marrying her!"

The blighter!

If he hadn't been so passionate, I might be an English Lord with a medieval castle and lots and lots of British pounds in the Garderobe (treasury room) for me to count!

And the legitimate right to bear and wear the Skottow coat-of-arms!

But they wed—John Augustus Skottowe became John Augustus McCarthy—and they moved to Perth County, Ontario, Canada, in 1832.

Their son, Thomas Britiffe McCarthy, was born in 1841—the first white baby born In Perth County . . . at the site of a future city—Stratford, Ontario.

The City of Stratford acknowledged this in the 1990s by naming a street after the McCarthy family—amongst Stratford's first settlers—'McCARTHY ROAD.'

And his son was my grandfather—John Augustus McCarthy.

My Mom gathered Dad's family history, gleaning information from anywhere and everywhere. She took a trip to England to research town, museum and church records and even spent the night at Great Ayton Manor in the room (not likely the bed, though) occupied by Captain James Cook as a boy.

(She later provided all the information to her son, my brother, Ken, who was a shift manager for a large printing company. He used his excellent skills to produce a large chart that shows the Skottowe/McCarthy lineage, as I have outlined above.)

Sally and I continued our trip around England. Her sister and brother-in-law lived in Diss, Norfolk, in south-eastern England.

We stopped to visit them, arriving just in time to dine with them at a local eatery, then we booked a room for the night at the famous Saracen's Head Pub.

My Amazing Hands remember two things from that stay—how lumpy the bed was and the floor.

The upstairs bedroom floor was made of hardwood slats about two inches wide. They must have suffered some water damage in the past, or maybe it was just 'old age,' as they were significantly warped.

The next morning, My Amazing Hands had breakfast served to us by the owner and his wife —in the kitchen! After I ordered, I was really tickled when he said, "Righty-ho, Guv'nor!"

Sally's sister and her husband were working, so Sally and I went on a short trip to the beach at Southwold Denes—about twenty-five miles away.

I couldn't pass up the chance to take off my shoes and socks, roll up my pant legs, and put my feet in another famous body of water...

THE NORTH SEA!

My Amazing Hands then drove us to Gatwick Airport, about an hour east of London.

We would be flying home from there the following evening, so we had some time for more adventures.

I didn't want to drive in London, so we returned the rental car, booked a room at Gatwick for the night, and took a train to King's Cross Station, the famous railway depot. That's where, in 1991, Harry Potter caught his train, the Hogwarts Express, on platform 9 ¾. <grin>

As I was still a supervisor/croupier at Casino Rama at this time, I was interested in checking out the casinos in England. I wanted to be able to say that I put down a few bets in England, but British law says I must be there so many hours before I could gamble. Something to do with laundering foreign money.

So I found a casino close to the train station and registered with them.

Also, as Sally and I were both VERY interested in theatre, we dearly wanted to see an old-fashioned play in London in one of the old theatres that still had raked seating and a raked stage. Raked seating improves the view and the sound for spectators, and the raked stage allows the illusion of perspective with the scenery.

This was typical of English theatre in the Middle Ages.

We had heard about this type of theatre. Now we had the chance to experience it.

My Amazing Hands and I just loved it!

After the show, we had a drink in an old pub nearby, just so we could say we did, then caught one of the many trains back to Gatwick for a good night's sleep.

Our plane departure was the following evening... so... we had time to go back to London so I could gamble And we wanted to sight-see this fabulous city.

I had to wait at the casino for about forty-five minutes for the required waiting time from when I registered the evening before. Sticklers... those Brits!

I played roulette, which is My Amazing Hands' favourite game to play, and 'deal.' Also, some blackjack—My Amazing Hands' second favourite game.

MY AMAZING HANDS

I believe I won enough to pay for the show the previous night, drinks, and dinner. Hooray!

Then we bought 'tourist' tickets on the double-decker bus route.

Tourist tickets mean that you can get on or off the bus at any stop to sight-see, then get back on for no additional fee.

The top deck on all double-deckers is open to the air. Some have 'guides' who point out landmarks as you go. Sally and I got off at St. Paul's Cathedral.

It is an Anglican cathedral—sitting on Ludgate Hill, the highest point in the City of London. The original church, dedicated to Paul the Apostle—largely destroyed by the Great Fire of London in 1666.

We went through the old doors that kings, queens, prime ministers, and military heroes—Queen Elizabeth, Princess Di, Winston Churchill—and many more notables have passed through.

I'm sure we could have spent the whole day there, but there was more we wanted to see, so we hopped on the next double-decker that passed by.

A couple of minutes later, we drove past Buckingham Palace. The Royal Standard is flown when the queen is present. If the Union Jack is flying, she is not in residence.

She was not in residence when we drove past.

I guess she wasn't expecting us! <grin>

We drove past the Parliament Buildings, then stopped and got off at Big Ben to shop.

Sally bought some things, and I bought my own souvenir, a tie depicting the palace guards. Do you know what one man on the tie is doing? He's wiggling his fingers with his thumbs in his ears.

Yes, I DID have enough nerve to wear it to Casino Rama when I returned to work. Ha! Ha!

The double-decker's route took us over the Thames River on London Bridge. Then east to Tower Bridge Road. Then north back over the Thames on Tower Bridge. We got off the bus at the Tower of London. This is the place where Anne Boleyn and many, many others were imprisoned and beheaded!

My Amazing Hands purchased a red leather bookmark at the tower gift shoppe with my last English money. I use it all the time.

We didn't have time to go inside, so we just walked the circumference of the Tower, where we saw the world-famous ravens.

Legend has it that at least half a dozen ravens must stay within the bounds of the fortress, or the monarchy will fall. There were over a dozen visible to us.

While there, on the banks of the Thames River, I took the opportunity to take off my shoes and socks, roll up my pant legs and put my feet in the Thames.

I had to maintain a McCarthy tradition!

Then, back to King's Cross Station, a train ride to Gatwick, into the plane, and back to Canada.

What an amazing ten days in England. Sally and My Amazing Hands enjoyed our trip to England tremendously!

2004

I wanted C.R.E.W. NITE LIVE 2004 to be perfect!

"What A Wonderful World," sung by Louis Armstrong, was my choice. Everybody liked Louis!

I couldn't obtain a karaoke soundtrack to sing along with, so I simply accompanied myself. My Amazing Hands played my guitar.

Another dealer friend, Frank, accompanied me on his trumpet while Trish played bass.

A pretty, talented gal dealer danced to our music—appearing and disappearing from the wings.

The audience loved us!

It went flawlessly.

We got a huge round of applause and even took a second bow!

Just like downtown!!

***

"OKAY! THAT'S IT! I'VE HAD IT!" I exploded in exasperation as . . . for what seemed like the hundredth time that day . . . I dropped my pick AGAIN!

My Amazing Hands were showing their age (over sixty and counting) as the pick was getting dropped more frequently now. But that wasn't the main problem!

The main problem was that, while I could reach down and grasp the dropped pick, the old knees weren't so good anymore, so it was getting harder and harder to get back upright again.

So, I had to play without the pick till the end of the song . . . not acceptable!

Then, one night, I was on the computer when I saw the guitar strap of my dreams.

I don't recall who the musician was, but he showed the host his new guitar strap.

It was hand-made of leather, had his name and a design engraved into the leather, and had a special pocket for the pick. (I called it 'My PICK-POCKET') <grin>

When the credits rolled around, I noted the name of the leather engraver who made the strap. He was located in Nashville—no wonder he could make such a beautiful 'western' guitar strap.

I went to bed early that evening and just lay there designing my own personalized strap in my mind.

The next morning, I put my dreams on paper, and, thanks to the glory of the internet, I found the engraver's address and phone number. A phone call later, I forwarded my sketches via that fantastic thing called email.

He called me back, and we discussed my new strap, which . . . at this point, was just a dream.

I told him about another innovation that I wanted on my strap. Here's the story . . . .

The cord that connected the guitar to the amplifier plugged into the bottom of the guitar.

In the heat of playing, it would be easy to step on the cord and unplug it . . . you would totally lose the ecstasy of the music and come crashing back to reality when you couldn't hear the guitar.

Not good!

So I invented a simple device—a small strap loop near where the bottom of the strap attached to the guitar.

The cord would go from the amplifier and through the loop thus formed before plugging into the bottom of the guitar.

Now, if the cord was accidentally stepped on, it would stay plugged into the guitar.

He phoned me to tell me that it was finished, and a couple of days later it arrived ... precisely as I designed it.

My little green pick fits in its own little pocket! (I *know* you remember—my PickPocket).

So I would always know where it was ... whether I sat the guitar down while I jumped on the drums for a song or two, or danced with my wife ... or if I took a break ... or just packed up to go home at the end of the gig.

AND...

Should I DROP the pick (heaven forbid!), or if my bass player should drop HIS pick, My Amazing Hand would have a spare pick available immediately!

No more hassles with my pick! YAY!

AND...

It has something that I invented ... a loop to hold my cord, so I don't accidentally unplug it!

AND...

It has my name on it.

Because the strap had a woodgrain look engraved into the leather, I told the engraver to keep the theme by having my name look like logs.

There are metal thingys at each end of the strap. They are quick-connectors that firmly lock the strap to the guitar. They prevented the guitar from coming un-hooked and were the latest thing (back then).

Man ... MY AMAZING HANDS LOVE THIS STRAP!

2005

While providing music for many, many events was profitable and fun, I disliked not personally performing—not singing or playing my guitar.

So I invented something called Guitar-Y-Oki.

It was the same karaoke equipment that I used with BLACK VELVET DISC JOCKEY SERVICES (see 1995), except I played my Fender Telecaster while karaoke songs were sung by me *and* by the patrons.

Not on <u>all</u> songs... but most.

The patrons thought it was pretty kool and it was fun.

A portable microphone had been purchased for well-wishing speeches by friends and relatives.

My business cards for Guitar-Y-Oki were designed by me and printed by Vistaprint.

As with BLACK VELVET, I made songbooks that listed about 2,500 karaoke songs and put copies on the tables, together with request slips, pens, and some business cards so the folks could request their personal favourites.

As before, I had songs for special occasions... like Hallowe'en, Christmas, St. Patrick's Day, New Year's Eve etc. I also had Italian tunes, Irish jigs, hymns, country & western, down east music, etc.

I had the music to fit the occasion, like birthdays, graduations, promotions, etc.

And I was playing my guitar—my own 'stage show.'

MY AMAZING HANDS

Folks loved the 'special-ness' of Guitar-Y-Oki.
And EVERYONE had a GREAT night—a LOT of fun!!

***

I LOVE to play golf, so I made a deal with the local golf course . . . I would provide Guitar-Y-Oki karaoke to the end-of-season league dance and also for the New Year's Eve gala in exchange for free golf for me and my guests.

A golf cart was included, and an outdoor locker . . . so I wouldn't have to transport my clubs whether I wanted to play just three, nine, or all eighteen holes.

Believe me, I took FULL advantage of this 'free' golf!

2006

Sally and I separated on February 7, 2006. Irreconcilable differences.

Not long after, I decided I had enough of working at Casino Rama. The weird hours and long daily drives had cost me my marriage.

I still needed a job, so drove over to Barrie to give my credentials to a company that found positions for executive types. Across the parking lot was a store called 'The Brick.' I had shopped there previously, so I had a pretty good idea of their line of merchandise. I knew that they sold all manner of furniture, appliances, and electronics, and their prices were highly competitive.

My Amazing Hands walked in, shook the manager's hand, and after fifteen or twenty minutes in his office, I had a job as a salesperson in the electronics department. I learned how to sell all sizes and types of televisions, radios, and all the paraphernalia.

When Sally moved away, she rented a small place for herself, and we agreed upon the furniture and household accessories that she would take with her. There were some household appliances and other items that I then had to replace.

The Brick was the ideal place for me to find employment, as one of the 'perks' of the job was that any of the employees could purchase anything on display on the floor at a substantially discounted cost. And if it were an item that had been discontinued for a quick sale to the public, it would also qualify for an *additional* employee's special manager's discount.

MY AMAZING HANDS

So My Amazing Hands tossed out a lot of older furniture and appliances and restocked my house with *brand new*.

I bought a queen-sized top-of-the-line bed, a smooth-top stove with a convection oven, a refrigerator, a microwave oven, a dishwasher, a fifty-eight-inch plasma television, a surround sound speaker system, and a black leather recliner chair with a footrest and a built-in power massager with a vibrator. The television sat on a glass 2-tiered table. The lower level was for the surround sound system and the new DVD player.

There was a sizeable three-sided shelving unit. The top was open shelving for speakers and knick-knacks, and was adjustable to the width of my new large tv. The end units had three glass-doored shelves on each side, with another cabinet at the bottom for the bass speakers.

To perfect the ambiance of the room, I also purchased 2 'display' leafy artificial trees, about six ft tall, and before installation, painted the wall behind the unit a medium gray colour to make all of the items in the cabinet stand out.

My mother had several hand-made pottery items, and I already had some similar items. All these precious items now had a home, behind glass, in my display/TV cabinet. I took FULL advantage of the employee discount on display items.

A 58" Plasma TV, the table with shelves that it sits on, and the wrap-around shelved sides with the additional floating shelf at the top were all 'display' items at The Brick. The control units for the TV, DVD, Stereo, Gaming Device, and Wrap-Around- Sound system, together with the assorted controllers, Bass Speaker, and various other purchased 'display' items, are on the shelves on both sides.

I had done some favours for the delivery guys . . . like coffee and donuts, etc. We were friends. They returned these favours by delivering, unloading, assembling, and preparing the items for me.

The Brick was a great place to work.

2007

I was driving to Collingwood one day, thinking quietly that my life had been blessed!

Then I thought to myself that I DO believe in Jesus Christ.

He has done *so* much for me, yet He is the one that I have been neglecting for way too long.

And that I would do something about that RIGHT AWAY! So I pulled over to the shoulder of the road, and I prayed! I praised God for all the GREAT things He had done for me! I thanked Him for giving us His Son, who died on the cross, to have all of man's sins forgiven.

I drove on, realizing that I had just been saved!

I'M A CHRISTIAN! I BELIEVE IN JESUS CHRIST! I'M A CHRISTIAN!

That Sunday, I drove to the nearest Baptist church, and a short time later, I became a member. And a few weeks after that, the pastor agreed to baptize me.

Accordingly, My Amazing Hands and I were baptized. I was totally immersed, as the Bible explains that total immersion in water is the only proper way. It says that that's the way John baptized Jesus.

I attended church regularly and particularly enjoyed singing hymns. I guess I might have been a trifle loud, as the pastor asked me to sing a solo during the church service the following week. I accompanied myself on my guitar. Every few weeks, I sang my heart out to my God! It was an honour to be asked!

MY AMAZING HANDS

Regrettably, we lost our pastor. He was an American citizen, and his work permit had expired.

So one of the Elders, my friend, Merv Gardiner, took over preaching the sermon weekly while we looked for a replacement pastor.

My Amazing Hands were asked to provide the music . . . pick the hymns for the congregation to sing . . . and lead them in singing them.

Every Sunday.

Then, one week I received a phone call from Merv.

He couldn't attend church that week, so he asked me if I would preach the sermon next Sunday.

What a tremendous honour!

I preached a sermon about musical instruments in the Bible.

I felt SO humbled to be able to preach the word of God.

A loud AMEN!

***

I struck gold again at one of the sales meetings at The Brick.

We often have company representatives join our meetings to promote their products. At this one meeting, it was the Sony rep. He showed us one particular model that was brand new to the public.

It was a twenty-seven-inch colour television. I don't know what was so special about it . . . but they wanted to promote it. If we sold one, we got points to spend on other Sony products. This promotion was just for store employees.

I had seen similar promotions and wasn't impressed. It was usually a lighter or a T-shirt—both with the company logo, of course.

On the second day of the promotion, I saw a sales buddy taking pictures. This was unusual, so I asked him what was up! He showed me his top-of-the-line, latest thing out . . . Sony Camera. He said he had sold two of those promotional TVs the day before and already had enough points to 'buy' this costly camera.

I didn't have a good camera, so the next person that asked me about a television—I walked them over to the new 27" promotion unit. After a bit of a sales pitch, they bought it!

It was a Friday, and I had nothing else to do, so I let one of the married guys go home early, and I stayed till nine. I sold three more promotional televisions!

One lady wanted a small television for her daughter's room. My Amazing Hands took her to the promotional unit . . . and she bought it! And this was repeated with two more televisions on Friday! And two more on Saturday!

One of them was a gentleman who wanted a big TV for his rec room. My Amazing Hands took him over to the promotional unit . . . *and he bought it!*

On Monday, I 'cashed in' my Sony credits and 'bought' four cameras . . . .all top-of-the-line . . . all brand new . . . all Sonys! One for me, one for my son Bill, one for my son Jim and one for a friend.

A couple of days of sales later, I 'bought' Sony's best CamCorder with more promo cash!

Then they discontinued the promotion!

Darn! I was doing my Christmas shopping early.

Sony's the BEST!!

2008

I was booked to play at one of the local Legions. It was Newfoundland Night, and we were asked to play down east music throughout the night.

So My Amazing Hands played *"Farewell To Nova Scotia,"* and *"Working Man,"* and *"The Squid Jiggin' Ground,"* and *"Jack Was Every Inch A Sailor,"* and *"Doin' the Newfie Stomp"* repeatedly.

We also had some guest singers, fiddle players, and 'gitar' pickers come up on stage.

About halfway through the evening . . . they had something special!

Anyone who wished to become an active member of the Royal Order of Newfoundland & Labrador Screechers could join tonight . . . FREE!

Membership was easy . . . you just had to KISS A CODFISH!

Prospective members lined up and KISSED THE COD!

YUP!—You guessed right—I DID, TOO ... I even got a certificate to prove it! It's hanging on my wall!

I've gotta tell ya . . . I'll swear that that damned fish tried to slip me the tongue. Lol!

***

My Amazing Hands and I decided that we would like a hot tub.

I was driving over to Barrie one day and noticed out of the corner of my eye that a no-name brand service station on the other side of the road had a whole whack of hot tubs all over the boulevard.

I was a half-mile or so down the road when My Amazing Hands pulled the steering wheel at a break in the traffic, causing me to make a U-turn! It turned the wheel into the service station with the hot tubs.

The next thing I knew, I was getting a sales pitch!

Next, I was arranging for a hot tub to be delivered—TO MY HOUSE!

Then I realized WHAT AMAZING HANDS I HAVE!

A couple of days later, guys in a truck that said 'HOT TUBS' on the side pulled up and asked me where I wanted mine. I took the men to the back of my house and pointed out the desired area. The vehicle was backed up near the spot, and gravel was shovelled onto the ground and levelled. Large squares of cement were laid down for the tub to sit on. They ran an outlet to the nearest wall and screwed it in place—ready to be plugged into.

Then they left.

A few hours later, they were back—with my new hot tub in the back of their truck.

They lifted it in place and started filling it with water. Then they left again.

They had shown me how full to fill it, plug it in and set it. It was easy to do. I put the insulated cover on it and waited until the next day. The next morning, I donned my bathing suit, went out to the tub, removed the cover, turned on the jets and lowered myself into my brand-new hot tub!

Oh-h-h! . . . What A Feeling!

. . . Delightful!!!

My Amazing Hands loved to just lay there, without a thought in the world - relax-x-xing!

Later that day, I put up a sign . . . 'CLOTHING OPTIONAL AFTER TEN P.M.'

Which leads to a whole whack of stories!

(But you're not going to hear them!)

Not too much later, I put up a canvas enclosure.

'Nuff said?

2009

My poker buddy, Cecil Brady, called me one day to ask a favour.

He had something he had to do that would prevent him from working on the weekend, and he asked me to replace him.

I didn't know that he and Patti, his wife, were working weekends.

Christmas was coming, so I assumed they were just earning some extra Christmas cash. Well, that was true. What I didn't know at the time, but I was about to find out... for many kids... he WAS Christmas!

You see, Cecil and Patti had contracted with the Collingwood Mall to work there on the weekends leading up to Christmas.

Cecil was **SANTA CLAUS**, and Patti was his elf! Who knew? I would never have guessed!

Patti, in her elf costume, would take pictures of the children on Santa's lap and provide copies of the occasion to the proud mama or daddy who brought their kids to see Santa Claus.

That's what elves are for!

However, on the upcoming weekend, he asked ME to replace him!

HE WANTED **ME** TO BE SANTA CLAUS IN HIS STEAD! YA-HOO!!

He told me that I would go there with Patti, and she would 'show me the reins!' so to speak.

As I had been acting/performing all my life, I thought I would be able to 'HO! HO! HO!' with the best of them! And I look good in red!

Cecil would loan me his Santa Claus costume, and Patti would assist me in the back room of a store which had generously donated space for Santa to change. So, Friday, around four p.m., there I was . . with Patti. . . in the provided changing room, for the first time in my life. . .putting on a Santa Claus suit.

Cecil's feet were a bit smaller than mine, so the boots pinched a bit, but My Amazing Hands managed to get them on, and I could walk okay if I took my time. Patti helped me squeeze into them.

That's what elves are for.

The pants just pulled on over a pair of my long johns. Cecil and Patti both warned me that it was imperative to use the toilet for <u>both</u> purposes before changing into the suit as there was no fly in it.

Then I pulled a bulky vest-like thing over my head. Lots of cotton batten instantly added inches to my slender frame. Next was the jacket.

Because of the cotton batten vest, Patti had to assist me in getting it on . . . but she didn't complain.

That's what elves are for!

Then My Amazing Hands pulled on a pair of white gloves.

Then . . . the . . . beard . . . .

You can't imagine the very peculiar feeling you get when putting a big, white, very hairy thing that you KNOW has been so intimately close to another man's face . . . on your own!

<u>ESPECIALLY WHEN YOU SEE DRIED-ON GREEN RESIDUE AROUND THE MOUTH AND NOSE AREA.</u>

So intimately close to your own mouth and nose!

So . . . had Cecil been chewing Chlorophyll gum last week?

Funny . . . it didn't smell like Chlorophyll gum!

I immediately sent Patti to a local craft shop to buy a small pair of scissors, then had her trim the inside of the beard to remove as much of it as possible. I let her dispose of the residue.

That's what elves are for!

I'll admit it . . . I almost quit right then and there!

There is only so much that the human male is capable of withstanding, and Cecil's residue wasn't part of that.

However, Patti reminded me of the long lineup of children waiting to tell Santa their most secret wishes and desires.

So . . . mustering up every ounce of self-control that my meagre frame was capable of, I took a deep breath . . . and put on the beard.

I can't say that I remember putting on the hat, with its attached white hair and floppy top with its big white pom-pom at the end. Then the spectacles, on the tip of my nose, of course!

And I only *think* I remember Patti applying some make-up . . . rosy cheeks and eye twinkle.

I don't remember walking down the mall's hallway to Santa's Throne, where an area had been specially set up for Santa Claus and his helper Elves.

Patti introduced me to a pair of helper Elves—girls from the mall stores—who volunteered to help Santa with the children.

But . . . I VIVIDLY remember the joy on each and every tot's face as they excitedly sat on my knee.

There, they would be asked if they'd been good this past year, chit-chat about Santa's reindeer, Santa's home at the North Pole, what they wanted for Christmas (repeated loudly so the parents could hear) etc.

The kids loved it!

Only a couple of kids looked at me and burst into tears. I was glad Patti or one of the other elves was handy to pass them to their mothers.

That's what elves are for!

I don't *think* any peed on me.

I tried to judge the child's maturity level so that I could chat with them accordingly. The older kids got to shake Santa's Amazing Hand! Then My Amazing Hands would give the child some donated treats, and Santa's elf would return the tot to the parents.

My conversations with them were punctuated by even more frequent Ho-Ho-Ho's.

That's what —Santa Claus— is for!

This fantastic experience didn't go without its negative side, though.

The suit was REALLY hot. And the beard itched.

And the boots pinched my feet.

All the Ho-Ho-Ho's were making me hoarse.

And I had to pee!

I told the children that the reindeer on the roof had to be fed, and they bought it!

EVERYBODY was smiling at me—and each other!

EVERYONE was wishing me—and each other—"Merry Christmas!"

EVERYWHERE there was Christmas joy! What FUN!

Patti and the Elves dispersed the crowd and helped me to get back to the changing room to cool off, to scratch, to take off my thick socks, to drink some water . . . and to PEE!

After a short break, we headed back down the corridor and repeated it all.

And when I put on the beard . . . I only thought about the young, happy, smiling faces that I was about to enjoy for the next couple of hours.

My Amazing Hands gave lots & lots of Christmas treats to lots & lots of happy boys and girls!

Thank you, Cecil.

Hope that your cold didn't last too long.

What a great day!

The afternoon flew by, and before I knew it, Patti and I were headed home again . . . however, this time, I had rosy cheeks, and my eyes twinkled!

Patti had handed me a pay envelope while still at the mall.

My Amazing Hands put it into a Salvation Army Christmas collection pot – unopened!

As the Salvation Army lady thanked me, I gave her a very croaky 'Ho!-Ho!-Ho!' in return.

She said I sounded just like Santa Claus!

HO! ~ HO! ~ HO!

I told her that . . .

SANTA'S AMAZING HAND SAYS . . .

Merry Christmas!

Signed . . .

Santa Claus

2010

A couple of days after Christmas, I went to the legion in a neighbouring city to play Euchre with a group of folks who played every Monday night.

I hadn't been feeling so hot all day.

My Amazing Hands flicked on the living room light when I got home—the bulb blew out with an audible 'pop'. For no apparent reason, this infuriated me. I retired for the night, tired from the long night and subsequent drive home. Then, after my morning ablutions, on Tuesday, December twenty-eighth, for no reason, I became infuriated again as I thought about changing that *&^%@$% light bulb.

Cursing under my breath (although I could have cursed out loud – I lived alone), I moved a table out of the way, then went out to the garage to retrieve a step-ladder off the wall. Banging this awkward device into doors and walls, I finally got the ladder into place under the light fixture, opened it up, and stepped up to where I could reach the bulb.

I read the wattage, then down the ladder, across the floor, down the basement stairs, get a new light bulb, back up the basement stairs using the handrails as I was surprisingly weak, then across the floor, and back up the ladder. Whew!

Suddenly, amid my fury, I saw big, round, very black circles, about four to six inches in diameter, floating in the air all around my head.

My Amazing Hands grabbed the phone and dialed 911.

My Amazing Hands dialling 911 saved my life!

Then I phoned a neighbour, Wanita K., who tended my two cats whenever I was away.

And I called my brother to let him know what was happening.

Then I unlocked the front door, sat down, and waited.

The police, fire department, and an ambulance all arrived very quickly, and I was laid on a stretcher and carried to the ambulance. We were on our way to the hospital.

I remember looking out the rear window and seeing cars pulling back onto the road behind us. I thought: *I've pulled over to let an ambulance by many times. Now it's MY turn.*

The ambulance staff carried me into Emergency, where I was given some pills and hooked up to a bunch of beeping machines.

My brother and his wife appeared but were helpless to do anything but comfort me. Just BEING there was enough, though! The doctor asked me if I'd had a helicopter ride before. He said I would get another today, as I was being transferred to Toronto General Hospital—renowned for its excellent heart facilities.

I was in and out of consciousness, so I had no idea how long it took to get to Toronto, but I recall the helicopter descending and seeing a lot of smoke-stacks before landing. I vaguely remember being lifted from one stretcher to another, then being on a bed where a tall Chinese gentleman told me... "Mr. McCarthy, you have had a heart attack. We will have to operate, and indications are that you will need a quadruple bypass". (It turned out that I only needed a triple bypass. Like that was MUCH better, eh?)

I asked his name.

He said, "If I stepped on your toe, you would shout 'YOW'! That's my name. Doctor Yau."

I read an article in the Toronto Star a year or so later saying that a top-level cardiac team, headed by Doctor Yau, had just accomplished a vital breakthrough. It went on to say that Dr. Yau was a cardiac surgeon and director of the cardiac stem cell therapy program at Toronto General's Peter Munk Cardiac Centre. And that he also holds a Chair in cardiovascular surgery research at the University Health Network. (ref. Toronto Star, Friday, January 27, 2012)

It is comforting to know that when your heart is (literally) in a doctor's hands, that he is the best!

MY AMAZING HANDS

I was still in the hospital over New Year's Eve, but I didn't have any plans, so that was okay.

My son, Jim Jr., travelled from London every day to stay with me.

I was released from the hospital on January 6, 2011, and Ken and Sharon were there to drive me home. What a family I've got!

I figured that God must have more for My Amazing Hands to do during this lifetime, as He saved me from the heart condition that took Nana, Grampa, and my mother from us.

Thank you, Father! Thank you, Jesus!

2011

Sally and I divorced on September 22, 2011. We were married for twenty-three years.

She chose to leave me five years before. She said our lifestyles just weren't compatible.

I'm a sociable guy, and I was missing feminine company.

So I dated Joyce for a while, who lived up in Midland, but she didn't want to move, and neither did I, and neither of us liked the long drive to the other's home, so we reached a stalemate.

We decided to part friends.

I had met her through a website called 'Plenty of Fish,' so I listed myself with them again. After a couple of coffee shop dates that I didn't want to pursue any further, as the ladies just didn't interest me, Darla phoned me.

When she told me that she lived in Bracebridge and worked in Toronto, I almost hung up the phone. But, something told me not to – so, thankfully, I didn't! She told me she really liked my profile on Plenty of Fish, was free the next night, and would like to at least MEET me, even if it didn't go any further.

My Amazing Hands just had to meet the owner of this enchanting voice.

I had arranged to see Grand Funk Railroad at Casino Rama the next night, and I told her about it. She said she loved their songs, *"We're an American Band"* and *"Locomotion"*! I did, as well!

MY AMAZING HANDS

We planned to have dinner when we arrived, get our show tickets, then gamble until showtime. I invited her to come, and she could leave any time if she wasn't comfortable. She said she'd love to. We arranged to meet in the lobby at sixish.

As planned, I accompanied some friends in their car when we went to Rama. Upon arriving, I anxiously scanned the patrons standing around the entrance doors. No single women were there except one very elderly Chinese lady, counting her money to herself. I knew THAT wasn't Darla!

So I went through the doors into the main lobby.

The only single woman in the lobby was this absolutely stunning woman who was obviously looking for someone as she was scanning everyone in the lobby. She knew what I looked like from my pictures in Plenty-Of-Fish, but often they don't look anything like the actual person when you finally meet them.

She, however, was even more gorgeous than her Plenty-Of-Fish photos.

I started walking towards her . . . our eyes met!

My Amazing Hands gently shook her dainty right hand as I asked, "Darla?"

She nodded that beautiful head in the affirmative.

And I fell instantly head-over-heels in love with this goddess.

I escorted her to dinner, but frankly, I don't remember much about the meal.

Later, as I stood behind her and popped coins into the slot machines that she chose, people around us must have thought I was nuts, as I couldn't get enough of the mixed aromas of her body and her perfume.

We found our seats and settled back to watch the show when it was time.

Suddenly I felt her hand reach out and clasp one of My Amazing Hands!

My Amazing Hands clasped hers.

And . . . WE KISSED!

I had found my *"Some Kind of Wonderful!"*

I sure wasted my money that night, as I hardly remember any of the show.

Afterward, we had a coffee in the casino, and my hot tub became the topic of conversation.

She said she had never been in one!

I'll tell you . . . it doesn't take this country boy long to know when the hay needs harvesting!

I invited her over to my house to try it.

She said she is VERY nervous driving at night, so she was just going to take a room at the casino, but, if *I* drove HER car, she would come.

I'm a gentleman—I told her I had a spare room if she didn't want to drive home late at night!

So, My Amazing Hands drove HER car, and we arrived at my home after an hour's drive.

Darla and I went into the house. I made each of us a drink! She made herself comfortable, making friends with my two cats, then asked about the hot tub.

I took her through the house and outside, where I removed the cover and started the bubbles.

I told her that I usually showered before taking a tub, and went indoors to do so, leaving Darla in the living room with a fresh drink.

When I emerged, Darla was gone. I imagined the worst!

The light from the kitchen window provided lots of light on the hot tub, and I hoped that Darla had gone out there to wait for me to get out of the shower before she stepped in.

Well, I was partly right—except she had waited for me IN THE HOT TUB!

Here is this absolutely gorgeous goddess... in MY hot tub... at MY house... in MY back yard....

And she had seen, and was obeying, the 'CLOTHING OPTIONAL' part of my sign!

YA-HOO!

And she liked my cats! And they just LOVED her... but not as much as I did!

2012

Darla didn't go home for a couple of weeks, and when she finally returned to Bracebridge, it was to pick up her belongings, as she had consented to move in with me! YA-HOO!

My Amazing Hands were absolutely delighted to have her—so were Sugar and Buddy—my two cats.

She spoiled all three of us! However, she still had an obligation to the company that she had contracted with until April.

She was the in-house cook for a crew of fifteen men. They all worked for a company that salted and/or sanded the ice on the streets of Toronto when they became slippery—and plowed and sanded them when it snowed. The men and Darla lived in trailers, and the site was called a 'winter camp.' The men were on call twenty-four hours a day, seven days a week, and Darla cooked for them. She provided three meals a day, plus feeding them if they missed meals or were just plain hungry . . . day or night.

The camp was open from October fifteenth until April seventh! Twenty-four hours a day! Darla LIVED there!

The personnel of the camp collected unemployment insurance during the off-season.

During this time, I worked for a man who lived near me.

Several companies required lands they owned to be surveyed before their development, and this man was a surveyor. He had lost his driver's licence, so he needed a driver to drive him on his job daily. He would have me drop him off at one end of a road, then go a mile or so down the road. After surveying down the road to the car, he would grab a coffee and do it again. And again! And again!

When we were in the Toronto area, we would visit Darla at the winter camp, and, of course, Darla and I would talk daily on the phone.

Finally, April arrived, and My Amazing Hands picked up Darla, along with all her belongings, and we drove home. Darla never went back!

And—she never left my home!

***

While Darla was still working at the winter camp in Toronto, My Amazing Hands started a fun little moneymaking venture—a recreational oxygen bar.

I don't think I have to tell you how healthy oxygen is for the human body.

It can:

- ~ increase energy levels
- ~ reduce stress
- ~ improve sports performance
- ~ provide relief for headaches and migraines.
- ~ stimulate brain activity
- ~ detox your blood
- ~ strengthen the immune system
- ~ improve mood
- ~ improve concentration
- ~ promote better sleep
- ~ aid forgetfulness
- ~ improve strength
- ~ prevent lactic acid buildup

The machine I used would remove the oxygen from the air and, using a cannula at the nostrils, would allow you to breathe 95% pure oxygen for twenty minutes. Skiers especially loved the burst of energy that the oxygen bar provided just before doing another downhill run.

I would route it from the oxygen generator, through bottles of distilled water with an assortment of scents, to the cannula. There was a variety of scents like vanilla, peppermint, chocolate, strawberry, lime, etc., that you could mix and match... e.g. you could have peppermint-chocolate if you wish.

A touch of a button would route the oxygen from the machine through a personal cannula (kept or discarded, as you wish), through your scent choice(s) to your nose.

I would charge the host establishment a basic fee and a small fee to the users.

I named my business 'IT'S A GAS.'

I ran this fun little moneymaker while Darla was still working that winter in Toronto.

2013

Have you ever shaken hands with some tall, muscular guy and, for reasons known only to him, he *crushes* your hand.

Man, that can *hurt*!

DON'T LET HIM DOMINATE YOU ANY LONGER!

Here's a kung-fu trick that I learned many years ago when I was in the Air Force, and it has saved me a *lot* of pain over the years.

So . . . it doesn't matter how big or how strong you are—male or female—fifteen or fifty—you can shake hands with ANYONE and not be hurt.

HERE'S HOW . . . HERE'S THE SECRET!

As I say . . . it doesn't matter how big or how strong you are—male or female—fifteen or fifty you can shake hands with ANYONE and not be hurt.

HERE'S HOW . . .

When Mr. TOUGH GUY extends his hand, (here's the trick) : →

PLACE YOUR INDEX FINGER IN THE MIDDLE OF THE TOUGH GUY'S WRIST AS YOU ARE SHAKING HANDS!

It doesn't matter how hard he squeezes your hand . . . you'll feel very little other than a mild pressure.

Give him a friendly smile, perhaps a wink, then, without changing position, give him some pressure back—along with more of your warm smile, and perhaps another wink!

Hold it until *HE* breaks the grip . . . and he will!

And he will be so disoriented that he will probably let you win.

I don't suggest you tell him, "A three-year-old has a stronger grip," though.

He could still punch you in the nose with his free hand! <grin>

MY AMAZING HAND HAS DONE IT <u>AGAIN!</u>

***

My Amazing Hands have always been handyman's hands.

To be a handyman, you must know about four things—electricity, plumbing, heating, and wood.

I know nothing about natural gas, so I ALWAYS get a licensed expert to 'do' things with my gas lines, gas furnace, etc. I don't touch the thermostat, either.

The RCAF taught me all about electricity, and over the years, I have expanded this knowledge to the point that I can totally rewire a house or make electrical repairs to vehicles and things like appliances, musical instruments, and other equipment whenever needed.

Over the years, I have accumulated the tools required to do all things electrical. I respect electricity, and the only shock I have ever received was from a static charge of clothing.

Regarding plumbing, I know my way around all my sinks, tubs, drains, water heaters, etc. I have installed <u>all</u> of them! I have also installed various water pipes to indoor and outdoor lines with shut-off valves. And I moved the hot water tank from one side of the basement to the other shortly after purchasing my house (see 1989).

My Amazing Hands have even totally rebuilt my bathroom. One day, as we were surveying, I spotted several boxes of ceramic tiles sitting at the side of the road by a garbage pickup point. I assumed that they were intended for anyone who would like to have them . . . take them, or the garbage man would! Whoever comes first.

When and if we decided to remodel, Darla and I thought of a brown motif, and . . . hey . . . the tiles I found were three different sizes and shades of brown. Perfect! Not knowing how many I would need, I took them all. I'm glad I did, as I just had enough of the two smaller sizes to do the walls in the bathroom and enough of the large ones to retile the kitchen floor.

And the nice man at the local hardware store told me and sold me everything else I would need to do the job myself—a special ceramic blade for my skill saw, grout, grouting tool, etc.

In the bathroom, My Amazing Hands removed the bathtub and installed a shower in the corner, which we much preferred. I never did like a tub . . . except my hot tub (preferably after ten p.m.).

I did the plumbing myself and glued towel racks on the glass.

I moved the old plumbing for the bathtub and rerouted them with the breather pipes to the roof by inserting them in the wall instead of leaving them in the middle of the floor.

Then I panelled the walls, relocated the sink to allow more room in front of the toilet and installed a brand-new one, with ornate faucets, where the tub plumbing used to be.

Mirrored tiles made the room look substantially more extensive.

And now I could wave 'hi!' to myself while sitting on the throne. <grin>

And it's easier to see to shave!

I installed a ceiling fan and built a big box over the sink and counter area. In this box, I installed adjustable overhead pot lights.

I laid linoleum on the bathroom floor with a pattern that resembled ornate rock.

It matched the ceramic wall tile that I installed from floor to chin.

So, My Amazing Hands expanded their skills to include plumbing and ceramic tile work.

The bathroom looked great when it was finished. So did the new kitchen floor.

That night, I went to my buddy Cecil's house for our weekly poker-playing get-together. He's the guy who chews chlorophyll gum while being Santa Claus (see 2009). . . LOL!

I immediately saw that he had also been busy.

During the past week, he had laid laminated flooring in two bedrooms and his dining room.

Of course, that got my brain going, and when I got home that night, I decided that the carpeting in my living area had to go, and that laminated floors in its place would look GREAT!

And if Cecil could do it . . . I was pretty sure that My Amazing Hands could, too!

I called him to ask for his advice, and he said he would come over the next day to get me started.

So ... My Amazing Hands ripped out the old, tired carpeting, and on the way back from the dump the next morning, we stopped at the lumber store to pick up everything I would need.

It turned out that laminating the floors was easy-peasy!

My Amazing Hands laminated my dining room, living room, hallway, office, and bedroom using three different styles and colours of flooring.

After another trip to the lumber store, I got the trim, floor strips, and everything else I needed.

The whole thing took me about three days of pure fun—laminating when I wasn't busy.

My tired old legs were starting to give me trouble now that I'm over 70, so I gave up golf.

I gave my son my clubs and the rest of my golfing paraphernalia. And, NO, I'm NOT senile! I knew I could borrow back whatever and whenever I needed to. I never needed to!

But I was having trouble getting up and down my porch steps. Each step was just too high. So when I had a friend over to help me put on a new roof, we took a morning, and I learned how to frame in, mix and pour new cement steps. It solved my problem. My steps are VERY safe to use now!

And after we finished the roof, I took advantage of his generosity by learning how to build an enclosed porch on top of the open cement one. I wired it for inside and outside lights and inside wall receptacles.

Then, we lucked out when I went to the local siding store to purchase new siding to finish the porch.

My friend there asked if I was interested in a large sheet of double-insulated glass that was left over from another job. It measures 5' X 4.5' (60" X 54").

One big double-thick window with no cross-frame pieces.

For the price I paid ... I *KNOW* I stole it from him.

My Amazing Hand installed it in the porch wall facing the garden that Darla had planted. Darla and I just love it. Our new cat, Buddy II, does too.

We can now sit on the porch and continue to be entertained by the menagerie of critters visiting us.

Our house is on the top of a hill bordered on the north by a wooded ravine with a babbling brook at the bottom. The brook is only about six feet wide but flows year-round.

Fish spawn up the little creek occasionally.

It's also home to frogs, garter snakes, tadpoles, Mallard Ducks, and Canada Geese.

I erected a split rail fence to keep the 'our ranch' feeling, and we are visited by many, many creatures, big and small.

We have had (Deep Breath Here) ... deer (a buck and, separately, a doe with fawns), coyotes, foxes, gray, red, and lots of black squirrels, cottontail rabbits (a young one this year, too), chipmunks, skunks, raccoons, opossums, and, of course, dogs and cats.

The monarch and cabbage butterflies love Darla's milkweed in a fence corner. We can watch them fluttering around through the huge window.

A myriad of birds flock to the feeders that she keeps well stocked, including:

(Another Deep Breath) Sparrows, wrens, mourning doves, chick-a-dees, flickers, finches, all kinds of woodpeckers, cardinals, blue jays, crows, blackbirds, turkey vultures, hawks, starlings, and (last but not least) different breeds of hummingbirds.

Darla also has a birdbath that she keeps filled with fresh, clean water daily, which birds and critters alike enjoy!

Also...

My Amazing Hands cleaned the basement's hot air and cold air heating ducts. Who needs those 'duct cleaning service' SPAM phone calls! Mine are done—by ME. After I tell them so, they remove me from their phone call list.

And then I did some renovations to the rec room—I removed a supporting wall and installed a steel I-beam to safely hold my upper floor up. I installed insulated ceiling tile and lots of fluorescent lights with individual switches.

My Amazing Hands also redirected the hot air to new heating outlets for the hot air flow.

Wood! One of the most accessible materials to work with.

Over the years, I have accumulated ALL the tools I need to complete some awesome projects.

MY AMAZING HANDS

In my estimation, the greatest project that I have completed, however, is Jesus' head with the crown of thorns that My Amazing Hands scrolled from very thin maple.

It is mounted on the wall so it can be seen as soon as you step into our home!

I had requests from friends and family to make them one.

So, My Amazing Hand hand-made five or six more to give to friends and family.

I was honoured to be asked to do so!

2014

Darla and I had been living together for a couple of years now, and we were both totally satisfied with our living arrangements.

What the heck!

We love each other! A LOT!

It seemed like we had been together for years . . . we fit perfectly.

I wanted to show the whole world how much she meant to me.

So . . . My Amazing Hands and I chose a pretty gold engagement ring that we just KNEW would look amazing on the third finger of her left hand.

We had arranged to get together with our friends, Terry and Rod, on the weekend for a meal at this quaint old hotel in this tiny country town located about halfway between our home and theirs.

The food there was knockout delicious . . . we knew this from a previous visit . . . and the staff was delightful.

So I called the owner, Katie, to reserve a table for four on Friday evening.

At the same time, after confirming that she would be working there that evening, I told her my plans, and she agreed to help me make our evening outstanding.

This is how it played out.

We arrived at the hotel at the same time as Terry and Rod.

Everyone had agreed to my request that we should wear country and western garb.

MY AMAZING HANDS

Nobody tweaked to my special request.

Nobody noticed that I waited for everyone to leave our cars and let them go ahead of me.

Nobody noticed the brown paper shopping bag that dangled from My Amazing Hands at my side, as unobtrusively as I could make it.

Nobody noticed when I slipped it under my chair as I sat down.

Nobody thought it strange that the owner, Katie, came over to our table to welcome us.

Nobody noticed the wink she gave me as she took our order for drinks.

Or thought it odd that the strangers at the nearby tables seemed to smile at us a lot.

The waitress who delivered our drinks offered us menus, but she left when we told her we were all going to have the daily special—locally grown beef and vegetables (I'm drooling just thinking about it).

After the meal, she cleared the table, took our coffee and dessert orders, and left.

I didn't say anything, just got up from the table. One of My Amazing Hands then took a framed document from the brown bag, went around the table to where Darla was sitting, got down on one knee, and read the poem that I had written to this beautiful woman who I had met through an online dating site called 'Plenty Of Fish.'

It was titled "SHE SAID YES!"

It went . . .

I STOPPED WISHIN'
STOPPED 'PLENTY-OF-FISH'N'
ON THE INTERNET
WHEN SHE SAID—<u>YES</u>

AND WHEN I ASKED HER TO GO
WITH ME TO A SHOW
AT RAMA
SHE SAID—<u>YES</u>

AND I THOUGHT I'D JUST FLIP
WHEN I ASKED HER TO DIP

IN MY HOT TUB WITH ME
AND SHE SAID—<u>YES</u>

AND WHEN SHE ASKED, "JIM
I'D LIKE TO MOVE IN
WITH YOU AND THE CAT!"
OF COURSE, I SAID—<u>YES</u>

I STOPPED BEING 'RAMBLY'
WHY, I EVEN LIKE HER FAMILY
AND THEY LIKE ME, TOO
THEY SAID—<u>YES</u>

OH, AND DARLA, ONE MORE THING
PLEASE ACCEPT MY RING
WILL YOU MARRY ME?
PLEASE SAY—-<u>YES!</u>

BUT SHE DIDN'T!!

She was so flabbergasted that it was a full two minutes later, with me still on my knees and all the people at the surrounding tables applauding and cheering that she realized what I was doing.

She was MORE than surprised... she was STUNNED!

However, when I took the ring out of my pocket and offered it to her... she FINALLY SAID...

"YES!"

My Amazing Hand slipped the ring on her finger.
WE WERE ENGAGED TO BE MARRIED!
YES! YES! YES! YES! YES! YES! YES! YES!

***

The surveyor didn't need me anymore, but I had a chance to do even MORE driving (read—'make even more money'), as I heard that a delivery service called Quicksilver Delivery in Wasaga Beach was looking for drivers.

I visited the owner, Ken... a really nice guy... and I was hired.

I started the next day on this new adventure.

MY AMAZING HANDS

For a small weekly fee, Ken would take calls, then phone me (cell phone), and I'd pick up and deliver whatever the customer wanted.

It was a cash business, and this is how I did it...

I'd get a call from Ken, let's say, for some beer for the customer.

I'd go to the beer store, buy the beer, and pay for it with a 'dividend' credit card. This type of credit card rewarded me with a cash bonus deposited to my account each December.

One year, my dividend was $1,487.00.

There's nothing better than 'free' money!

I'd deliver the beer or whatever to the customer and charge a seven dollar delivery fee.

For the first year, it was a 'strictly cash' business, and I got a lot of three-dollar tips.

Then I discovered a device that would let me 'swipe' the customer's credit card on my cell phone.

Less cash for me to handle.

I used to keep my cash in a bright blue pencil case, and one day I was about fifteen minutes from my latest delivery when I noticed it wasn't beside me on the seat, as it usually is.

Oh! Oh!

I whipped the car around and raced back, watching the other side of the road for that familiar blu I was about half a block from the customer's house when there it was, bold as brass, lying in the middle of this busy street, with people walking and kids playing nearby.

The float and the sales in it contained close to five hundred dollars! WHEW!

A prayer of thanks, fervently felt, and I carried on with my deliveries.

I never lost that blue pouch ever again!

***

I came to know some of my regular customers and became friends with many of them.

One regular was Jumpin' Joe Lawrence.

'Jumpin' Joe Lawrence was well known in the billiards community in Canada and the USA.

He played all manner of the game but really shone at 9-ball.

JAMES E. MCCARTHY

He was the Canadian 9-Ball Pool Champion of 2000, amidst other accolades. A gentleman, a friend, and . . . a good tipper!

2015

My first wife, Dorothy 'Glenda' McCarthy, died on March 28, 2015.

This lovely lady, my wife of seventeen years, had raised our five children and was Grandma to many more over her too-short lifespan.

For a good deal of those years, she was on her own, as I was away earning money necessary for our family's welfare.

Everyone loved and respected her.

Our son, Bill, lived with her through the years she suffered from cancer until her demise.

Thank you so much, Bill!

She is missed by her children and grandchildren, friends, and acquaintances!

And me!

***

Then, another family member died.

My sister, Cheryl Lynn (I called her Sherry), died on Monday, June 5, 2015. She had a lethal form of cancer.

We were close when we were young.

I was her 'big brother' (remember the story back in 1950?), but we drifted apart over the years.

I was in the military, then got married and raised children.

And I was involved in various businesses . . . and, of course, my musical career.

Meanwhile, she married Paul Agroff and had children of her own. Consequently, we lived many miles apart for most of our adult lives. But I never stopped loving my little sister.

***

—{DARLA AND I GOT MARRIED ON JUNE 20, 2015}—

My Amazing Hands want you to know that our wedding was ABSOLUTELY AMAZING!

Because we and most of our friends were 'into' country and western, we decided to have a western theme for our wedding.

So, after completing the wedding list of guests, I designed, then made, and mailed out . . . our Invitations. I made them in the shape of a big heart, folded them in half, and mailed them in a regular envelope. When received, the front had a design of hearts. When opened up, the heart unfolded, and the details of the country wedding were then visible.

The back was an invitation to come to our home the following day, Sunday, for an afternoon of 'Live Music, Guitar-Y-Oki, Bar-B-Q, and horseshoes. Bring lawn chairs and b.y.o.b.

Inside the invitation, I yelled 'Howdy!', then 'Y'all are invited!' because Darla McCauley and James McCarthy is 'Gittin' Hitched on Saturday, June 20, 2015'. It included a notice to 'Please Attend Church Dressed Western . . . Cowboy Hat, Blue Jeans, and Boots and Come to the Reception and Dance Dressed the same'.

A prominent notice at the bottom said, 'SORRY, NO CHILDREN OR SPURS.'

The pastor at the church allowed us to wear cowboy hats in the church because 'It is a Wedding service, not a more solemn Church service'. My Amazing Hands provided the pastor with a top hat that he wore with a black suit and string tie and, with his white mustache, looked the very part of an old country minister.

I had a friend who was a sound technician and, together with a volunteer from the church who provided music and graphics as required, played up-tempo country and western music that I had provided as the guests arrived.

The guests were 'danced down the aisles' to their seats by the hombres in our wedding party!

At most weddings, the guests sat down to chat with family and friends.

MY AMAZING HANDS

Not at OUR wedding!

Nope!

When they got to their seats, they stood up, turned around, then clapped to the good old fiddle and country guitar tunes as the next-in-line guests were danced to *their* seats. When everyone was seated, the music stopped, and the parson got everyone's attention to the start of our wedding by ringing an old-fashioned iron triangle dinner bell.

Then my wife-to-be was escorted down the aisle to the strains of "Here Comes the Bride" and thunderous applause by everyone in the building.

She looked absolutely stunning in her white lace gown with veil, train, and all the trimmings.

My Amazing Hands helped her up to the pulpit.

She read her vows to me, and then I <u>sang</u> my vows to her. The words appeared on the overhead as I sang.

My brother, Ken, accompanied himself on his guitar and sang a lovely song to us as we signed the register.

Then one of My Amazing Hands escorted my brand-new bride down the aisle and out of the church to the strains of *"Happy Trails To You"* . . . performed by Roy Rogers and Dale Evans on the overhead projector.

We stopped on the way home at a beautiful spot for pictures. Then a stop at our house for Darla to pick up her blue jeans. Then we were off to our western-Style Wedding Reception!

We held our reception at the Angus Legion. I had played on this stage many times, both with my guitar and with karaoke. Now it's MY turn to "Dance to the Music."

And what great music it was . . . ALL COUNTRY MUSIC—ALL NIGHT LONG!!

After a delicious meal provided by the Legion ladies and as they cleaned up, Darla and I went to the centre of the dance floor. Darla was seated! I pretended that I was having trouble biting her garter so I could take it off her pretty leg, so My Amazing Hands pretended to take my teeth out and used them to grab her garter. I had secreted a spare set of teeth in my pocket.

The crowd loved it!

Then we traditionally gathered the single ladies, and Darla threw her garter over her shoulder.

We had hired a special guest, Tyler Garbyson, a 'country-style' dancer. After dancing solo, he led my guests with some good old boot-stompin', high-kickin' LINE DANCIN'! Tyler was a pro and taught all the dancers some new steps!

This is written in 2021, and folks are STILL talking about our Amazing 2015 Country Wedding!

2016

My Amazing Hands were getting older—and feeling it as time passed!

It got to be a chore to carry the equipment out of the house, into the car, into the gig, set it up, and have the weight of the guitar around my neck all night.

It made my back ache.

I loved it when Ken or a patron would take the guitar for a song or two.

Then, at the end of the evening, we would tear it all down, carry it to the car, then move it into the house.

Then do it all again for the next gig.

So I decided to drop the guitar (figuratively, of course. I LOVED my guitar).

So . . . Guitar-Y-Oki got replaced by MOSTLY COUNTRY KARAOKE.

***

About this time, Darla got breast cancer. Treatment saved her life and reversed that nasty, nasty disease!

DARLA IS A BREAST CANCER SURVIVOR! YA-HOO!

DARLA GOT TO 'RING THE BELL' AT THE HOSPITAL! YA-HOO AGAIN, <u>LOUDER</u>!

Thank you so much, Royal Victoria Hospital staff!

Although the chemo and radiation therapy made her VERY ill, she was always smiling and keeping my coffee cup full and hot for one of My Amazing Hands!

And singing along when we had karaoke night, always smiling with the rest of us!

Ken took over as sound technician on all our gigs.

He has a natural aptitude for all things musical, so he knew exactly how to set the controls to make us all sound GREAT, instead of merely good.

I was slowing down my career rapidly . . . not being so active in promoting my musical talents. but still managing a few gigs.

Here's a story . . . Mostly Country Karaoke was performing at Gravenhurst Legion.

A patron asked me if I had Johnny Cash's *"One Piece at a Time."*

I didn't have it but promised him I would have it the next time we played there.

He said I would have to buy a round for the house if I didn't.

I countered that HE would buy the house a round if I did have it and sang it for him!

Well . . . we played there a month or so later, and there was my buddy . . . the Johnny Cash fan.

My Amazing Hands started the evening off with, you guessed it, *"One Piece at a Time,"* and dedicated it to him. As the song ended, he made his way to the bar and came good on our bet—HE BOUGHT A ROUND FOR THE HOUSE, AS PROMISED!

I found an honest man in the Legion bar in Gravenhurst. Bravo!!

So, I added a few bucks to my pension income. However, the equipment was getting harder and harder to carry and set up. And I was getting very few phone calls for gigs.

My Amazing Hands retired from working a day job after fifty-seven years.

Just did karaoke!

Here's another story . . . .

We were booked at the Legion in Darla's hometown—Port Loring.

During the evening, I met more of her family.

Someone suggested that we should perform at the Open Country Singing Contest held in North Bay. It was sponsored by the Nipissing Country Music Association and was open to anyone. You could compete in the category of your choice for a nominal entry fee. There were cash prizes and beautiful trophies for first, second, and third place.

I entered the male fifty-plus category.

The first day, Friday evening, was the contest.

The next day, Saturday afternoon, the top three in each category performed, followed by handing out the trophies and cash prizes.

I performed my favourite song, "*The Auctioneer*", and thought I sang it pretty well.

I got a lot of positive comments.

But I didn't realize how important it was to stay within a time limit.

Apparently, it's EXTREMELY important!

I just sang the whole song, as I have done for many years, but I RAN OVER THE TIME LIMIT!

I won third—AGAIN!

If you want to thumb back to 1953, you will recall that the only other music contest that I had ever entered was the Kiwanis festival when I was eleven, when I thought I had won, but I placed third.

I've heard that history repeats itself.

Back then, I said . . . "UGH!"

AND NOW—SIXTY-THREE YEARS LATER—ALL I CAN THINK OF TO SAY IS ANOTHER—

"UGH!"

At least this is a beautiful trophy, not a paper certificate like the 1953 one was.

OH, WELL!

We had a LOT of fun and met many friendly folks that day.

I wasn't able to make it in succeeding years.

Maybe next time . . . I'll pick a short song and only sing one verse!

2017

Chris, the leader of the house band from North Bay who had supplied the background for the talent contest, had made a CD with the rest of his group as backup. My Amazing Hands were given a copy of their CD. Darla and I played it in the car on the way home. We loved it.

We still had fun jammin' every Tuesday night at seven at my house.

We would move the furniture back to make room for Dennis, who carried his portable keyboard and amplifier into the house and back to his car afterward. The others would bring their guitars and microphones. Ken had his guitar and amp. I had a spare microphone that he used. And, of course, I had my guitar and mic and provided the speakers and power board. Darla also enjoyed singing and provided rhythm with the eggs, tambourine, and maracas.

I gave each a big thick black book where we could put the song sheets I prepared, and I cued in the chords to make it easier for everyone. We had over a hundred songs in the book, and everyone would pick their favourites for all to play. Occasionally we would have guests . . . other musicians or folks that just wanted to sing along.

I hated to see it end.

However, there was something I have always had a hankering to do!

I wanted to see if I really was as bad a singer as the song sounded—the time when I heard myself sing using professional studio equipment, way back when we did that rushed song at RCA. That was back when we got stomped by Stompin' Tom. He got held over, and we went home.

Maybe I have been fooling myself into thinking that I was, and still am, a darned good singer.

I wanted to record again. I wanted to make a CD.

So . . . I DID!

I'm SO proud of it!!

This was something that I had wanted to do since back when I recorded at the RCA studios in Toronto.

But I swore I would be better prepared for it if I ever got a chance to record again!

I thought to myself, "I can do that!"

I thought I would perform with my karaoke songs as a backup . . . who needs a band? Besides, that should be a LOT easier to record if I don't have to get the background music organized. That means I can record more songs in the same time.

As I rented the studio by the hour (complete with a sound engineer), it would cost me MUCH less and give me a better quality result.

To make a long story short, I booked the studio. Darla and I and Ken and some friends, Terry and Rod were there. I gave Rod the camera and said, "Here! Take LOTS of pictures and videos!" He did!

It's intimidating . . . but my experience at the RCA studios prepared me, and we laid down some pretty decent songs— eleven tracks altogether.

Ken sang harmony with me on an Everly Brothers song and played some lead guitar.

And I arranged with the engineer that I would come back a few days later after he did his magic—'mastering' the tracks. This means that by using equalization, compression, limiting and enhancing stereo, he balances the sonic elements of a stereo mix to optimize playback across all systems and media formats.

When I left our 'mastering session', I was the proud owner of my very first CD tracks. But I wasn't anywhere near done yet.

I waited till I got home; I rushed into my computer room, one of My Amazing Hands put the disc in, and Darla and I listened to me sing . . . ON MY VERY OWN CD! WOW! What a THRILL!

I called it "JIM McCARTHY SINGS."

I couldn't wait to let Ken and his wife, Sharon, hear it, but I decided I wouldn't give it to anyone until it was ready!

On the way home, I had stopped in a store and picked up some blank, printable CDs, together with a package of empty CD cases. Over the next few days, I designed the front cover, which, when folded, was also the front inside, which listed the songs on the CD. I put on my 'cowboy hat,' and Darla took some pictures. I chose one that I liked and, with the help of Photoshop, tweaked it until I was satisfied.

I also used Photoshop for the background colours and the text, along with the back cover, containing a list of all 11 songs.

Oh . . . thank you, computer guys, for Photoshop!

I found a program called Acoustica CD/DVD Label Maker. Using this program, I downloaded some images of musical notes, added the picture of my head with the cowboy hat, some graphics that showed the title of the CD, rolled up my sleeves, and . . .

I burned the songs on printable CDs on my computer. Next, I printed the top of each printable CD using my special printer.

Then I printed the front and back of each CD, cut them to size, folded them, then inserted them in each CD case. Finally, I added the CD, threw in a business card for good measure, and voila . . . CDs that were as good as the stores carried. (I thought so, anyway). I proceeded to distribute them.

Of course, I gave many away to family and friends! Even sold a few at the gigs when we performed!

I decided to do another, considering the first CD's *worldwide* (I wish) success.

So, I called my brother and my son, Jim Jr., when I found another recording studio MUCH closer to home, which also has an excellent reputation. A phone call to discuss rates, etc., and we booked a day suitable for all to record. We got together, practiced the songs we would do, and met at George's recording studio. It was in a garage, but George had done a LOT of work making it into a very professional recording studio.

Jim Jr sounds amazingly like Randy Travis, and I already mentioned that Ken is a great musician.

When we were done, George mastered the songs and gave the finished product to me a few days later.

He did a great job.

MY AMAZING HANDS

Then I used my skills to design and print the CD. I was thrilled with the result. We all wore a BIG smile and . . . our cowboy hats.

We had a LOT of fun laying down those songs. I burned and printed a few copies each and a bunch to sell at the gigs we were playing.

I wanted to sing with my wife, Darla, on a CD.

She, too, has a great voice and loves to do a solo or duet when she accompanies me on gigs, and I love to sing with her. She's a good singer, an amazing woman, and a fantastic wife.

I was proud to accompany her on this CD.

I gave copies to friends and family and sold them at our gigs, as I did the other two CDs. Everyone raved about how good Darla was. I was jealous.

Maybe, when she makes it big and has her own CDs, she'll let me sing one song for old time's sake.

Great fun!

We gave a copy to a friend—a lady who works at the local LCBO store. She just went on and on about how good Darla was and almost swooned when I introduced her to Darla when we were at the store picking up some wine one day.

We get all the empty packing boxes we want

2018

I came into this world with nothing, owning nothing and owing nothing. I want to leave this world *the same way*.

This is my wife, Darla's, second marriage.

When her first husband, who she loved very, very much—passed away— she wasn't prepared to manage any of the family's financial affairs. She had issues that she was unable to deal with.

I wanted to have our affairs in order so she wouldn't have to endure these horrors again, should something untoward happen to me.

So, My Amazing Hands signed a 'reverse mortgage.' Neither of us would have to make any mortgage payments as long as one or both of us were still living. When we both died, the house would be sold by our executors to satisfy the claims of the mortgage company.

The balance would be settled with our estate and distributed as per our will.

The only stipulation with the RM (Reverse Mortgage) was that the taxes and insurance on the house had to be paid when due, and the house upkeep had to be maintained—snow and leaves removed, re-roof when required etc. Stuff that we would do anyway.

We were able to obtain RM cash, deposited directly into our bank account, that would not only pay the balance owing on our car but would give us the cash to pay EVERY OTHER DEBT THAT WE HAD. So, we were able to eliminate about $1,800 per month in payments.

Also, we could purchase things that we needed but couldn't afford till now, like an electric elevator between floors, so I didn't have to climb the basement stairs any more, a three-seat couch that had two of the seats electrically operated to recline at the push of a button, full size electric heated blanket on our bed, improved drinking water filter system etc.

More importantly, I had the peace of mind that Darla wouldn't have to worry about a place to live or a car to get her around. We also had money in the bank, and . . . I got this book published right away instead of the much slower method of submitting it to an agent, who re-submitted it to a publisher who only published the best submissions.

That left, however, our deaths.

***

I didn't want either of us to be burdened with details should we lose our partner.

So . . . I purchased a plot in Avondale Cemetery in Stratford.

We each expressed our desires for a memorial stone, and based on that, My Amazing Hands designed ours!

The great folks at Stratford Memorials took my sketches and brought them to life.

This is how our tombstone looks . . .

As I have been a musician most of my adult life, My Amazing Hands depicted my trusty old Fender Telecaster at the top of the stone. Darla's love of birds and flowers is reflected in the hummingbird sipping nectar and the roses that are not only engraved on the front but also sculpted life-size on the side. And the cross reflects our respect for our God, who has loved and protected us—throughout our lives!

After completing it, they placed our memorial stone on our actual cemetery plot.

The funeral home has been paid—so that my body could be sent to them when I die.

They will clothe me in attire as laid out in my will, delivered to them by my son, Jim Jr., who will collect the clothes from my home and deliver them to the funeral home.

I also paid the funeral home to contact the company in Toronto from whom I purchased a casket and ensure it is delivered to them. They will then insert my body after clothing it, and deliver it to Avondale Cemetery in Stratford.

Of course, my executor and/or Darla's executrix will contact the memorial company to fill in the dates on the memorial after we die.

Darla's wish is to be cremated, so her ashes can be half with her previous husband and half with me.

So we contacted the funeral home and paid for their services to have Darla's remains cremated.

We ordered two ornate hardwood urns. The funeral home will put half her ashes in each box and give them to me, if I'm still alive, or to her daughter, her executor, if I'm not.

I will ensure that one urn is buried in my cemetery plot, and her daughter will arrange that the other urn is buried with her dad, James McCauley, Darla's previous husband.

***

I decided that the name Mostly Country Karaoke would limit the folks who would patronize me, thinking I was 'just' country music, which I'm not, so I changed the name to GOODTYME KARAOKE.

I designed and printed new business cards and hand-painted the table poster on the back of the old Guitar-Y-Oki table poster, as I knew I wouldn't be using it again. Hard to throw it out, though.

Darla was still not well and wasn't getting any better. Back and stomach problems.

My legs were getting painful if I walked more than a few feet, especially when carrying musical equipment. I was a little overweight, which didn't help.

Ken was a real trooper. He never complained, even though he carried speakers, power boards, boxes of songbooks, etc., to the couple of gigs we had.

Our last couple of jobs were for a lady from our church who was having a family reunion at a country restaurant, and an outdoor get-together in a friend's backyard.

We have nothing else booked in our immediate future.

But Ken comes over most Wednesdays to sing some karaoke songs!

And I am STILL adding songs to my KJ repertoire . . . just in case!

It's hard to let go!

2019

Ken performed with various combos over the years, and today he MAKES electric guitars.

As difficult as that is, they are incredibly professional. They all have Ken's unique touch, and they sound GREAT!

He's in the process of making one that resembles a Stratocaster.

I know that when it gets finished, it, too, will be amazing.

He's a darned good singer, a great guitar player, and a terrific frontman.

He has a knack for conversing with an audience, as I believe I do.

Did I mention... he's a GREAT brother, too!

Also... did I mention... I HAVE AN ELEVATOR IN MY DINING ROOM!

I'm seventy-seven years old now, and my legs aren't what they used to be.

So I bought an elevator that travels from a corner of my dining room down to my rec room.

Just get in, close the door, and push the button.

It sure makes it easy on these poor tired legs of mine.

Leaves all of my strength to sing some karaoke songs in the rec room.

Sometimes I grab up my Telly and do a little pickin', too.

Sometimes I chase Darla around the room... but not so much anymore! Lol!

As I mentioned previously, my brother, Ken, came over most Wednesdays, and we would have fun singing karaoke in my rec room.

We sometimes sang some songs solo. (Try saying THAT after a couple of drinks without sounding like Mel Tillis).

One Wednesday, we each had two or three drinks, and our glasses were empty... so I headed upstairs to get refills for both of us.

Eight stairs went straight up to a small landing that opened to the backyard through a back door. To get upstairs, you would have to turn right, then go up three more stairs, then turn a handle and enter a door into the kitchen.

That night though, I made it to the landing, turned right, reached for the handle, and passed out.

Around ten-thirty that evening.

I came to my senses at five o'clock the next morning... in the hospital.

The hospital staff was cold to me (you will find out why in a minute), but they phoned my wife at home, who came to get me.

I didn't think much of it.

I had twisted sideways when I fell and landed on my shoulder.

It was sore for a few days, but that was the only after-effect of my fall.

I thought!

A week or so later, I was driving and had to make a left turn.

The traffic light had turned orange while I was in the intersection, so I accelerated slightly to get around the corner before it turned red.

I noticed another car coming behind me, which was also accelerating.

I also noted a young mother with a couple of kids, one in a stroller, on my right... impatiently waiting to cross... trying to beat the pedestrian 'walk/don't walk' sign.

And a couple of cars were coming toward me in the opposite lane.

As drivers are wont to do, I intended to release the pressure on the steering wheel with my left hand so it would slip through my fingers and straighten the wheels—completing the turn.

However, MY LEFT HAND WOULDN'T LOOSEN ITS GRIP!

I didn't want to cause an accident, and I certainly didn't want to hit that mother with children.

Fortunately, I have been blessed with the ability to react with lightning speed without having to think about it.

For example, if I accidentally knock something off a table, My Amazing Hands can react so quickly, I can usually catch the object in mid-air before it has fallen more than a few inches.

Ken tells me he is blessed with the same ability.

So . . . my right hand reached across the steering wheel and pulled my left hand off it.

The wheel straightened up, and I pulled into a nearby parking lot to take stock of things.

Then, I did something stupid.

I drove home.

The Lord was looking after me that day, though . . . I made it home safely!

But, wisely, I then had Darla drive me to the same hospital where I had been the week before.

This time, they took more tests, then, without telling us much, said that I didn't have time to wait for an ambulance . . . Darla should immediately drive me to Barrie's large district hospital.

They phoned ahead to tell them to be prepared to receive and treat me!

When we arrived, we were rushed into the Intensive Care Unit, where I was told that I had a blockage in the Carotid Artery on the right side of my neck.

It was blocking the blood flow from the heart to the left side of the brain.

I met the surgical staff, who prepared me and, after surgery, took me to the recovery room.

The artery had been opened up, cleaned out, and closed back up again with dissolving stitches.

Everything appeared normal at first, but I soon discovered that I couldn't remember a lot of things.

I forget the names of well-known television and movie actors and people's names shortly after being introduced, for example.

Sometimes I stutter as my brain struggles to remember a word or phrase that I KNOW I know!

Usually, though, I eventually remember—a while later, it will just pop into my head!

On my return visit a few months later to see the surgeon, after everything had healed, I found that the hospital that I initially went to didn't do anything on my first visit other than the blood test for alcohol.

The medical staff thought I was drunk, so they didn't do further tests.
I HAD A STROKE!
And, because they didn't pick up on that stroke—a week later—
I HAD ANOTHER ONE!
Fortunately, no one was injured as a result of their ineptitude.

***

MY FISH MUG

My sons bought me this coffee mug after I had taken both boys out for a day's fishing.

That was about thirty-five or forty years ago.

I still have it, and still use it every day, and have, pretty well every day, since I got it.

Thousands upon thousands of cups of coffee later.

It has pictures of Smallmouth Bass swimming in blue waters on both sides.

I Love It!!

2020

The year of Covid-19. 'Nuff said about that horrible year.

Real estate values took a sudden leap over the last couple of years, so My Amazing Hands were able to get even more equity from my house by signing an upgraded 'reverse mortgage.'

We had steadily been paying down some credit card amalgamation debt, bank overdraft debt and the cost of Darla's hearing aids that we purchased on time.

However, NOW... thanks to this 'reverse mortgage', we are totally debt-free!!

We paid all of our debt down to $0.00.

Hallelujah!! Thank you, Lord!

For the first time in our adult lives... DARLA AND I OWE <u>NOTHING</u>!

ZERO!! ZILCH! ZIPPO!! NADA! NUTTIN'!

Or, in the great words of CROWBAR, ♪ " *Oh! WHAT A FEELING—WHAT A RUSH-H-H*" ♪

My Amazing Hands have put a few bucks in our bank account (just a few, mind you) that we can spend as we wish, without a worry.

When either Darla or I die... the other will be able to grieve in peace.

As it says on our monument, 'IT'S BEEN A GREAT DANCE.'

MY LIFE IS & ALWAYS HAS BEEN & ALWAYS WILL BE... TRULY...

<u>'AMAZING'!</u>

— IT *REALLY HAS BEEN* A GREAT DANCE —

Sadly, I think my musical career is over.

Oh, my brother still comes over once in awhile, and we sing some karaoke in my rec room.

And both Darla and I sneak down there to do a few tunes ourselves occasionally.

Sometimes I get out the guitar, play, and sing.

Just like in the good old days when I did so to thousands of people on a stage.

But my back starts to ache from the weight of the guitar.

And My Amazing Hands get sore and crampy.

And I have trouble getting back up if I drop a pick and bend down to get it.

My legs are too sore.

But I'm not complaining.

It has been a lifetime of friends and fun.

And I got to TRAVEL, have ADVENTURES, raise an AMAZING family, and meet SUPERSTARS!

WHAT

MY AMAZING HANDS

HAVE DONE HAS BEEN

SIMPLY

"AMAZING"!

Epilog

INSTRUMENTS I HAVE PLAYED:
1=very well, 2=somewhat, 3= occasionally

PERCUSSION:

    Full set traps (1) Various groups and orchestra
    Snare Drum (1) Military and Town Bands
    Bass Drum (1)
    Cymbals (1)
    Bongos (1)
    Maracas (1)
    Tambourine (1)
    Eggs (1)
    Claves (1)
    Cow Bell (1)
    Cajon (box, sounds like drums) (2)

BRASS:

    Trumpet (1) Town and Military Bands
    Cornet (1)
    Saxophone (faked playing on Casino Rama stage) (minus 4)

JAMES E. MCCARTHY

STRINGED INSTRUMENTS:

    Electric Guitar (1)
    Acoustic Guitar (1)
    Bass (non-upright) (1)
    Steel Guitar (2)
    Violin (3)

KEYBOARDS:

    Organ double keyboard w bass pedals (3)
    Piano (3)

VOCALS:

    Sing Lead (1)
    Sing Harmony (1)
    Sing with Choir (1)
    Sing Bass (3)

MUSICAL ACCOMPLISHMENTS:

- Performed on Casino Rama Entertainment Centre Stage six times
- Recorded at RCA Studios
- Recorded, designed, and printed three CDs
- Played all over Northern Ontario
- Performed to houses up to approx. 3,500 patrons
- Performed musical theatre
- Trophies for musical competitions
- Performed on Television
- Performed on Radio
- Assorted Karaoke businesses spanning over 20 years
- Various live bands over 60 years
- Played with Mariachi Band in Mexico

CELEBRITIES I HAVE MET:

Chapter numbers will show where they are in my book (Sorted alphabetically)

Burns, Pat (1991)
Captain Highliner (1994)
Clark, Wendel (1991)
Davis, Geena (1994)
Doyle, Judith (1993)
Eagleson, Alan (1991)
Eikhard, Shirley (1974)
Elliott, Sam (1988)
Feagan, Ronald (1956)
Gill, Vince (2000)
Gretzky, Phyllis & Walter (1983)
Gretzky, Wayne (1991)
Harlin, Renny (1994)
Hutt, William (1951)
Jeffrey, Larry (1956)
Keenan, Mike (1991)
Lawrence, Jumpin' Joe (2014)
Lewis, Jerry Lee (1972)
Lindros, Eric (1991)
MacInnis, Al (1991)
Mariachi Band (1978)
Mercey Brothers (1974)
Neilson, Roger (1991)
Rexe, Steve (1978)
Shanahan, Brendan (1991)
Sky Low Low (1974)
Smith, Steve (1991)
Stephen Truscotte's brother (1960)
Sovine, Red (1972)

Sutherland, Donald (1980) – I mixed him a drink but didn't actually meet him. My wife, however, did. She was his hostess at the restaurant where I was bartending
Wally K. Orchestra (1961)
Watt, Tom (1991)
Wregget, Ken (1991)
Yau, Doctor Terrence (2011)

ANIMALS I HAVE RIDDEN

Saddle horses
Bareback horses
Trotters and Pacers with Sulky
A cow

VEHICLES I HAVE DRIVEN

Tricycle Scooter (foot powered)
Scooter (gas powered)
Pink and non-pink bicycles
Farm tractors
Harvester
A vast assortment of trucks from half-ton to five-ton.
School Buses
RVs (Recreational Vehicles)
A vast variety of cars, very, very old to brand new.
Fast cars (Porsche) to slow cars (1923 Model T)
Big cars (stretch limousine) to small cars (Morris Mini)
Go-Karts
Taxicab
Railway steam locomotive
Railway diesel locomotive

MOTORCYCLES

from Honda 90 to a Honda Goldwing Aspencade 1200
I'm still licensed to drive a 'cycle.

AIRCRAFT I HAVE PILOTED:

Cessna
Piper Cub
Cherokee
Beechcraft
Huge Glider

WATERCRAFT I HAVE DRIVEN/SAILED/ROWED

Cardboard Box Boat
(sailed in nana and grandpa's kitchen when I was 2).
Raft
Punt
Pedal boat
Rowboat
Sailboat NK class
Various Outboard-driven Power Boats
Various Inboard Power Boats up to and including 24 ft. Yacht

WINTER: VARIOUS SNOWMOBILES I HAVE DRIVEN

From Arctic Cat to Ski-doo to Polaris to Yamaha.

HEAVY EQUIPMENT I HAVE DRIVEN

International Harvester
'Champion' Road Grader
Huge Crane with Big Demolition Ball
Giant Fork Truck used to move Cement Kiln sections
Crane to load Huge Cement Kiln sections onto an ocean-going cargo ship.
D10 bulldozer.

WATERS I HAVE HAD MY FEET IN

CANADA:
All Great Lakes lakes and rivers adjoining them except Lake Michigan,
Thames River at London, Ontario,
Avon River in Stratford, Ontario
Ottawa River
Lake Timiskaming
Nottawasaga River

U.S.A:
Mississippi River at New Orleans,
Gulf of Mexico
Pacific Ocean

ENGLAND: River Thames at London, North Sea, Irish Sea, English Channel

FRANCE: Seine River at Paris

BAHAMAS: Atlantic Ocean

MEXICO: Pacific Ocean – Acapulco de Juárez

MY AMAZING HANDS

WHERE I'VE LIVED

(all in Ontario, Canada—Sorted alphabetically)

Aylmer
Belleville
Chatham
Clinton
Goderich
London
Niagara Falls
Stratford
Toronto
Trenton
Wasaga Beach

OTHER FEATS

- Stood at centre stage at Stratford Shakespearean Festival

- Drove up Mount St Helens far above the treeline a year after its eruption

- Preached sermons to the congregation in church

- Music Director at my church

- Performed in Church
  —in choirs
  —sang solos with and without guitar
  —performed a duet with Lisa S.

JAMES E. MCCARTHY

- Actor in film 'Wasaga' with a spoken part

- Actor in film 'Long Kiss Goodnight

- Director, Actor, Singer, Props, Lighting, and Sound for many Amateur Theatre performances in Wasaga Beach and Collingwood.

And Last But Certainly Not Least . . .

MY AMAZING HANDS *WERE* . . . SANTA CLAUS!

WHAT

MY AMAZING HANDS

HAVE DONE HAS BEEN

SIMPLY

"AMAZING"!

About the Author

JAMES E. (JIM) McCARTHY was born in 1942 in Stratford, Ontario. WWII was raging, and, while his father was overseas, Jim and his mother lived with her parents in Stratford. When the war was over, dad took his family to live in Chatham, where Jim attended public school (he skipped a grade), then Goderich, where Jim attended high school. In 1959, Jim joined the RCAF. His Top Secret rating led to MANY adventures.

Jim married, then had children. He learned to play drums and guitar, and played with various bands. Later, he was a DJ and a KJ. Over the years, he lived in Stratford, Chatham, Trenton, Niagara Falls, Goderich, Clinton, Belleville, London and Wasaga Beach (now residing there). His interests are in theatre, music, plumbing, electrical, and carpentry...learned while renovating his home.

He is now (2023), age 81, a devoted Christian and thanks God profusely for his wife, Darla, and peaceful retired life.

CPSIA information can be obtained
at www.ICGtesting.com
Printed in the USA
LVHW071937160623
749591LV00004B/20/J